African Women
South of the Sahara

Edited by
Margaret Jean Hay and Sharon Stichter

Longman
London and New York

Longman Group Limited
Longman House
Burnt Mill, Harlow
Essex CM20 2JE
and Associated Companies
throughout the World

Published in the United States of American by Longman Inc.

First published 1984

British Library Cataloguing in Publication Data

African women south of the Sahara.
1. Women—Social conditions   2. Women—
Africa, Sub-Saharan
I. Hay, Margaret Jean   II. Stichter, Sharon
305.4′2′0967   HQ1121

ISBN 0-582-64373-2

Library of Congress Cataloging in Publication Data

African women south of the Sahara.

Bibliography: p.
Includes index.
1. Women—Africa, Sub-Saharan—Economic conditions.
2. Women—Africa, Sub-Saharan—Social conditions.
3. Women—Africa, Sub-Saharan—Political activity.
I. Hay, Margaret Jean.   II. Stichter, Sharon.
HQ1788.A57 1983 ⏐ 305.4′0967   83-7905

ISBN 0-582-64373-2 (pbk.)

Set in 10/11 Times (Compugraphic)

Printed in Hong Kong by
Commonwealth Printing Press Ltd.

Contents

Preface

Academic interest in the study of women in Africa has grown enormously in the last few years. At the same time, among policy-makers, there has been a growing recognition of the importance of women's past and present contributions to African development. A large body of scholarly literature on African women has emerged, and university courses in African history, society and development, and in black studies and women's studies, are beginning to incorporate material on African women.

It has been a challenge, however, to make the fruits of this new scholarship easily available to undergraduates and to the general reader. Much of the best work on African women is scattered in journals which are difficult to obtain or is still unpublished. In addition, most of it consists of detailed and specific case studies, which make the task of generalization somewhat daunting. There has long been a need for a general work on sub-Saharan African women, which would give an overview of the subject, would incorporate and synthesize the best insights of the new scholarship, and would at the same time be accessible to undergraduate readers.

We hope that the present volume will meet this need. It is an introductory, interdisciplinary text, written from the perspective of a number of disciplines but set in an historical context. Each chapter is written by a specialist familiar with the issues in that particular field. Each introduces a topic in clear and straightforward terms, and attempts to point the way towards deeper study of the area discussed.

A note is in order on our definition of the subject matter. While focusing on the present, most of the chapters in this book also present a picture of African women in pre-colonial society, along with a consideration of the major changes occuring during the colonial era. Further, the information on women in South Africa has been integrated into the thematic discussion. We have not, however, included material on women in Africa north of the Sahara, since the body of relevant scholarly literature is, unfortunately, still quite distinct from the materials and issues explored here.

The work reflects a combination of group effort and individual expertise. We think that the combination was a fruitful one. Although each chapter remains the individual creation of its author, each was written within editorial guidelines which attempted to insure continuity and comprehensiveness. The prior circulation of outlines and drafts among contributors facilitated discussion and interchange, and in the end, contributed greatly to the book's internal cohesion.

Editorially, the work has been a joint effort in the fullest sense, both of us having worked together on all phases of the project. As editors, we would like to thank all the contributors for their hard work, patience, and good-humored willingness to accommodate revisions. Iris Berger, Nancy Hafkin, and Christraud Geary also deserve thanks for their assistance with particular aspects of this project. And finally, our appreciation goes to our editor, Peter Warwick, for his wise editorial advice and enthusiastic support of the project.

Margaret Jean Hay
Sharon Stichter

African Studies Center
Boston University

List of tables

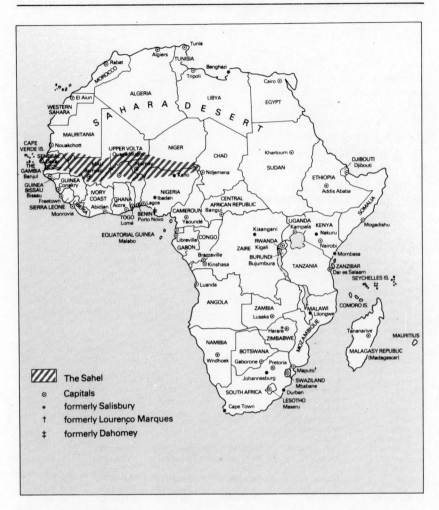

Contemporary Africa
Source: Africa Report Magazine, *publication of the African-American Institute, updated in Jan. 1980 by M. Wiley, Michigan State University.*

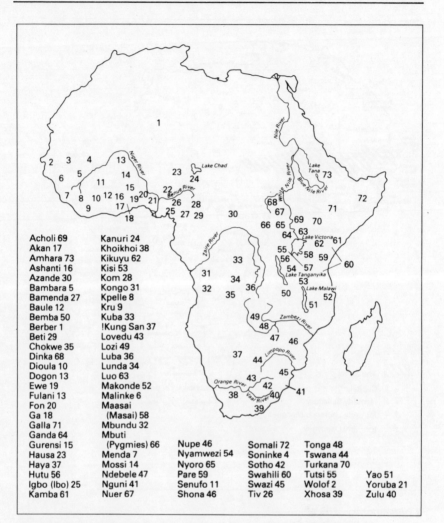

Acholi 69
Akan 17
Amhara 73
Ashanti 16
Azande 30
Bambara 5
Bamenda 27
Baule 12
Bemba 50
Berber 1
Beti 29
Chokwe 35
Dinka 68
Dioula 10
Dogon 13
Ewe 19
Fulani 13
Fon 20
Ga 18
Galla 71
Ganda 64
Gurensi 15
Hausa 23
Haya 37
Hutu 56
Igbo (Ibo) 25
Kamba 61

Kanuri 24
Khoikhoi 38
Kikuyu 62
Kisi 53
Kom 28
Kongo 31
Kpelle 8
Kru 9
Kuba 33
!Kung San 37
Lovedu 43
Lozi 49
Luba 36
Lunda 34
Luo 63
Makonde 52
Malinke 6
Maasai
  (Masai) 58
Mbundu 32
Mbuti
  (Pygmies) 66
Menda 7
Mossi 14
Ndebele 47
Nguni 41
Nuer 67

Nupe 46
Nyamwezi 54
Nyoro 65
Pare 59
Senufo 11
Shona 46

Somali 72
Soninke 4
Sotho 42
Swahili 60
Swazi 45
Tiv 26

Tonga 48
Tswana 44
Turkana 70
Tutsi 55
Wolof 2
Xhosa 39

Yao 51
Yoruba 21
Zulu 40

Approximate locations of major ethnic groups mentioned in the text
Source: *based on Map 2 in Phyllis M. Martin and P. O'Meara,* Africa
(Bloomington, 1977).

Introduction

As one of the world's major cultural regions, sub-Saharan Africa has been distinguished by the prevalence of shifting hoe agriculture and lineage-based societies. Here, in contrast to pre-colonial societies in many other parts of the world, women traditionally played a major role in food cultivation and trade, in addition to food preparation and child-rearing. In some, though not all, African societies, women enjoyed control over the fruits of their labor and wielded substantial political power.

Even in Africa, however, women's power and status were always in some major ways less than those of men. In this book we will explore the range of variations in women's social position in Africa, taking into account not only the great diversity of traditional social arrangements, but also the overlay of outside influences, from European colonial conquest in the late nineteenth and early twentieth centuries to the Arab/Islamic penetration of earlier eras. The contemporary situation of women has been shaped by all of these historical forces.

The first three chapters of this book look at the role of women largely from the point of view of their economic position and their economic roles. Conceiving of 'the economic' in a broad sense, these chapters describe the work women do in production, distribution, and reproduction, as well as their degree of access to economic resources such as land, livestock, and trade items, and to education, skills and wage employment.

Chapter 1 opens with the observation, also underlined in later chapters, that African women do the bulk of subsistence labor in agriculture, yet do not control much of the surplus generated from this labor. To explain this situation, Jeanne Henn elaborates a view of the traditional African household as embodying the control of labor of women and junior males by senior men.[1] Women are economic and social dependents of males; yet they are expected somehow to provide all the food for their family's daily consumption. The many modifications which are introduced into these relationships in state and stateless societies, slave-holding societies, matrilineal and patrilineal kinship systems, and pastoral and hunting and gathering societies are also delineated.

This account of the traditional African household as a patriarchal economic unit differs from earlier formulations which focused solely on women's and men's work roles in the pre-colonial area, emphasizing the functional complementarity between the two. Instead, this approach calls attention to who controls productive and reproductive labor and who benefits from it.[2] It also provides a starting point for the analysis of women's position in the society as a whole, since in many societies household and lineage were the most important political and economic units. Yet there is a danger in this view of representing African women as mere pawns in the hands of 'patriarchs'. That such a conclusion would be erroneous is suggested by much of the material in subsequent chapters. The problem of the relative powers of men and women is taken up in Chapter 4 on the family, and in Chapter 9 on politics.

A second theme introduced in Chapter 1 is the complex and contradictory effects of colonial rule on African women's economic position. On the one hand, women's workload increased in many areas because of male out-migration for wage labor. Women's legal rights to the land were circumscribed in the change-over to Western systems of individual land tenure, and men controlled the proceeds from the new and lucrative cash crops such as coffee, cocoa, and cotton. The strength of patriarchal households was broken down in some ways and reinforced in others. Chapter 1 also emphasizes, however, that in some areas of personal rights, women's position improved as a result of colonial changes.

In Chapter 2 Jane Guyer provides a detailed look at some of the contemporary variations in women's rural economic role, variations which are linked to the differential impact of the world economic system on varying local structures. Three rural economies are described, each attached to the world economy in different ways: (firstly) through limited participation in regional economic relationships, (secondly) through cash-crop production for the world market, and (thirdly) through men's wage work for national industrial and agricultural enterprizes. A fourth case, illustrating female wage work in large-scale plantation agriculture, is also discussed.

The first case is the West African system of savannah agriculture among the Senufo, where the complex balance of men's and women's roles has not been much affected by outside forces. The important role of men in growing staple food crops here constitutes an exception to the more general situation in Africa of female predominance in subsistence agriculture. The Senufo also illustrate the case of matrilineal society where women inherit limited but secure access to land and incomes.

The second case examined is the well-developed cash-crop economy of the Ewe of Ghana, where cocoa-growing resulted in a male monopoly of the proceeds from that export crop and the transfer of nearly all food-producing functions to the women. But not all export-oriented economies have followed this pattern, and some sources of variation in women's position in other cash-crop producing areas are ably analyzed. The third case examined is the labor reserve economy of southern Africa, where the majority of men migrate to wage jobs elsewhere. In these areas, agriculture stagnates, and women remain heavily dependent on male remittances if they do not migrate themselves.

African towns of colonial origin were previously the temporary homes of male labor migrants; today, they are witnessing a more rapid immigration of African women. Towns of indigenous origin always had a more balanced ratio between men and women. Facing job discrimination and generally high unemployment in towns, women often join the 'informal labor market', where their activities range from small-scale trading of all sorts to semi-legal activities such as beer brewing and prostitution. In Chapter 3 Claire Robertson describes the various occupations of urban women, making use of the life histories of a market trader in Accra, a domestic servant in Johannesburg, a prostitute in Nairobi, a leader of the women's movement in Nigeria, and a secretary in Lusaka. The insights into the personal lives of urban women graphically illustrate many of the themes developed in Chapter 4 on the family. The importance of looking at women's position in the class system as separate from that of men's is also emphasized in this chapter.

The picture of urban women presented in Chapter 3 is supplemented by a statistical Appendix, compiled by Sharon Stichter, which presents selected data on women's economic participation and education in African countries. The Appendix also introduces the widely used concept of the 'labor force' or 'economically active population' and discusses its limitations when applied to women's work. The accompanying tables document some of the main variations among African nations with regard to women's labor force participation, wage employment, occupational distribution and educational attainment.

Chapters 4 and 5 consider the position of women within the family and kin structures of traditional and modern Africa, and the various forms of women's associations outside the family. In Chapter 4 Luise White emphasizes the importance of all women's relationships within the family—with siblings, parents, and in-laws, for example—and not just the bond between husband and wife, which has been the focus of most of the earlier work on women in African families. She describes the relation of kinship systems to economic organization, and discusses polygyny, family work roles, age at marriage, divorce, woman-woman marriage, and women's decision-making roles within the family in both pre-colonial and post-colonial eras.

The division of men's and women's roles in which women are confined to the domestic sphere while men monopolize the 'public' sphere, common in some parts of the world, seems to have limited application here.[3] Africa has a particularly rich tradition of women cooperating in groups, rather than being restricted solely to a 'private' or domestic domain. Community participation ranges from rural work groups and secret societies to modern cooperatives, from urban associations of women traders and professional women to those of beer brewers and prostitutes. Audrey Wipper provides an overview of these groups in Chapter 5, contrasting the indigenous associations, in which membership was largely ascribed, to the modern ones, which are based on voluntary membership. The variety and power of women's associations in some traditional societies suggest that in these cases women had considerable autonomy in the areas of special concern to them, such as farming, trading, female rites of passage, childbirth and the education of young girls. Women's groups made rules and enforced social control in these areas of their own societies.

Today many rural cooperatives and self-help projects are primarily composed of women. Some represent grass-roots initiatives, while others are government-sponsored, and still others combine both characteristics.

The problems and potentials of some of these associations are discussed both here and in Chapter 11, which focuses primarily on the officially-sponsored development efforts.

Women in many of the urban occupations described in Chapter 3, particularly the self-employed, have formed occupational associations to protect their interests; perhaps most famous are the market women's groups in West Africa, which have also played important political roles as outlined in Chapter 9. A variety of urban business enterprizes have been undertaken by groups of women who pooled their meager capital resources. In West Africa such groups have a longer tradition and are based on kinship as well as other social ties; in East Africa they are a newer and more fragile phenomenon.

The portrayal of women in religion, ideology, and the arts, as well as women's own expressions in these spheres, are the concerns of Chapters 6, 7, and 8. In Chapter 6, Margaret Strobel gives a full and incisive account of women's roles in African traditional religions, in Christianity and in Islam, and of the gender ideology expressed through those religions. She notes that the traditional female rites of passage, so prevalent throughout Africa, transmit the ideology of female inferiority to the initiates and socialize them to their proper roles as wives, while at the same time giving them a sense of value and the importance of womanhood. The rites often express or mediate the contradiction between autonomy and submission inherent in women's roles. The widespread participation of women as ritual specialists, spirit mediums, and members of spirit possession cults in traditional Africa is related to the struggle to compensate for inferior status, as well as to the real physiological problems encountered by women. Such roles illustrate another avenue through which some women could acquire influence and wealth in traditional societies.

The advent of Christianity, with its own version of the proper spheres for men and women, initiated conflicts between African beliefs and imported ones; many conflicts revolved around women's roles. Christianity condemned such practices as polygyny and clitoridectomy; many African separatist churches defended them as critical aspects of tradition. Islam, too, brought its own tenets regarding women, including specific legal rights for women in marriage and divorce, 'purdah' or the seclusion of women, and the exclusion of women from formal religious office. It mingled perhaps more successfully than did Christianity with indigenous cultures, but not without many internal tensions.

Contemporary secular ideology about women exhibits a great deal of ambivalence. Negative images of 'town women' are often invoked by male opinion leaders, who appeal to African tradition to support their views. In contrast, there is the positive advocacy of women's liberation by political leaders in such countries as Guinea-Bissau and Mozambique. The negative viewpoints recounted in Chapter 6 form an important counterpoint to the progressive ideologies chronicled in Chapter 10 on national liberation movements.

A special feature of this text is the inclusion of chapters on women and the arts, areas which are too often omitted from discussions of social change. The plastic and verbal arts both express and illustrate many of the themes which emerge from the other chapters. Narratives, songs, and praise poems reveal much about social life, and women are as important as creators and practitioners of these arts as they are as subjects. In Chapter 7 Deirdre LaPin contrasts the 'sweetness' of traditional women's narratives with the 'sharper edge' to be found in contemporary writings by women. In Chapter 8 Lisa Aronson notes the separateness yet complementarity of women's and men's arts, a reflection of the complex interrelationship of men's and women's work. Similarly, the domestic orientation of many women's arts reflects the large proportion of labor time spent in domestic activities. Nonetheless, some women's arts, such as pottery and weaving, can be highly professionalized and have considerable religious significance and economic worth in the 'public' domain. Groups of potters and weavers protect their craft skills and marketing channels, much as do the other sorts of women's occupational associations discussed in Chapter 5. As might be expected, changes in marketing opportunities can promote changes in women's arts.

The last three chapters concern women as political actors and as objects of public policy. Chapter 9, by Jean O'Barr, returns to the question of women's power raised in Chapter 1, looking at it in the pre-colonial, colonial, nationalist, and post-colonial contexts. Noting that power is an aspect of all areas of social life, she reminds us that it is particularly difficult to separate the 'political' from the economic and the religious in pre-colonial African societies. She argues that African women's power was often indirect, encompassing such strategies as withdrawal, evocation of the supernatural, and manipulation through men. In addition, however, in some societies women had substantial amounts of direct power, selecting leaders in women's spheres, holding public office, acting as members of women's pressure groups or as individuals wielding resources for desired ends.

Several striking instances can be found of the use of women's traditional powers and associations as vehicles for protest during the colonial era; here the discussion in Chapter 9 builds upon that in Chapter 5 on associations. The predominant theme for the colonial era, however, is women's loss of power and status, paralleling the setbacks in the economic sphere. Women in public office were ignored in the new colonial hierarchies; and customary rights like 'sitting on a man' among the Igbo were outlawed.

Women played critical roles in many of the anti-colonial nationalist movements. Chapter 9 analyzes differing styles of participation and varying outcomes in several types of nationalist movements: Nigeria, where the movement was early and relatively nonviolent and where market women were an important pressure group; Algeria, where a war was fought against an entrenched settler regime and where women participated in the conflict but were not rewarded afterwards; Guinea, where the movement adopted a more socialist ideology and where women were rewarded for their participation with substantial gains; and South Africa, where the struggle has been long and success is not yet in sight.

These cases show both parallels and contrasts to women's roles in the contemporary armed liberation struggles in Mozambique, Guinea-Bissau, and Angola, as described in Chapter 10. For these cases, and to a lesser extent for Zimbabwe and Namibia, Stephanie Urdang discusses the movements' ideological commitment to the liberation of women, their strong emphasis on the political mobilization of women, and women's important roles in the armed resistance. In some cases these factors have led to important roles for women in the post-independence governments, but in most cases it is still too soon to tell whether women will retain their power and how the proposed changes in production will affect women.

In most African countries today, African women lack political power. Chapter 9 points out that as the locus of power has shifted from village and lineage to the centralized nation-state, politics have become even further removed from the arenas in which women have had influence. Less than two or three percent of the top leadership in African countries is female. One political forum for African women's issues is the national women's association or the women's branch of the national political party. The strengths and limitations of these organizations in articulating women's interests are discussed in Chapters 9 and 5 .

Despite women's lack of power, public policy continues to have an enormous impact on women's status. Two factors have led to increasing concern among policy-makers with women's issues: the crisis in African food production and the pressure of the international feminist movement. Yet policies designed to increase food production may affect women farmers either positively or negatively, depending on how control of production and the rewards of labor are divided between men and women. In discussing this problem, Chapter 11 returns to the theme of the sex division of labor in agriculture elaborated in Chapters 1 and 2.

In Chapter 11 Barbara Lewis summarizes the impact on women of land tenure changes, settlement schemes, extension services, disaster relief, and technological innovations. Technological change is a particularly complex subject and deserves to be better understood. Lewis points out that innovations such as cooperatively owned corn mills have in some cases lightened women's labor, yet in other cases machine-powered mills and presses have threatened to displace women's vital cottage industries and create unemployment, since women have neither the capital to own the new mills nor access to alternative jobs. Finally, Chapter 11 compares three current development projects: one which has worked to the disadvantage of women and two which promise, despite obstacles, to benefit them. The factors which lie behind the differing outcomes are analyzed. The book concludes with the hope that African planners and international aid donors will make more extensive efforts to design projects which will bring genuine benefits to Africa's women.

Notes

1   The major source for this was is Meillassoux (1981).
2   For a full discussion of this issue and a review of recent literature in the field, see Strobel (1982).
3   This division of men's and women's roles was first proposed as universal by Michelle Rosaldo, 'Woman, Culture and Society: A Theoretical Overview', in Rosaldo and Lamphere (1974).

PART ONE
African women in the economy

1 Women in the rural economy: past, present, and future

Jeanne K. Henn

The great majority of African women are farmers. Most days they must work in the fields from four to eight hours, aided only by a simple hoe, in order to provide their families' basic food. They must also work a second labor day fetching firewood and water, and drying, shelling, storing and cooking the food from their gardens, all the while caring for their children.

The rural woman's labor day has changed little since the pre-colonial era, except that today it is longer and therefore harder. The social constraints which shaped a woman's economic and domestic work in the pre-colonial period still hold, although modified by the colonial integration of African rural economies into international economic systems. This chapter examines the impact of pre-colonial socio-economic structures and of colonial changes on today's rural African women and on the work they do.

Readers should be aware that research into pre-colonial traditions is a hazardous exercise. Social systems and cultural practices were obviously changing throughout the period due to internal contradictions, the interpenetration of different societies, and a millenium of long distance trade with the outside world. Source materials on African societies in the pre-colonial era are both scarce and problematic. Written records of eighteenth and nineteenth century observers are mainly reports of outsiders such as travelers and European anthropologists. There are more studies from the colonial period which are often informative but also limited by the biases of the colonial mentality, especially racism and sexism. Finally there are more recent studies by both foreign and African scholars based on oral history and interviews with old people who can recall various traditions from the early twentieth century. All these sources have their limitations, as informants sometimes attempt to reinterpret 'tradition' to support their own positions in social struggles, such as those between men and women.

Pre-colonial period

Economic systems

Food farming in pre-colonial Africa was almost everywhere a system of shifting hoe culture. A new field of one to two acres was cleared in forest or bush land once or twice a year. After two or three crops had been produced, the field was abandoned or left to fallow for 15 to 20 years. This type of farming system required either low population density and plenty of virgin land or the periodic migration of the community to new areas when the land was exhausted. The perpetual need for new farm land and also the episodic dangers posed to small stateless societies by expanding or slaving states made migration a perennial feature of most people's lives.

Men's role in extensive hoe agriculture was commonly limited to the heavy land-clearing phase, but they also played a military role in defending and acquiring land—a relatively frequent requirement with shifting agriculture. Women usually carried out all the major farming tasks— breaking up the soil, planting, weeding, harvesting, and carrying the harvest home—with little or no male help. African shifting agriculture is commonly referred to as a woman's farming system (Boserup, 1970).

In contrast, a small number of African societies practiced an intensive form of hoe agriculture, fertilizing their land or fallowing for very short periods. Intensive agriculture was found in mountainous areas where volcanic soils had high natural fertility, and in areas where invaders or aggressive neighbors had pushed smaller groups into limited landspaces. Due to the use of organic fertilizers, the terracing of slopes, the maintenance of water control systems, and systems of crop rotation involving close planting and more careful weeding, intensive farming systems usually demanded more labor than women could supply alone. Thus combined male and female food farming (usually with a sexual division of specific tasks) was more common among intensive than among extensive farmers.

Farming systems in which men performed the bulk of the work with little or no female help were rare in pre-colonial Africa. Male hoe farming was found in the savannah region which forms the southern border of the Saraha desert, for example among the Senufo described in Chapter 2, and among the Yoruba peoples of southwestern Nigeria and Benin (Dahomey). In some of these cases, Islamic women lived in household seclusion (purdah), while in the Yoruba case they worked in food processing, trade, and handicrafts. Oxen-plow cultivation was even more rare in the pre-colonial period, but where it existed, for example in Ethiopia and in a few cases in southern Africa, men sometimes took over most of the agricultural labor.

We can get an impression of the relative importance of women's, men's, and mixed sex farming systems from Map 1, originally published by Hermann Baumann in 1928. Baumann studied the sexual division of labor in 140 African societies described in anthropological studies and travelers' reports from the pre-colonial and early colonial periods. He found that women did all the field work, except clearing, in 40 percent of the cases, men did most of the work in 15 percent, while mixed sex farming systems prevailed in 45 percent (Baumann, 1928: 308-16). Women's farming systems dominated in tropical rain forests such as the Congo basin and were also common in Central, Eastern, and Southeastern Africa.

2

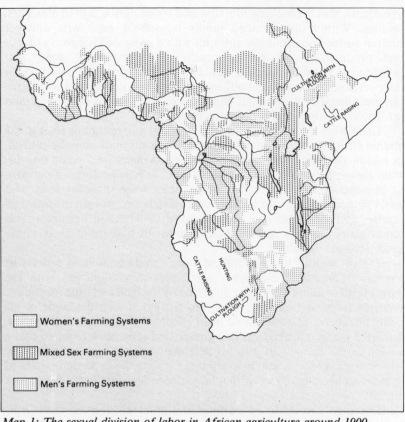

Map 1: The sexual division of labor in African agriculture around 1900
Source: *Hermann Baumann, 'The Division of Work according to Sex in African Hoe Culture',* Africa, *1, 1928, 293.*

Agriculture was combined with cattlekeeping in many societies of east and southern Africa. Women usually took the entire responsibility for food farming while men herded the cattle and cleared the land. In strictly pastoral and nomadic societies such as the Masai of East Africa and the Fulani of the West African savannah, men herded and women milked the cows and produced butter. In hunting and gathering societies such as those of the forest dwelling Pygmy peoples and among the San peoples of the Kalahari Desert, men hunted and women supplied the regular diet of roots, berries and fruit.

The household and the state

African political systems ranged in structure from small stateless communities to vast hierarchial empires. There was, however, an element of continuity: all were based on the extended family as the funamental socio-economic unit. The polygamous household, headed by one man with several wives and unmarried male dependents or, alternatively, composed of a group of married brothers and sons with their wives and

3

dependents, was the basic production and consumption unit in almost all societies. Within the extended family household, each wife and her children formed an economic sub-unit with a separate kitchen, fields for food production, and perhaps cattle. Each extended family was embedded in a socio-political structure characterized by networks of wider economic and political obligations based on kinship ties. Nonetheless, most households were self-sufficient economic units producing their own food, housing, and other necessities.

There were three basic categories of social and economic roles in the internal structure of the household: the top position of household head, the middle position of temporarily dependents males who would one day attain the position of household head, and the base position of permanent dependents. The permanent dependents were those persons who would never become heads of their own households: women in almost all societies and men who had been enslaved or who had become clients (economic or military servants) of a powerful household head whose protection they sought.

The division of labor in the extended family household reflects its structure. The household head, sometimes in conjunction with the lineage head or clan chief,[1] controlled the use of land and other economic resources (such as tools or cattle). He also controlled the labor of his family members. The household head allocated food fields to his wives, instructed them to feed clients and guests, and sometimes required that a portion of the harvest go into his personal granary. He distributed the field clearing, herding, and military tasks among the dependent males of the household. A patriarch with a large dependent family did little work himself.

The 'men's work' in agricultural and pastoral societies (land clearing, house-building, herding, and military tasks) was usually performed entirely by the dependent males of the household—the sons, younger brothers, nephews, clients, and slaves of the family head. 'Women's work' included food production, storage, and preparation, the manufacture of pottery, baskets, mats, clothing and other household goods, care of children and the sick, and a wide range of domestic and personal services for children and for men, especially for their husbands. This traditional sexual division of labor in the family has been reproduced in ideology and in practice for centuries. One of its most important legacies is the contemporary expectation that African women must feed their families, either by growing the food themselves or by earning the money necessary to buy it. Since most African women have enormous difficulties developing a sufficiently large cash income to purchase their daily food, either in town or in the countryside, the great majority are forced to spend the bulk of their labour time in subsistence food production.

During the pre-colonial era, women played important roles in the social and political reproduction of households and kin groups. When women were exchanged as wives, they provided their fathers and husbands with social, economic, and military links to other lineages and clans. The alliances created by marriage ties were important to the political prestige and the military strength of households and their heads. As Gayle Rubin points out, however, it was men who became the partners in these relationships, while women were but the means by which they were created (Rubin, 1975: 174).

As wives and mothers, women also provided their husbands with the most valuable category of dependent—children. A large progeny was the key determinant of a man's social prestige, political power, and economic prosperity.

In most African societies, the key measure of a man's wealth was the number of dependents in his household (Meillassoux, 1964; Laburthe-Tolra, 1977: 154). The association of wealth with persons rather than with material goods is explained by the conditions of production. Unlike many other world areas, labor—not land—was the scarce factor of production in Africa. A man's ability to expand his control over land and his production of food and livestock depended crucially on the number of dependent men in his household and on the number of women farmers whose agricultural and domestic labor he could mobilize.

With control over people as the key to political power and economic accumulation, control over marriage was a vigorously defended patriarchal privilege. Until he was married, a young man remained a dependent who owed total obedience and economic service to his household head and patriarch (O'Laughlin, 1974: 313). No man could arrange his first marriage on his own, he had to wait for his father to 'give' him a wife. Marriage was the beginning of a man's social and economic emancipation. Once married, he could control the labor and output of his wife and eventually exchange his daughters in marriage for new wives. Marriage allowed men to accumulate dependents and social status; for women, marriage marked the transfer of dependence from father to husband.

Stateless and state societies

Many pre-colonial African societies had no permanent political structures above the household level. Socio-political linkages were formed on the basis of kinship, but positions of leadership or political power were rarely vested in a single person or group. In most stateless societies the ideology of equality among all household heads was widely respected. While differences in wealth and prestige inevitably emerged as heads of households and lineages strove to become 'first among equals', the basic rules of political and social organization were designed to diffuse political power. Decisions on important social and military matters requiring inter-household cooperation were made in a council of elders which grouped all the household heads concerned with the matter at hand. Because women were rarely heads of households, they took no part in the society's primary political structures, although women often formed similar, but less powerful, social and ideological organizations.[2]

The line between stateless and state societies in pre-colonial Africa cannot be clearly drawn. We find societies sometimes described as stateless in which the principle of equality among household heads was routinely violated and particular lineages gained political and military dominance. When lineage or clan chiefs were exacting both military allegiance and economic tribute from subordinate households and lineages, it no longer seems appropriate to call their societies stateless.

State societies in pre-colonial Africa ranged from hierarchical lineage systems to complex empires grouping several different societies under a single political center. Expanding states integrated subjugated peoples into a unitary polity in several ways: tribute systems in which ivory, slaves, and women had to be given to the king or ruling group; feudalistic labor service systems in which conquered peoples worked for the ruling family or for all members of the dominant ethnic group; and systems of direct slavery. In any state society there was a clear economic differentiation among households: the vast majority of families provided an economic surplus which was expropriated by the dominant strata.

The study of women's economic roles is more complex in state societies because household relations intersect with the social class and tribute relations of the wider society. An excellent example of the dual effect of patriarchal and feudal relations is provided in Ethel Albert's fascinating discussion of women's roles in the kingdom of Burundi (Albert, 1971). Here the conquering Tutsi king distributed land and cattle among his male kin. The king's relatives (called nobles) had the right to demand tribute and labor service from Tutsi and Hutu commoners. The pastoralist Tutsi looked after the cattle of the king and the nobility, while the agricultural Hutu worked the farms of the Tutsi as serfs.

Women's economic roles varied significantly with the class position of their husbands. The 'noble' Tutsi wife merely supervised the agricultural labor of male Hutu serfs. The 'commoner' Tutsi wife had to clean the cattle kraal, churn butter, and do a great deal of farming herself. The Hutu wife, her husband being continually away farming for the Tutsi, was left alone to provide all the food required for the survival of her family.

The feudal relations of the Burundi kingdom originated in the pre-colonial period, but they remain to oppress the lower class to this day. Albert remarks, 'most of the women of Burundi . . . must work to the limit of their strength so that they will not die of hunger. This is because most Rundi are of the inferior castes where men and women share the wretchedness of the poor' (Albert, 1971: 181). Like his wife, a Hutu man is exploited and impoverished. He is, nonetheless, a patriarch in his own family where his wife must 'kneel before him when she offers him his gourd of beer' (Albert, 1971: 187).

Slavery

Slave relations existed in both stateless and state societies. In most cases slaves were integrated into the household social structure. Female slaves were often designated as wives of the household head who claimed all their children as his own. To become the wife of the patriarch did not necessarily give a female slave any greater security than a male slave— both could be given as payment on a debt (this was often true of 'free' wives as well), and slaves of either sex were subject to serve as human sacrifices, especially at the funeral of an important master (Laburthe-Tolra, 1977: 1283-96).

In most African societies slavery was limited to a few slaves per household (MacCormack, 1977; Miers and Kopytoff, 1977). On the other hand, in some state societies such as the Muslim sultanates of the West African Sahel, the wealthiest families might own hundreds of slaves who were either settled in agricultural villages or integrated into the patriarch's household as concubines or servants (Fisher and Fisher, 1971).

The topic of slavery in Africa and its relation to the various inter-continental slave trades is the subject of a great deal of recent research.[3] Rather than try to review this literature, I will simply make three obser-vations which are particularly pertinent to the themes of this chapter. First, the Atlantic slave trade of the sixteenth to nineteenth centuries contributed to the growth of highly centralized and militarized African states against whose slave raids the traditionally stateless societies had little protection except distance and rugged terrain. Second, in the slaving societies which practiced slavery themselves, the majority of retained slaves were women, due to higher prices paid for males by the Atlantic slave traders, the fear that male slaves could be hard to control in great numbers, and the fact that the traditional economic roles of women and children made them highly useful in African agriculture and as household servants (Meillassoux, 1981; Manning, 1981). Third, some of the 'male farming systems' described earlier, such as the Hausa of the West African Sahel, made extensive use of both male and female slave labor in agriculture.

Kinship systems

A person's position in the family largely determined his or her economic role. This section will discuss the impact of kinship relations on work and economic position by examining the differences between patrilineal and matrilineal societies.

The majority of agricultural societies and all pastoral societies in nineteenth-century Africa were patrilineal, that is, societies in which the most important kinship relations are traced through the male line. At marriage a bride moved to her husband's village where she was expected to remain for the rest of her life. A woman's marriage usually established or reinforced an alliance between the heads of her own and her new husband's lineage. Nevertheless, for a long period the bride was con-sidered a 'stranger' by her husband's kin (Paulme, 1971: 12). The stranger had to prove her fidelity to her husband's family by bearing several children for their lineage and by producing many good harvests.

In patrilineal societies a woman's economic security was more precarious than in matrilineal situations, because a wife farmed her husband's land and did not have firm land rights in her natal village. If the marriage was harmonious, all was well. But if the marriage was bad, a woman would not only lose her land rights if she fled from her husband, but she also risked losing those land rights for her children. Many women farmers still face this dilemma today.

When a man died in these patrilineal societies, his eldest son usually inherited his social position as household or lineage head. With his brothers, the heir also inherited land rights, cattle, material possessions, and, most important, the female and slave dependents of the deceased father. Daughters inherited little or nothing from their fathers; wives never inherited from husbands. Widows and their unmarried daughters were themselves inherited by the deceased's heir. Thus, even after the death of her husband, a woman still belonged to the patrilineal family which had paid her bridewealth. She was part of a man's wealth, and society was organized to press her into accepting that role.

A widow had important incentives to accept her inheritor as her new husband. If she did so, she continued to enjoy the social acceptance and land rights her former marriage had provided. If she refused, she had to leave her husband's village, an option which put her sons in danger of losing their rights to the land she had farmed. Furthermore, if her children were beyond the age of seven, a departing widow could not take them with her; the children belonged to the father's lineage.

Matrilineality refers to the practice of tracing kinship allegiance and inheritance rights through the mother's family. In matrilineal societies, men inherited land and social positions from their maternal uncles rather than from their fathers. Maternal uncles also made the marriage arrangements for their sisters' children. But matrilineality didn't change the fundamental domestic principle of patriarchal rule. Men, rather than women, still controlled land, marriage, dependents, and politics. As in patrilineal societies, a woman was not consulted about the arrangement of her marriage, and marriage involved the same obligation to work in the husband's interest. When the husband inherited land, his wives were obliged to farm it for him, an obligation which often required abandoning their own fields in their maternal villages.

On the other hand there were several aspects of matrilineal customs which tended to improve women's economic and social security. First, a woman did not necessarily have to move away from her maternal village when she first married. If her husband had not yet inherited land from his maternal uncle, he would establish a household and farm in his wife's village. Second, if the marriage broke up, a divorced woman could reactivate land rights in her maternal village much more easily than divorced women from patrilineal societies (Hill, 1978: 221). Finally, if a woman divorced, her children remained with her because they 'belonged' to their maternal rather than to their paternal kin. One matrilineal society, the Senufo, is discussed in the next chapter.[4]

Pastoral societies

African pastoral societies were patrilineal and patrilocal. Five or six independent households usually grouped together in small villages which were moved twice yearly between wet and dry season pastures. Each household head, often the husband of several wives, was the social equal of the other household heads in his village. Each wife had her own one room house inside the village compound. In contrast to the prevailing practice in agricultural societies, in most pastoral groups women were the housebuilders whereas men built the thorn fences which surrounded the village and formed a protected kraal for the cattle at night (Dupire, 1971).

For men, economic and political rights were determined primarily through membership in clan-wide age groups. A young man normally passed from junior dependent status in his twenties and thirties to senior elder status in his forties and fifties. Younger men were the primary herders and warriors while the elders, upon whom the junior males were dependent, directed the herd movements, negotiated water rights with other groups, controlled raiding and military activities, and arranged marriages (Hedlund, 1979; Reisman, 1980; Jacobs, 1975).

As in agricultural societies, women were social and economic dependents first of fathers, then of husbands (Bryceson and Mbilinyi, 1980). Women's access to cattle, the primary means of subsistence, was based on the fulfillment of their obligations as wives and mothers. A woman had to use her 'marriage cattle' to feed her family. The milk and butter she produced were shared among a wide network of kin and friends because the socially regulated use and sharing of food were vital to the reinforcement of communal relations and territorial cooperation with respect to land and water rights. A woman's cattle could also be used to provide bridewealth for her sons. In fact a woman had no effective personal claim to 'her' cattle because she had to hold them in trust for her sons (Dupire, 1971: 86). On the other hand, Dupire suggests that pastoral women were considerably less restricted than most women in agricultural societies on matters concerning choice of residence and choice of sexual partners. Still, like their agricultural counterparts, today's pastoral women work harder and longer than their husbands or sons in order to complete the tasks which are considered the social obligations of their sex (Reisman, 1980).

Hunting and gathering societies

While most agricultural societies engaged in hunting and gathering, only a very small number of African peoples, principally the Pygmies of the dense tropical forests and the San peoples of the Kalahari Desert (often called Bushmen), relied on hunting and gathering for their entire subsistence. Because these groups depended entirely on finding food supplied by nature, communities were small and highly mobile. Current research among the !Kung San of the Kalahari found groups averaging 35 people (Draper, 1975). Both men and women range far from the camps when seeking food. The camps themselves are moved at intervals of several days to several weeks.

In the pre-colonial period and even to this day, hunting and gathering societies had no apparent hierarchical domestic structure or patriarchal rule within extended family relationships. Marriage tended to be relatively impermanent. Wives could leave husbands or even the community itself with little difficulty, taking their children and simply joining another group. It was generally accepted that children 'belonged' to their mothers although neither boys nor girls were controlled in their economic and social behavior by parents in a manner comparable to patriarchal control over dependents in patrilineal and matrilineal societies. It is important to note, however, that !Kung women's rights in children apparently diminish when hunting and gathering groups begin to settle in villages (Draper, 1975: 108).

The egalitarian relationships among men, women, and youth in hunting and gathering societies contrasts strikingly with the subordinate position of women in other African societies. Kjaerby (1979) attributes this to the fact that the labor of women and youth was not mobilized by men to produce a surplus product. It is also significant that people's total dependence on nature's products for food made it largely impossible to form large, stable communities. The possibilities for reproducing a strong patriarchal hierarchy were thereby reduced. Still, more research is needed if we are to understand how women in hunting and gathering societies escaped the economic and personal subordination which was so common in other African societies.

Colonial period

The process of linking African rural economies with non-African markets began long before the colonial era. Africans exported gold, ivory and slaves from the early Middle Ages, but prior to the colonial period, European and Arab merchants were largely confined to the coasts while the interior circuits of Africa's long distance trade were controlled by African patriarchs and state rulers.

During the nineteenth century increasing trade in natural rubber, palm oil and other industrial raw materials heightened the interest of European capitalists in Africa as a source of cheap industrial and consumer goods. Soon factory owners joined merchants in calling for colonial conquest, and by the late 1880s Britain, France, Germany Portugal, and Belgium had established claims to nearly all of Africa.

Colonial conquest fundamentally changed the pre-colonial economies. Under colonial rule African societies were forced to produce the agricultural raw materials Europeans wanted: peanuts, cocoa, palm kernels, cotton, and coffee. For most part, the new crops were grown by women and dependent males in traditional villages. In some areas, particularly in Central, East and southern Africa, large-scale European plantations were established. A labor force was created by pulling traditionally dependent men out of the villages and setting them to work in the foreigners' trading houses and plantations. To impose such sweeping economic changes, the colonists first had to break the widespread military resistance to foreign rule. After two decades of warfare, the colonists consolidated their political dominance over traditional state rules and lineage heads.

The contradictory effects of colonial changes on women

The process of conflict and accommodation involved in the colonial restructuring of traditional economies had a significant impact on women's economic activities and social options. On this all scholars agree. Nevertheless, to categorize the effects of colonialism on African women is to enter an unsettled debate.[5] Some scholars (Boserup, 1970; Van Allen, 1974) suggest that the combination of capitalist exploitation and European ideas about appropriate economic and domestic roles for women all but destroyed the economic independence and traditional form of social authority exercised by African women in the pre-colonial era. Others (Huntington, 1975; de Thé, 1970) question the idea that women had significant independence in the pre-colonial era. They point out that in many societies colonial intervention gradually weakened traditional patriarchal control over women, lessened the possibility of torture, slavery or death as punishment for female rebellion, and for the first time made divorce available to women who were attempting to escape an intolerable personal or social situation.

During a recent discussion on the question, 'which life was better for women, that of the past or that of today', Cameroonian women emphasized the importance of today's greater personal security:

(Marguerite-Marie) In the past women were terribly mistreated, especially widows. Some were killed and others severely beaten. They were subjected to very painful insect bites. Really, one cannot see that it was better in the past for women.

(Micheline) There was no means to unite among women. And if you ran away, they caught you and beat you.

(Vincent, 1976; 74-5)

Still, evidence from other societies shows that not all women were without defense against such harsh treatment (Obbo, 1976). Igbo women, for example, developed effective women's self-help and mutual protection associations during the pre-colonial era which could carry out public ridicule and even group punishment of men who seriously mistreated women. These associations are described in Chapters 5 and 9.

Generalizing across societies is still very difficult, a situation which indicates the need for more research on the relationship between women's socio-political status and their economic roles both in the past and in the present. On one issue, however, all researchers agree: during the colonial period, African women's workload increased, in many cases significantly.

The colonial extraction of economic surpluses from the African rural population (via high taxes, forced production of export crops, food levies on the villages, and removal of young men to work on European plantations or as forced labor on state railways and mines) was the basic force behind women's rising labor burdens. Colonial economic policies fundamentally changed the context in which African household and kinship relations functioned. The traditional powers of patriarchs and chiefs were reconstituted, as colonial states attempted to strengthen the power of those household heads and chiefs who could 'produce' what the colonial powers wanted: export crops, taxes, laborers. At the same time, by acquiescing to colonial demands, African leaders lost traditional legitimacy. At the household level, the great majority of patriarchs were economically and politically weakened under the weight of colonial tax and forced labor policies.

The result was a gradual breakdown of the socio-economic linkages tying traditional male dependents to patriarchal households and linking smaller households into larger economic units. As sons were drawn away from the villages, as household slaves were freed, and as most village headmen lost ritual and traditional punitive powers, extended family households began to break up into man-wife-children units. As a result of these changes, traditional cooperative relations in farming activities also broke down: women lost younger male help, and everyone's labor time was diverted from food and craft labor to work on colonial crops.

On the other hand, colonially favored headmen and chiefs reconstructed past social hierarchies in the changed context. Many of the chiefs and village headmen approved by the colonial state were given extensive powers of tax collection as well as unofficial but virtually unchecked authority to mobilize less favored villagers to do unpaid work on their private farms. At the other end of the social hierarchy, pre-colonial clients and slaves continued to be denied access to sufficient land, and they therefore tended to become the poorest peasants, the forced laborers, and, in a few areas, the landless rural proletariat of the colonial era.

As property rights became individualized under the influence of colonial legal changes and the planting of tree crops, African men who had been powerful in the pre-colonial era were able to accumulate much of the best land. Women's access to land for subsistence farming and especially for market farming was highly circumscribed: women faced the encroachment of private male claims to land they had traditionally used for food farming or gathering, but they were barred by tradition rather than by colonial law from becoming landowners.

Colonial policy was contradictory in the matter of women's personal rights. At times European missionaries and colonial administrators intervened against what they considered excessive oppression, for example the killing of widows, the use of women and children as collateral on a debt, or child marriage. On the other hand, colonial authorities recognized the role of patriarchal power in mobilizing the labor of women and youths. When conflicts arose between the need to keep women working both on food farms and on export crops and the desire of the state or church to protect women from excessive oppression, the basic economic logic of colonialism prevailed: patriarchal power over women was upheld in the interests of colonial profits. In the end, contradictory colonial interventions produced no fundamental change in women's status as social and economic dependents of their fathers and husbands.

To state that women were economic dependents is not to say that they were incapable of supporting themselves and their children. On the contrary, nearly every investigation of African women's farming and craft activities shows that they were always physically and intellectually capable of economic independence. But this evident capacity was repressed by traditional and colonial practices of land and crop control, ideological restrictions on rights to mobilize 'family labor', which gave such powers primarily to patriarchs, and customs defining women as dependents. Such socially constructed and socially reproduced constraints on a woman's ability to make economic choices and investments remain a fundamental frustration to millions of African women today (Remy, 1975: 370).

Against this general background, let us look more closely at two major forms of colonial economic change which had lasting effects on rural women and their work: the production of export crops and the development of rural and urban capitalist enterprises requiring wage labor.

African production of export crops

At the beginning of the colonial period and again during the great depression of the 1930s, there was little reason for self-sufficient African households to produce export crops because European merchants offered so little in return. To break down the widespread resistance to the growing of export crops, colonial governments required African households to pay heavy taxes in colonial money. In many areas, this cash could only be earned by producing colonially specified crops and by selling them at official prices. During the 1920s and again in the 1950s, prices for African produced crops improved, and this induced many household heads voluntarily to divert increasing amounts of family labor to colonial crops even though some types of subsistence foods and crafts had to be neglected or abandoned. African villagers thus became increasingly dependent on cash to purchase European cloth, hoes, salt, soap and cooking pots, goods they continued to need in some measure even when price relations turned drastically against them as they did during the 1930s and 1940s.

The transformation of the African household from a self-sufficient production/consumption unit into a peasant farming or pastoral unit which was obliged to produce some crop or other commodity demanded in world markets represented a profound alteration to the traditional African rural economy. A form of international capitalist dominance over the rural household was established in the colonial era which has not been lifted to this day. Colonial interventions had far-reaching effects on the labor time of both men and women and on the social relations of production between them.

The production of export crops altered the sexual division of labor and significantly increased the total labor time of all members of the rural household. The increased workload fell hardest on women. Men commonly withdrew from food production tasks to concentrate on export crops; women not only took up the slack in food production but also helped with the new colonial crops (Bukh, 1979; Stichter, 1976). This process is described for the Ewe of Ghana in the next chapter. Among the Beti peoples of southern Cameroon, for example, during the depression year of 1934 when cash crop prices were extremely low and taxes high, women had to work over 70 hours a week as compared to an average of 46 hours in the pre-colonial period. The corresponding labor time for men in 1934 was 25 hours a week for household heads and 55 hours (or twice their pre-colonial average) for the dependent males of the household (Henn, 1978: 80, 140).

Heads of households, although obliged to meet various colonial demands, still retained their general control over family farming operations. In the Ivory Coast, for example, when cotton, which in the pre-colonial era had been grown by women to meet family clothing needs, became a cash crop, heads of households began to require that the portion of the crop which would be sold must be grown on their personal fields, a practice which established the head of household's ownership of the product (Etienne, 1980).

As cash transactions became widespread during the colonial period, household heads attempted to maintain their tight control over family cash resources in an effort to minimize the economic independence of their male and female dependents. Young men often managed to escape patriarchal dominance by seeking wage work outside the village, but fathers could still prevent them from growing cash crops on their own (Laburthe-Tolra, 1977: 880). Patriarchs were even more anxious to prevent their wives from earning cash incomes, fearing that a woman might try to initiate a divorce by repaying her own bridewealth (Kaberry, 1952: 146). The colonialists recognized the danger to export crop production should senior men lose control over dependents or so-called 'family labor'. Hence, colonial land regulations, tax and inheritance laws, crop marketing systems, and even agricultural extension practices all facilitated the control of the household head over the cash resources generated by peasant family labor (Conti, 1979). With men firmly in control of land and cash, women were hard put to challenge the new patterns of labor and income distribution which so drastically increased their working days while often seriously diminishing their welfare.

African wage labor in colonial enterprises

The most important and universal characteristic of African jobs in colonial factories, mines, and plantations was their extremely low wages. African earnings were rarely adequate to allow the worker to sustain himself, much less a wife and children. Wages had to be supplemented with food and other goods and services from the peasant household (Hay, 1976: 87; Guyer, 1978). It was the unpaid labor of rural women which subsidized the colonial wage.

Because inadequate wage levels were exacerbated in many cases by harsh working conditions (whippings, long hours, dangerous environments), Africans often resisted work on state construction projects and European plantations. In cases of serious 'labor shortage' the state was quick to resort to force, sometimes kidnapping villagers into forced labor but more often simply presenting the village or territorial chief with the required number of laborers to be 'recruited' (Manga Mado, 1970). Forced labor was used by the colonial state right through the Second World War, first to provide men and women to serve as head carriers (porters) to provide transport of goods for state officials and merchants, then to build roads, railroads, administrative centers and state enterprises such as factories and mines. Forced laborers were also made available to private European enterprises (Nzula and others, 1979).

It was primarily dependent males who were sent by their household heads or chiefs when the colonialists requisitioned forced laborers. Their mothers and wives were then required to produce their food and carry it by headloads to the state construction sites (Guyer, 1978: 580). Women were also obliged to feed the huge gangs of porters who regularly passed through the villages and to supply food to colonial administrative centers.

In addition to its mobilization of forced labor, the colonial state helped private European agricultural and mining enterprises recruit wage laborers in what came to be known as the migrant labor system. African men would enter contracts for six months to two years to work for wages which barely kept them alive and then provided a small bonus if the contract was completed. A migrant laborer often worked hundreds of miles from his home hoping that at the end of his contract the bonus would be sufficient to pay his bridewealth and start him on the road to economic independence in his own village. Unfortunately, in many areas —southern and eastern Africa in particular—a single labor contact was usually neither sufficient to complete the bridewealth nor to meet the cash needs of a rural homestead. Married men were therefore forced to leave their households many times over in search of wage work, especially in those areas where the colonial states attempted to insure large supplies of wage labor by prohibiting or discouraging the growing of cash crops.

Wives of migrant laborers were left to care for the children, the cattle, and the farm with little or no male help. But even though they had to manage the household economy on their own, wives rarely had the authority to make decisions regarding sales, loans, or gifts of economic resources traditionally controlled by men (C. Murray, 1977). Jean Hay (1976) has described a case in which Luo women nonetheless managed to cope fairly well with male absence by adopting new trading strategies and new agricultural techniques, but the more common result of the continual absence of a high percentage of working age males was a gradual and significant deterioration of rural family welfare (Brown, 1980). Indeed, the extremely impoverished female headed households of South Africa, Botswana, Lesotho, Swaziland, Zambia and Mozambique are the contemporary result of more than a century of South African capitalist 'growth' based on migrant labor (Cliffe and Moorsom, 1979; C. Murray, 1979; Sibisi, 1977). The situation in Botswana and the Transkei is described in the next chapter.

Wage jobs open to women were rare in the colonial period. European plantations sometimes employed women on a seasonal basis, especially for crop processing such as shelling or bagging, but these jobs were normally limited to women living in the immediate vicinity (Bryceson, 1980). In some areas a wealthy class of export crop producing peasants emerged and provided seasonal 'wage work' for women, but more often than not this work brought only a small payment in food or landclearing services, or the promise of a gift when the harvest was sold (Cliffe, 1976: 119; De Thé, 1970). In all cases a woman's return for wage work was considerably lower than the meagre amounts paid to men (Elkan, 1957).

The gradual development of urban labor markets during the colonial period provided very limited economic opportunities for women (see Chapter 3, below). Urban wage jobs were almost entirely restricted to men, especially in government and industrial enterprises. A rural woman who accompanied her husband to town could attempt to fulfill her traditional obligation to feed the children by trading food, brewing beer, or producing cooked food to be sold on the roadsides, but a woman's earnings from these so-called informal economic activities, even when combined with a man's wages, were nearly always too low to allow the family to survive in the city. Thus, the great majority of workers' wives remained in the villages where they could protect their husbands' land rights, feed their children, and provide a refuge for the workers in times of sickness, unemployment, or old age. Rural women's agricultural products and the extensive services they are traditionally required to provide for their families have become virtual subsidies for the extremely low wages paid to the semi-proletarianized African working class.

The past and the present

The past is still very evident in the contemporary working lives of African women. The relations of patriarchal dominance in the household economy combined with continuing practices of rural exploitation through low crop prices and high consumer goods prices constrain a woman's economic options and confine the great majority of rural women to a life of heavy labor and limited welfare. Recent evidence on the emerging food crisis in Africa (USDA, 1981) and on the alarming balance of payments and foreign debt situations in many African countries gives us little hope that rural women's lives are changing for the better. Women's economic problems are directly related to changes in their nation's and the world's economic systems, but they are also strongly rooted in the socioeconomic traditions of the pre-colonial era and the colonial policies discussed in this chapter. For a report of African women's own analysis of and struggle against this 'double exploitation', see Chapter 10 in this book (see also Urdang, 1979).

Change is needed on two fronts. The larger economic forces which act to privilege industrial and urban development over agricultural investment and rural modernization must be redressed. The rural areas are no longer capable of providing cheap labor and export crops to finance urban and industrial growth without serious attention to providing the kinds of investments and expertise which can raise agricultural productivity and rural living standards. This is the first front. But change here is not enough.

Women's specific problems of low productivity in food farming, lack of cash to invest in modern inputs, lack of time and money to provide adequate nutrition for their children, and, in most cases, extreme overwork are also related to long-standing traditions which operate at the household and village level. This is the second front. The problems here are more subtle, commonly ignored or denied by national and local male leaders, and perhaps even more difficult to deal with.

The patriarchal household remains a prominent feature of African rural economies. Husbands manage the family farm. Men keep the proceeds of export crops under their own control and expect that their wives' food crops and small cash earnings will be used to meet most of the family's daily consumption needs. Unfortunately, women's harvests and incomes are often inadequate to meet the heavy responsibilities thrust upon them. Furthermore, a woman's attempts to increase her earning capacity by engaging in independent economic activities is severely limited by lack of time (traditional subsistence and domestic obligations take up eight hours a day) and by customary prohibitions against a woman's right to own or control economic resources.

Although women's earnings are much smaller than men's everywhere, many men still attempt to control the use of their wives' cash in what seems to be a deeper struggle to retain control over female labor. For example, in the 1950s Phyllis Kaberry wrote that among the Bamenda peoples of West Cameroon 'women can keep small sums of money, but the question of rights to money becomes crucial when larger sums are at stake. Bamenda men insist on the husband's right to cash earning' (Kaberry, 1952: 146). In many places a husband can still forbid his wife to travel, trade, or work for wages. Even in socialist Tanzania the power of 'custom' can thwart a woman's attempt to gain economic independence. In the late 1970s, a man convinced the management committee of a village communal farm to turn over his estranged wife's annual earnings to him even though he himself had been living and working in another village with his second wife. The husband apparently wanted to control his polygamous household by having most of the food and clothing come from him; he returned a small portion of his wife's earnings to her to cover his own estimate of her food needs (May Matteru, personal communication).

Traditional practices such as the payment of bridewealth, predominantly male inheritance of land, and the belief that children 'belong to' their father's lineage in patrilineal societies all continue to limit the freedom of choice and the economic independence of African women. Although modern legal systems offer the formal possibility for the inheritance of land by widows or a woman's right to shared custody of her children in divorce, actual legal judgments commonly defer to the 'traditional customs of the area' which routinely deny a woman's right to land or parental custody. Ignorance, poverty, tradition and outright male opposition are formidable barriers to women's ability actually to obtain the legal rights they have on paper.

Contemporary state institutions, such as producers' cooperatives and export crop marketing agencies, reinforce patriarchal dominance over the labor and earnings of women. Often only heads of households are accepted as members of cooperatives. In this case most women do not receive the seeds, credit, agricultural advice, and crop payments which are dispensed through the cooperatives (Conti, 1979: 86). In Tanzania's newly formed cooperative (*ujamaa*) villages, a family's membership, land rights, and communal labor obligations and work points are usually all registered in the name of the head of the household (Storgaard, 1975-76; Brain, 1976). No married woman is recognized as a household head. If a woman divorces, she must battle for the right to be recognized as the head of a separate household with a right to land. The outcome of such a battle is still not predictable.

Contemporary development policies affecting women are discussed further in the last chapter. If future rural development programs, agricultural research, and village level investments are to benefit women and children equally with men, the delicate process of removing patriarchal constraints on women without demolishing their traditional family and community supports must go on. Women's economic problems are, in some ways, basically the same as men's—but they are, in many other ways, harder to solve simply because one of their root causes is thousands of years of male privilege.

Notes

1 Lineages are groupings of several extended families all directly related to a single ancestor three to five generations in the past; clans are similar groupings of lineages related to an ancestor further removed, where all the intervening steps in the genealogy may not be directly remembered.

2 For a contrasting opinion and counter-examples, see Hoffer (1972, 1974).

3 Recent publications on slavery and the slave trade of special interest for this discussion are Wright (1975), Manning (1981), Miers and Kopytoff (1977), Gemery and Hogendorn (1978), and Klein and Robertson (forthcoming).

4. Bukh (1979) provides a highly readable description of women's work and status in a patrilineal society. Discussions of women's position in matrilineal societies are found in Poewe (1978), Gessain (1971), and Brain (1978).

5. Mullings (1976) and Tiffany (1978) provide a review of this debate. For sympathetic critiques of Boserup's important work, see Huntington (1975) and Beneria and Sen (1981).

2 Women in the rural economy: contemporary variations

Jane I. Guyer

Two themes recur in analyses of women's positions in the rural areas of Africa: enterprise and autonomy on the one hand, and poverty and over-work on the other. In almost every region women have access to some kind of productive resource or a particular market which provides them with an income of their own. And yet almost everywhere that income seems limited and earning it absorbs time and effort which has to be inte-grated with housekeeping and child care. This situation is clearly not simply 'tradition'. Every rural economy has been affected in a more or less profound way by production for national and international markets, the migration of its people as wage workers to areas of high labor demand, or integration into regional market systems. And yet in many cases it is still versions of indigenous customary law which define the ac-cess of each sex to productive resources. In order to understand women's present position, one therefore must understand the way in which the demands of the wider economy and the possibilities and constraints of local systems interact.

During the past two decades a wealth of basic research has been done which documents the main components of women's economic lives: what, in any particular ethnic group, women are responsible for; what land rights they may hold; how they spend their time; what they do with their income; what they can expect from fathers, husbands, brothers, sons; and the whole range of ethnographic questions which illuminate how they make a living and contribute to the livelihood of others. In its detail each ethnography can be highly particular. The purpose of comparative work is to explore major themes which may lie behind the particularity and variability, in order to go beyond *what* is happening and suggest possibles reasons *why*.

The criterion used here to group cases for comparison will be the nature of the links between the local and the wider economic systems. During the last hundred years the commodity economy penetrated into African agriculture in three major ways: (1) through the growth of export crop production by small-holder farmers; (2) through expansion of employment outside the small-holder sector; and (3) through the more diffuse effects of the extension of trade. For most of the colonial period these modes of domination tended to be pursued in different geo-graphical regions. For example, in southern Ghana, Nigeria, and Senegal small-holder farmers expanded production to include crops for the export market, but wage employment was very little developed and in some cases was deliberately limited by the colonial governments, eager to maintain high levels of agricultural output. By contrast, the mines of South Africa and Northern Rhodesia (now Zambia), and the plantations of Kenya withdrew labor from the rural areas, whose own production for the market was constrained by a battery of discriminatory legislation.

Finally, throughout the colonial period there remained areas which were more remote or less strategically important, from which people and goods were occasionally requisitioned, on whom taxes were levied, but whose local economies were infiltrated rather than transformed. One might characterize the attachment of these communities to the world economy as (a) through commodity production for international trade; (b) through wage work for national industrial and agricultural enterprise; or (c) through regionally specific economic relationships.

This chapter is an ethnographic exploration of women's position in ethnic groups falling into each of these three broad categories. This initial division provides a useful starting place. However, one modification needs to be made at the outset, and that is to include historical change. Since the end of the colonial period African economies have become far more complex. Some of the colonial states which depended on export agriculture, Nigeria for example, have since developed substantial mineral resources, leaving agriculture far behind as a source of revenue for the government or income for the individual. In others, like Ghana, Senegal and Tanzania, small-holder agriculture remains the basic resource of the national economy but serious concern has developed on the part of the government about stagnant levels of production, and on the part of the farmers about low prices and high levels of government control. In yet others, like the Ivory Coast (on a large scale) and Cameroon (on a much smaller scale), plantation agriculture has been expanded with the partial aim of by-passing the smaller-holder sector. Some rural economies have continued to supply workers to other sectors but under changed conditions of demand because industry and mining now require a more highly skilled, permanent labor force. Others, as in parts of Kenya and Tanzania, have been converted into cash crop regions. In all cases there has been expansion of non-farm employment, particularly in the public sector, and with this has come a heightened appreciation of the importance of regional production and marketing systems, to supply the urban areas with food. As a result the constraints and possibilities for particular rural economies and the people working in them have become more complicated, and in many places local balances of manpower and resources have been seriously affected by political crises, price fluctuations, demographic pressures on the land, and natural disasters.

In this situation it is hardly realistic to cling to three stereotypic cases and compare them in a static framework. Instead, each selection will describe women's position in a particular case, trace its direction of change and then briefly compare and contrast this with others falling roughly into the same category as the sun set on imperial rule. Because of the element of change, a fourth case has been added to represent a very small, but possibly growing, area of female employment, namely full-time wage work in large-scale plantation agriculture.

Each case study will include a general description of what women do, and close attention to a set of particular issues: first, the sex ratio in the rural areas and the forces which determine it; second, the proportion of women who are managing the day-to-day requirements of their families single-handed; third, the kind and amount of resources women control relative to men; and finally, the value of their work by comparison with the value of men's work. Having described these local, or 'micro'-level questions, we now need to return to the broader 'macro' issue of how they fit into a wider economic system.

A final caution: with a few exceptions, agriculture is not a major growth sector of African economies. The people who work in it, both men and women, are generally aware that incomes and opportunities are better in other occupations. But agriculture still employs up to three fourths of the population. Some of the poverty and frustration which case studies describe is not, therefore, particular to women, although it is experienced by women in particular ways.

Case 1
A peripheral economy: the Senufo of the northern Ivory Coast
(*Source:* SEDES, 1965)

The Senufo people are known for their skillful farming and outstanding wood-carving. They grow a variety of staple food crops (yams, rice, maize, millet, and some cassava) in a complex and productive farming system. Maize and cassava are crops imported from the New World in the centuries before colonial rule and they have been successfully integrated with the indigenous staples. Export crops, however, were resisted and finally rejected. The French colonial government made great efforts to introduce cotton and groundnut (peanut) production, without long-term success. Senufo men were also recruited in forced labor for the privately owned plantations of the coastal region, and many young men still migrate in search of paid employment. A detailed study done in 1962 presents the picture of a population still primarily concerned with the provision of its own needs: two-thirds of the total value of goods consumed was provided directly from subsistence production (SEDES, 1965, **5**: 57), and only about one-third of total production was sold on the market (SEDES, 1965, **5**: 27). The sex breakdown of the population was 48 percent male and 52 percent female, indicating a limited amount of out-migration by men.

The Senufo live in large villages, in open savannah countryside. The farming system is still relatively intensive hoe agriculture, as described in Chapter 1, with fields being left to fallow one year out of three if possible. Both men and women farm, but the staple food crops are primarily managed by men. The villages are composed of several 'quarters', many of whose inhabitants trace their descent from a common ancestor in the female line. In the past the members of each quarter farmed collectively and the quarter chief administered the food supplies for the whole group. The farming unit today is the compound, a smaller group composed of a set of brothers, their sisters and/or wives and their children.

In the Senufo matrilineal kinship system, women retain the right to live in their natal compounds throughout their lives, and many of them do stay, even after marriage. If husband and wife come from the same village, they can keep up the obligations of marriage without living together in the same compound. The women who live in a compound therefore include wives who have moved in and sisters who have chosen not to move out. The compound members grow the main staple, millet, in a collective field, and every adult has his or her own personal plot to cultivate and a personal granary. Thus each woman has rights in land either through her natal kin or her husband's kin, and she has the right to be provided for from the collective plot.

In whichever compound they live, brother's or husband's, women take care of the children, cook the food, fetch wood for fuel and water for washing and cooking. Domestic work accounts for almost half of their total work time (SEDES, 1965, 3: 125) which is a very similar proportion to findings of time-allocation studies in many African rural societies. For Senufo women, water and fuel provision are particularly time-consuming because of the relatively dry climate and savannah vegetation.

The remainder of women's work time is divided between farming, associated tasks of porterage and storage, processing farm goods for sale, or marketing. One form of processing which gives women a regular income is brewing beer from millet, which they can sell either within the village or at a local market. All small-scale marketing is done by women, although any large transactions are handled by middlemen from a neighboring ethnic group, the Dioula. The goods which women sell in the market consist of produce from their individual farms or crops sold on behalf of their menfolk. Forty-one percent of women's work time is spent on the farm, and nine percent in processing and marketing.

How does this compare with men's work? First of all, men spend a greater proportion of their time in farming and related tasks (72 percent), which in absolute amounts of time, is about twice the time which women devote to agriculture. Their next most important time-consumer is house-building. By comparison with women they spend much more time on schooling, religion and rest. This last category accounts for 27 percent of men's days, and 17 percent of women's (SEDES, 1965, 3:, 125). Findings very similar to these emerge from studies of men's and women's work the world over because of women's primary responsibility for what is generally called 'domestic work'.

Many of men's and women's tasks are complementary and con-tribute to collective welfare, but there are some areas of separate responsibility. In the Senufo case, men and women are responsible for different crops in the farming system. The traditional staples, millet, yams and now maize also, are assigned to the men. Women help only with weeding, harvesting and transport of the crop from field to village. The women's personal fields are devoted mainly to rice and groundnuts. The important question then becomes: are rice and groundnuts mainly subsistence crops contributed to the compound for its food supply, or are women free to sell them? And how does this compare with the use to which men put their own crops?

The data are striking. Among the Senufo it is rice and groundnuts which are commercialized and men's crops which are devoted in the higher proportions to subsistence (SEDES, 1965, 5: 28, 38-9). Women also earn cash incomes by doing agricultural labor for others. The study does not tell us how men's and women's total cash incomes differ. Probably men still earn more because they sell livestock, wood carvings, and a small proportion of their farm products. What is important to note is the freedom of women to earn their own incomes, separate from the joint endeavors of their compound.

Their involvement in day wage work points up the final critical comparison to make between men's and women's economic positions: the value of their work. At the time of this study, the daily wage for men was 150 francs, for women it was 75 francs. Looking back at the value of the crops which men and women produce, a similar discrepancy is apparent. A day's work in yam, maize or millet cultivation is worth three times as much in the value of the final harvest as a day's work in rice or groundnut production (SEDES, 3,197) Women's activities are confined to products whose returns to labor are low.

Comment and comparison

In much of Equatorial and East Africa women supply far the greater labor input into agriculture. They are the mainstay of the subsistence food supply system, in contrast to the Senufo, where the men have a larger role. The Senufo system is particular, but it does show very clearly some of the potential strengths and weaknesses of women's position. Women have control of certain resources, and they have access to personal incomes, but the value of their labor time is lower. For the moment, compound organization and staple food farming by men protect women from having to support themselves completely from this disadvantageous position. In many cash-crop and labor-reserve areas the protection afforded by this kind of system has begun to break down without significant improvement in the terms on which women earn an income.

Case 2
An old cash-crop economy: The Ewe of southern Ghana

(*Source:* Bukh, 1979)

The old cocoa region of southern Ghana in the 1930s was one of the richest areas in West Africa. Vast cocoa groves provided incomes high enough to finance schooling, housing, and investment funds for other endeavors. People live in large villages, set in wooded countryside, accessible by motor transport, and with some modern amenities and services. Almost all of their children attend school, many people travel to the cities and hold jobs in the non-agricultural sectors of the economy. But in the long run the rural areas have ceased to be an important source of high personal incomes. By the second generation land suitable for cocoa was less available and cocoa prices began a long, slow decline to a trough in 1964-65. Under these circumstances men began to leave the countryside to search for better paying work, but the rapid inflation of the 1970s left many of them without an income adequate to support a family in an urban area.

To deal with this situation Ewe people relied on the ability of women to keep the food supply system functioning without much help from men. During the cocoa boom they had reorganized family work in a way which is echoed in many other export-crop areas: men turned all their attention to cocoa, while women took over the cultivation of basic food for the family. In the economic crisis of the 1970s, women and children remained in the countryside because it was the only place where they could be sure of food supply. Many women are now forced to do what Senufo women do not, that is, provide for themselves and their children. According to Bukh's study, 65 percent of women over 18 are solely responsible for their children's daily nutrition. Women form 58 percent of the rural population, and are the heads of 40 percent of the households (Bukh, 1979: 37, 111). Men do contribute to certain aspects of the economy, but under the circumstances women have to be prepared to support their dependents on a day-to-day basis.

Although expressed in different terms than the Senufo study, the advantages and disadvantages of women's position to achieve this are brought out clearly. By comparison with their own menfolk women are at a clear disadvantage in providing for a family. Cocoa is still the best source of cash income but women own only four percent of the total cocoa acreage. Women's food farms are smaller and on poorer land than men's because women working alone find it difficult to do the heavy work.

The advantages seem few but they are striking by comparison with other cases. As in other patrilineal societies, Ewe women do have rights to land, and the local market for the goods they sell is strong enough to provide a cash income. Sixty percent of women over fifteen years old are farmers, but half of them combine farming with petty retail trade, processing, wage labor, and artisan work to bring in the money necessary to cover personal and household expenses. Like other women they devote large proportions of time to domestic duties including two hours per day cooking. The total work load adds up quickly when it includes three occupations. Bukh gives an example of a widow supporting her aged father and seven children by working from 4 a.m. to 10 p.m.

One of the most important resources which women have to draw on in meeting these demands is the help of their children. Children look after each other, run messages, take care of small livestock, fetch water, wash dishes and later take part in the more difficult work which contributes to income more directly. Luo women in western Kenya, who also combine farming with small-scale trade, depend heavily on children to cover many of the daily duties (Okeyo 1979, 1980a). In West Africa, children are often fostered in order to provide women with help or an apprentice in their craft.

Bukh does not calculate the value of women's labor relative to men's; in fact, this is extremely difficult data to collect. But their control of resources is poorer, and in particular the low fertility of the land which they cultivate is bound to mean that their work is relatively poorly rewarded.

Comment and comparison

Certain aspects of the situation Bukh describes are very common results of the integration of export crops. As described in Chapter 1, many peoples have intensified the old division of labor by sex so that food production has become primarily a female responsibility. Margaret Haswell shows a similar pattern in a groundnut-producing village in the Gambia. The men have entirely given up cultivation of millet, the traditional staple, in favor of groundnuts, and the women cultivate rice amost exclusively for the family diet (Haswell, 1975).

But again, there are marked variations. In another old groundnut-producing area, northern Nigeria, women do not work on the farm whatsoever because of the observance of Muslim seclusion (Hill, 1969). Men farmers have to provide both the food and the export crop, or buy food from cash incomes from the sale of other crops in the market. A similar pattern without the influence of women's seclusion, has developed in the cocoa-producing areas of southern Nigeria. Women are not, on the whole, responsible for much farm labor either on their own or on a family farm. In both these areas women's niche in the economy has become, to a far more extreme degree than any of the other cases discussed so far, the processing of agricultural goods and small-scale trade. Even in purdah, Hausa women manage to earn an income through trade, the sale of cooked food, or the production of groundnut oil and other ingredients of the local diet. Yoruba women more or less monopolize their regional food marketing and distribution systems. Some are wholesale traders on a large scale, while others practice much more marginal and intermittent businesses.

For these women, their primary income is in cash, and not in farm products for direct family use. It is possible, but rare, for women to earn higher cash incomes than their husbands. They earn enough to take care of many expenses for their children, and may have to support the family during the season when men have no incomes from their farms. But again, the economic survey data suggest that women's occupations give low returns to labor input, relative to men's within the same system.

Women's work in the cash-crop economies tends to cluster around two occupations: food farming for the family with small amounts sold on the market, and entirely market-oriented activities in processing and trade. The question then arises of whether there are any systematic differences between these two kinds of situation, either in the systems themselves or in women's level of welfare. The response of different rural areas to the stagnation of export-crop incomes may give a partial answer.

Southern Ghana is an area where export crop production brought relatively high incomes at one time. Women's subsistence food production was one element in the ability of male farmers to take the risks of expansion. As prices fall men search for other alternatives, again using women's food production as a cushion against the volatility of national and international economies. Women who have access to land cling to food production as a source of security. Men's occupations differentiate, and women's remain relatively uniform. By contrast, in economies where women are primarily in trade, when they need to take over greater responsibility for the family income, they have to exploit the regional market, become more enterprising and more mobile. The active marketing system which already exists provides this possibility, and with it, all the risks and potential rewards of the cash sector.

Women farmers may also prefer to specialize or diversify their activities, but there are major constraints: the tradition of subsistence maintenance by each domestic group, the intensification of subsistence values by the export-crop economy, and the unavailability of non-family labor to supplement on the food farm. Their problem is compounded because in economies where women did little trade in the past, the successive governments have encouraged the development of other kinds of marketing systems: shops owned by foreigners, cooperatives, or marketing authorities. In some areas no significant internal market system for peasants to trade with each other has ever developed because of low peasant incomes, government policy, domination of a single cash crop and the commitment of female labor to subsistence farming. For example, an authoritative study of the Senegalese rural economy states that the 'primordial place occupied by groundnuts in the rural economy . . . has prevented the organization of an internal market, turned peasants away from seeing each other as potential consumers . . .' (Pélissier, 1966: 897). In this situation it can be difficult to create local marketing institutions strong enough to compete with entrenched interests in the more lucrative wholesale sectors.

The whole issue of economic differentiation in Africa's rural areas is complicated and understudied, and women's position within it is even less clear. The straightforward occupational differentiation discussed so far is just part of the more profound issue of income differentiation. The old cash-crop areas have been in the commodity economy for long enough to begin to develop and consolidate class differences, which makes it somewhat misleading to discuss women's economic role in terms of the average man and the average woman. Where some farmers of cash crops are able to cross the critical Rubicon from use of family labor to extensive use of wage labor, the position of women may be quite fundamentally altered.

A 1973 study of Ganda cotton and coffee farmers shows how critical the farm owner's wife may be to the management of the entire farm (Richards and others, 1973). In this part of Africa women can be successful managers of agricultural enterprises as long as they have access to the same resources as men. It appears, however, that they rarely own and manage land in their own right. What happens to these farm-wife-managers in case of divorce or widowhood is not clear, whether they can continue to work the farm, or have to move out and possibly down in the class hierarchy. To get a complete picture of the relationship between class and gender one would also need to know about the status of the kinswomen of wage laborers. The economic life histories of men and women may be quite different from one another if women cannot accumulate productive resources on their account.

To summarize briefly, women's activities are primarily geared to local demand for locally produced goods and can expand when the possibility of occupational differentiation does exist. Although theories of economic growth expect local markets to grow as producers become more involved with export-crop production, this has happened in some areas to a much greater degree than others. The growth of the internal market appears to have been particularly slow where women are committed to subsistence food production, not because of women's 'motives' but because of the constraints on their range of choices.

Case 3
Labor reserve economies: Botswana and the Transkei
(*Sources:* Brown, 1980; Lucus, 1979; Leeuwenberg, 1977)

Botswana and the Transkei were brought within the orbit of South African industry during the last years of the nineteenth century. Their rural areas consist of open range land where the local populations once herded cattle and kept farms for their staple food. The cattle economy went into dramatic decline in the 1890s as a result of an epidemic which killed off large proportions of the herds. Since then, the reconstruction of rural life has been directly influenced by South Africa's needs for migrant workers in the gold and diamond mines and in industry.

In areas treated as 'labor reserves', cash cropping was deliberately limited by colonial governments and subsistence production was maintained; the need for a cash income would force out the employable members of the population, and the subsistence farming would feed the rest at no cost to the wage-earner. In this way wages could be kept as low as possible. The implicit assumption behind such policies was that the mutual obligations between kin could be activated at intermittent points during a worker's life without being reinforced by the day-to-day reciprocity implied in co-residence.

In the long run this policy has left the rural areas extremely vulnerable, subject to many demands and very few inputs. Subsistence farming on limited land is simply not flexible, and the farmers in these systems have no other alternatives: little possibility to expand production for the market, little access to the (low) wages of distant migrants, and few resources to cope with ecological problems, production fluctuations, or population changes. As a result the last twenty years have witnessed a steady decline in subsistence maintenance. In a rural survey of Botswana (reported in Brown, 1980: 5), the poorest 50 percent of households depended on cash transfers and employment as their primary sources of income. The situation in the Transkei is much worse. Only ten percent of the households in the survey produced enough from their farms to feed themselves, and two-thirds of all food consumed was imported from outside. But sources of cash income within the Transkei were almost nonexistent. Cattle ownership is very unequal, there are virtually no cash crops and only ten percent of the adult population, mainly men, is employed for wages. In both these cases rural households need wage remittances from their kin in order to hire labor and ox-teams to plough the land, and just to buy the food they need to live on. Almost by definition, this kind of system leaves the women and children disproportionately in the rural areas. At least 25 per cent of all adult men are absent in both of these regions. In the Transkei 67 percent of households are headed by women, a far higher porportion than any of the other cases (Leeuwenberg, 1977: 2-8).

So far these two cases have been discussed together, but in the last ten years their situations have diverged. Jobs for unskilled migrants are less available as South Africa's industry becomes increasingly capital-intensive. Brown's survey in 1978 suggests that 48 percent of men from a rural area in Botswana are employed but only one third of them now rork on South Africa (Brown 1980: 4). Burdened with most of the agricultural work, but suffering from the level of poverty which keeps land and equipment ownership for female-headed households much lower than for males, women are exercising the other option which is to give up farming altogether. Brown found that 25 percent of women from the rural area in which she worked were employed, a far higher proportion than in any of the other economies discussed here (Brown, 1980: 4). The out-migration of women has the effect of redressing somewhat the sex ratio in the rural areas.

Women in the Transkei, however, cannot leave the rural aeas. As the farming system declines further, the male migration rate rises and the ratio of men to women falls still further. How these women manage is a tribute to human stamina and ingenuity but the costs in declining standards of nutrition and climbing child mortality are very high. As in the cash-crop areas, children's work is a significant addition to the family labor force especially in female-headed households (Lucas, 1979: 37). On the other hand, one fact stands out in studies of both countries, and that is the determination of women to educate their children to make them employable outside the rural areas. Even at the low levels of living in the Transkei, families spend anything from 20 percent to 70 percent of their cash incomes on education (Leeuwenberg, 1977: 15; see Alverson, 1978).

Comment and comparison

Studies in other areas of Southern Africa give the same impression: 60 percent of households headed by women, heavy dependence on remittances, lack of income-generating activities for women within the reserves and limited avenues to leave them. However difficult women's lives seem in the rural areas further north there are always some mitigating factors. Land may be scarce but there are trading opportunities; employment is limited but the land is still fertile enough to provide the basic necessities; women are less often faced with making a living alone and some kind of money-earning work can be pursued year round to offset the relatively poor returns per day.

Case 4
Female plantation workers in Cameroon
(*Sources:* De Lancey, 1977; Koenig, 1977)

In a very few areas of Africa, women are full-time employed agricultural workers. The cases discussed here are very large, partly state-run enterprises which have been in existence for a long time. The rubber and palm plantation at Dizangué was founded in the 1920s and worked by forced laborers as late as the Second World War. The vast plantations of the Cameroon Development Corporation (CDC) on the slopes of Mount Cameroon occupy some of the most fertile soil in Africa and have been producing tropical products for the world market for almost a hundred years.

The workers for both these plantation systems were imported from other regions of the country first by force and then by recruitment. The CDC workers in particular are now an established proletariat through two or more generations. Since they are not local by origin, they have less access to land and the opportunity for developing 'peasant' farming than the local populations. The workers are organized and work under the protection of the national labor code. Since the two cases are a little different they will be discussed separately.

The women working at Dizangué turned to wage labor 'in times of extreme need', as a way of supporting their children (Koenig, 1977: 258). The average age is a little over forty, but only 28 percent of these women are currently married. For the most part, they are rural women who have migrated to the plantation as an alternative to trying to manage alone in subsistence farming. Once at the plantation, they form a small sector of the total labor force (20 percent) and tend to cluster in jobs with lower pay and no productivity bonuses (Koenig, 1977: 94). However, when the daily wage is computed it appears that women earn about three-fourths of the average male salary. As we have noted earlier, this differential is considerably smaller than the differential in returns to labor in the peasant sector.

The workers on the CDC tea plantation appear to be even better off. Although the data are not precisely comparable, De Lancey shows that the employed women had double the cash income of a sample of married women working in the peasant farming and marketing sectors. They had higher savings levels and, significantly, invested heavily in their children's education.

Comment and comparison

The Cameroonian plantation workers, as an example of rural wage workers, benefit from certain advantageous conditions. In large enterprises the conditions of work are public knowledge and government regulated. By contrast, employment conditions and wages can be highly variable in the small-holder sector, depending on local and seasonal levels of demand for laborers. Secondly, the work on tea and forest crops is not as distinctly seasonal as, for example, coffee or sugar, so that workers have some degree of job security. Many of the women in both samples had been employed continuously for over five years. One hesitates to generalize from this kind of employment to seasonal farm labor in South Africa or the whole range of work arrangements with local farmers. It is not wage work per se which makes the difference, but the conditions of year-round commitment to wage work, visibility and organization.

Conclusions

Table 2.1 summarizes our findings from the cases studied, with respect to the four criteria set up in the beginning.

In Africa women account for a high proportion of the work involved in food supply: in the farming itself, in processing, drying, storage, and in both retail and wholesale marketing for local and regional trade. In the poorest areas this is a supportive, subsistence farmwork to supply food to their own households. But in many countries large urban populations depend on this female labor force for the regular supply of their daily food through complex marketing systems.

Women's access to resources appears to be inferior to men's, in one way or another, in all cases: smaller farms, less fertile land, less opportunity for occupational mobility, less wage employment. On the other hand, women's access to income can, in the short run, sometimes be more secure than men's. In many cash-cropping areas men's incomes from agriculture are seasonal, whereas women can earn small incomes from local trade year round. Men's crops may be more subject to the volatility of world markets or state pricing policy than women's food crops. In areas where high population density has affected access to land, the poorest men may be unable to get the resources to put themselves to work, whereas their wives may find ready markets for the bean cakes they make, the groundnut oil or the baskets. Until agriculture becomes a more productive occupation than it is at present, the existence of other options may make the difference between managing or not. For women who have little or no access to a man's income the ability to put themselves to remunerative work on a regular basis is critical, even if they are forced to do it on disadvantageous terms.

The evidence suggests that women's work is everywhere valued less than men's. But is women's labor really less productive than men's? The evidence is, at best, ambiguous, because in most areas the kind of work which each sex does is different. In places where certain tasks are common to both sexes one finds either narrower gaps than one might expect, or further factors to explain the differential. Kathleen Staudt found that Kenyan women farmers, for example, had significantly

TABLE 1 Women's position in four African economies: summary

Sector	Senufo	Ewe	Xhosa (Transkei)	Dizangué Plantation
	Food: farming and sales	Food: farming and sales	Food: subsistence farming (insufficient)	wage work
Rural sex ratio (women per 100 men)	108	143	144	20 (labor force only)
Female-headed households (%)	0 (?)	42	67	n.d.
Resources	Land: market sales	Land: small, no cocoa market sales	Land: insufficient, little capital, no employment	Employment
Ratio of returns to labor (m:f)	2:1	4:1 (Nigeria 1952) 2:1 (Cameroon 1964)	1.8:1 (Botswana 1976)	1.3:1

Sources: SEDES, 1965; Leeuwenberg, 1977; De Lancey, 1977; Guyer, 1980; Lucas, 1979. In the absence of data from Bukh, data from comparable West African cocoa economies has been used.

poorer access to advice and credit from the agricultural extension system (Staudt, 1975). Lucas's analysis of men's and women's farming in Botswana shows that production *per acre* differed hardly at all, even though women's resources were significantly poorer (Lucas, 1979: 4, 47). Finally, Dunstan Spencer's (1976) discussion of rural wage rates in Sierra Leone suggests that productivity differences between the sexes are mainly task specific, and therefore not constant across the board. In his case the daily wage rate reflects this: women receive even a slightly higher wage than men for rice harvesting but only two-thirds of the men's wage for land preparation and planting, and even less for 'other farm work'.

The data are too locally specific to be used to draw major conclusions. But they allow us to raise the possibility that differentials between men and women in returns to labor are highest in the small-holder, cash-crop economies and lowest in the fully proletarianized populations. Over and above the likelihood of women's marginally lower physical productivity and the established fact of their poorer control of resources, there appears to be a further determining factor which derives from the system of labor control and labor valuation in the wider economy.

The wider system

When one examines women's economic position in the context of national and international economies one needs to go beyond the fact that much of the rural women's work provides security, inexpensive food and the next generation of workers. On the basis of slender evidence, there seem to be some characteristic sets of contradictions for women which differ according to the dominant source of wealth in the economy. In the case of peripheral market involvement, the possibility of more equal access to resources between men and women may exist in certain indigenous social systems; but its preservation is purchased at the cost of a static level of living. Production of cash crops for the market appears to intensify the disparity between the value of men's and women's labor and their access to productive resources; on the other hand, the concomitant growth of market trade and general occupational complexity often provides regular employment opportunities for women under conditions which can be integrated with domestic duties. Women in these systems are anything but under-employed. Where the labor force is proletarianized, the wage disparity between men and women may narrow; the critical problem for women then becomes differential access to limited wage employment.

For the moment, the majority of women in rural Africa live and work in the peasant sector, involved with the wider system to a greater or lesser degree depending on the region. Their work will continue to be the backbone of the food supply system, but under shifting conditions. The urban areas are growing extremely quickly while agricultural productivity remains stagnant. At a time when the fact of women's key position in food supply, painfully and slowly forces itself on policymakers, many of those women are trying to educate their daughters for occupations other than agriculture. A literate female farming population is one possibility for the future; but so is a female rural exodus to match the male migrations of the past two generations.

3 Women in the urban economy

Claire C. Robertson

Cities in black Africa occur in many types, reflecting the diversity of a huge area. Some are primarily mercantile in origin, some administrative, and a few are industrial. There are old cities whose founding dates preceded the beginning of continuous European contact in the fifteenth century. For instance, some towns along the East African coast like Mombasa and Malindi grew up as part of the vital Arab trading world, while in West Africa towns on the edge of the desert, like Timbuktu, functioned as the hubs of ancient empires. Some West African coastal towns also pre-dated European contact. Cape Town in South Africa was founded in the seventeenth century by Dutch settlers. There are also relatively new towns, however, whose formation was a product of changes wrought by the colonial powers; these include most of the big cities of Central, inland East, and southern Africa.

A common way of analyzing African cities has been to divide them up according to their indigenous or foreign mode of origin (Southall, 1961). This division has been extended to their inhabitants, so that those who are migrant and those who are indigenous are thought to have significantly different characteristics. In the 1950s and 1960s analysts often concentrated on the social dislocation experienced by the migrants, while later scholars went on to talk of the reintegrative functions of ethnicity and voluntary associations in an urban context. Because most cities were viewed as being relatively new, and because the majority of the inhabitants of even the old cities are migrants, these studies did not show much about the effects of long-term urban residence on indigenous city-dwellers.

It is becoming evident that whatever the presumed differences are between migrant and indigenous city-dwellers (for example, that the latter would be in a more stable socioeconomic situation), they do not apply to women. Whatever their origins, urban African women are experiencing the same sorts of changes, many of which are detrimental to their well-being. The fact that most women share similar pressures and crises raises questions concerning not only the impact of sexism on their fate, but also the impact of class formation. This chapter will explore some of these ramifications.

Class formation is progressing rapidly in black Africa, with African elites occupying the niches formerly reserved for colonial administrators. The persistence of white minority rule in South Africa makes that country an exception. This differentiation by economic status is graphically expressed in the physical aspect of many cities. For instance, in Accra, the capital of Ghana, there is an old, very densely populated pre-colonial central city composed of mud and cement houses with corrugated zinc roofs. Further inland from the shore is a colonial elite neighborhood now mainly occupied by upper-class Ghanaians. Further north still are some extremely posh suburbs where large houses are surrounded by compound walls and shaded by palm, mango, and frangipani trees.

Near these villas are the packed squatter settlements so characteristic of Third World cities, where electricity, running water, and toilet facilities are scarce. These differences are mirrored on the roads where, behind slick new Mercedes, the *tro-tros* (open-backed trucks) bump along, carrying as many people as can fit on their benches. In Lagos, Nigeria, the same situation exists on a bigger scale because of the recent influx of oil wealth, and in Abidjan, Ivory Coast, there is even a luxury hotel with an ice-skating rink as well as a swimming pool—a surrealistic phenomenon in a tropical climate.

In South Africa the class differences are even more dramatic: laws prescribe that blacks live in dreary, poverty-stricken government-owned developments outside the cities, while whites reserve for themselves a luxurious urban life-style maintained by the cheap labor of blacks. In parts of Central and East Africa, the situation is similar, although the contrasts are perhaps not so stark.

In discussing urban women and class formation, a first requirement is to rid ourselves of the tendency to submerge the women's identity in that of the men. That is, in too much of the literature, women's socioeconomic status is presumed to be the same as that of their husbands or fathers. Under certain conditions this may be a permissible assumption, especially when women are wholly dependent on men for their support, as in some Western situations. Even here, however, the assumption ignores power relations within families and the differential access to family resources. In the situation of sub-Saharan Africa, women often have property, and rights to property, quite distinct from that of their husbands, and women perform work outside the home which is vital to the economy. In most rural areas, women provide approximately 70 percent of subsistence needs by growing or gathering food, and in cities this function often continues as women are responsible for feeding their families. It becomes important, therefore, to distinguish women's money from men's in determining socioeconomic status, as well as in discussing economic change.

A second pitfall best avoided is the use of the 'traditional/modern' dichotomy in analyzing socioeconomic change. This model is ahistorical, because change is continuous in all societies, making it impossible to fix on one (usually apocryphal) point as having been 'traditional', and another as being 'modern'. The underlying goal of change is usually assumed to be Westernization, that is, patterns of change that duplicate the Euro-American experience. Here, rather than assuming that socioeconomic change necessarily involves only the imposition of Western-type structures from above, I will consider it to be a continuing series of adjustments and reactions within indigenous African social structures, for which outside forces can act as catalyst but not as instigator.

A third problem frequently encountered in the literature is the routine underevaluation of women's work. The official statistics on women's economic role, presented in the Appendix and in Table 2, frequently reflect this limitation. As the Appendix points out in more detail, a woman who works eighteen hours a day trading, housecleaning, and childrearing may be classified as 'underemployed', or the importance of earning wages may be stressed, and self-employment ignored or deprecated. Gross Domestic Product statistics are compiled which omit the value of domestic or unpaid labor; women's work is sometimes assumed to the valueless because it is done by women. Fortunately, we now know better. This chapter is a brief introduction to the knowledge about the work of urban African women which we have gained in the past several decades.

Women's occupations

Women in sub-Saharan African cities work inside and outside the home in a variety of occupations. Whatever the origins of the women, the occupations they pursue tend to fall into certain categories because of women's differential access to education and the constraints imposed by the sexual division of labor, both colonialist and indigenous. Although most black African nations have enacted laws that forbid discrimination on the basis of sex, only very few women have been able to overcome the socioeconomic constraints which keep women illiterate, poorly paid, or marginally self-employed.

Whatever the causes of female inequality, the results can be seen in Table 2, which describes the occupations of female and male residents in ten black African cities. (For the statistical sources of Tables 2 and 3 see page 50). Analysis of Table 2 makes a good beginning for the explanation of women's economic roles in urban Africa. First, the paucity of the data shows just how little is known about the exact situation. The Nigerian censuses are difficult to obtain and unreliable. For Khartoum and Abidjan, 1955 was the most recent date for which detailed information was readily available. In Bamako in 1960 the census-takers assumed that most women were exclusively housewives. Housework was not considered to be work and was lumped together with 'unemployment' in Bamako and Cape Town.

Second, the data in Table 2 sometimes include only wage-earning workers and omit the self-employed. Most women are self-employed, since discriminatory hiring policies and the lack of training often bar them from available wage-paid jobs. For instance, only the 1960 Ghana census inquired about self-employment in detail and made a thorough attempt to count the self-employed in each type of occupation. In that census, 24.5 percent of the working men were self-employed, compared to 79.8 percent of the working women (Republic of Ghana, 1960: 71, 115). In Nigeria in 1966/67, some 81.4 percent of the employed women in urban areas were self-employed, compared to 59.2 percent of the men. In addition, 12.4 percent of the women were unpaid household workers or apprentices, compared to 8.6 percent of the men. The remainder earned formal wages (Republic of Nigeria, 1966/67: 20-1). Self-employment, even if the census takers ask about it, is sometimes not mentioned; sometimes it is illegal. In South Africa and in Kenya illegal beer-brewing provides employment for many urban women. Prostitution is usually illegal. When governments insist on licenses for traders, women who

TABLE 2 Occupations of adult[1] African urban dwellers by sex, 1955-1976 (percentages)

Town	Year	Professional, technical, and related workers		Administrative, managerial, clerical workers		Sales workers		Service workers		Agricultural, forestry, and related workers		Production, manufacturing and maintenance workers		Home-makers		Other workers		Unemployed		Total	
		F	M	F	M	F	M	F	M	F	M	F	M	F	M	F	M	F	M	F	M
Abidjan,[2] Ivory Coast	1955	0.0	1.3	7.5	8.5	70.0	21.4	5.0	15.2	0.0	3.1	7.5	38.8	—	—	7.5	5.9	2.5	5.6	100.0	99.8
Accra, Ghana	1960	2.3	4.4	2.3	16.8	35.3	12.9	3.0	11.5	0.5	4.4	6.0	24.4	32.1	0.2	9.6	14.8	8.9	10.5	100.0	99.9
Bamako, Mali	1960	0.0	1.0	0.0	3.1	1.0	20.4	0.6	23.3	1.0	9.8	1.5	5.0	—	—	2.0	30.7	93.9[3]	6.7	100.0	100.0
Mali-all urban	1976	1.4	5.6	1.0	3.3	1.9	8.9	1.3	5.0	2.4	26.9	1.5	26.1	88.7[4]	20.9[4]	1.3	1.1	0.8	3.9	100.3	101.7[5]
Cape Town, South Africa[2]	1970	1.2	0.3	0.1	1.0	0.3	1.6	22.3	5.6	0.1	4.9	0.6	58.3	—	—	9.9	3.9	65.5[3]	24.3	100.0	99.9
Dar-es-Salaam, Tanzania	1967	2.0	4.2	3.5	13.6	1.0	9.0	7.6	26.7	2.2	3.2	2.1	22.2	76.7	0.4	1.7	22.0	2.6	4.3	99.4	105.6[5]
Fort Lamy, Chad[2]	1962	0.3	10.2	0.0	1.8	11.1	13.3	0.2	39.0	4.3	11.4	0.3	15.5	76.5	0.0	6.2	0.3	8.2	8.0	99.7	99.5
Khartoum, Sudan	1955/1956	1.6	4.8	1.4	12.3	2.6	8.0	2.6	17.8	0.1	2.9	1.7	21.5	81.9	—	22.3	7.2	10.4	25.4	100.0	99.9
Lusaka, Zambia[2]	1970	1.1	3.1	0.1	0.7	2.9	10.4	1.5	5.6	1.1	9.8	0.4	4.8	67.6[6]	13.7[6]	1.8	29.4	23.6	22.4	100.1	99.9
Tananarive, Malagasy Republic	1960	--	--	1.6	17.9	3.3	13.4	7.8	10.5	0.1	5.3	2.1	16.5	—	—	0.1	7.8	84.8[3]	31.6	99.8	103.0[5]
Yaoundé, Cameroon	1976	4.0	8.0	5.1	11.6	2.9	9.1	2.8	9.8	1.3	1.5	5.3	38.4	66.0	0.6	6.8	7.7	5.8	13.1	100.0	99.8

Notes:
1 Aged 14-15 or older.
2 Bantu population only, or African population only. Lusaka figures differ from Hansen's because of the inclusion of homemakers.
3 Housewives included.
4 The Mali 1976 census differentiated economically inactive from unemployed, putting most women in the former category under homemakers, but it probably also includes retired persons.
5 Percentages may add up to more than 100 because some categories overlap; people may have multiple occupations, or different censuses used different categories, that is, sales workers in one census may have included some clerical workers but not in another census.
6 Included also students and disabled.
— Not given, or impossible to discern.
-- Included under administrative, managerial, and clerical workers.

cannot afford them, or who wish to avoid paying for the licenses, will say that they are housewives. Because of the prestige which is occasionally attached to being a housewife (a luxury few families can afford), some women will report that they are housewives while they will not mention their hairdressing or their vegetable-selling businesses.

Third, the data are inconsistent. This table should be used with caution, because the census takers' categories were often different. I have tried to make them comparable, but it was not always possible to ascertain the definitions used. The figures are therefore more reliable for making comparisons of labor force participation by sex within a city than across nationalities.

Despite all these reservations, Table 2 still shows us something about female labor force participation. It is clear that there is a far greater percentage of men than women in professional, technical, administrative, and clerical jobs. Although women sometimes do slightly better in the 'professional' category alone, because of their roles as teachers and nurses, the male/female differential is particularly striking for the administrative, managerial, and clerical workers. The variations between African countries in women's access to the various categories of white-collar work are treated more fully in the Appendix, Table 7.

High-ranking urban white-collar workers are, of course, the most powerful group in African countries today, and they are as over-whelmingly male in sub-Saharan African countries as they are elsewhere. In Table 2, where the figures most approach equity in Abidjan, the women's figures are artificially inflated by the omission of homemakers as a category. Certainly, one can find a female High Court Justice or UN ambassador here, and a female senator there, but these are exceptional cases. As described in Chapter 9 below, pre-colonial African societies had women rulers with real political power, but during the colonial era women lost this traditional status and have not regained it in the modern sector.

One area of women's pre-colonial authority was in market trading, which has a long history in West Africa. The results for 'sales workers' in Accra and in Abidjan in Table 2, and in urban Nigeria where 59.7 percent of the employed women were in sales in 1966/67 (Republic of Nigeria, 1966/67: 20-1), show the dominance of coastal West African women in trade. In inland East and Central Africa, where few towns existed before colonial rule, women generally were more recent partici-pants in market trading. Where Islam prevails, men are more likely to dominate trade, as they do in Bamako, Dar es Salaam, and Khartoum. In Kano, Northern Nigeria, on the other hand, Muslim women are still active as traders despite their tradition of seclusion — they use inter-mediaries, like their children, to sell for them. Even in this area, women's trade has generally been concentrated in the preparation and sale of foodstuffs; the more valuable long-distance trade in gold, ivory, kola nuts, and slaves was usually, but not always, dominated by men.

Because of their restricted access to credit and capital, management problems, and family obligations, few women have been able to manage large-scale trade or businesses on a long-term basis. Getting start-up capital is becoming more and more difficult as kin-based women's work groups are breaking down in the urban setting, and also partly as a result of the advent of universal primary education (see below). Also the introduction of intermediate technology, as described more fully in Chapter 11, may deprive women of the means of acquiring capital without substituting alternative employment. In some areas, for instance, hand corn-grinding was carried out on a piecework basis, with poorer women working for women with large food-preparation businesses. The introduction of male-owned and operated gas-powered corn mills helped the large traders, who could afford to pay for machine-ground corn, and deprived the smaller ones of the means of getting capital. The profits from corn-grinding then went into the male sector. The case of Naadey, whom I encountered in Accra, illustrates some of the problems faced by traders.

Naadey is a vigorous 41-year-old woman living in the center of Accra. She, her grandmother, and her mother were all involved in selling fish; she is now teaching her daughters the trade. In fact, her eldest daughter is 20 and in the process of taking over some of the business. But her younger daughters do not want to do it. They went to school and are unsuccessfully looking for clerical positions. Meanwhile, the business is not prospering because, due to the mechanization of the fishing industry, and discriminatory policies by the government and large foreign-owned corporations, the fish supply is becoming concentrated in a very few hands. A few women, aided by their powerful male governmental connections, are making things extremely difficult for most fish traders.

Naadey finds that her alternatives for employment are extremely limited, since monopolistic conditions are increasingly prevalent in other commodities as well. Her clerk husband, who is supposed to be paying for the education of her four youngest children (three boys and a girl), has taken another wife who is young, attractive, and educated. He has a house in a suburb and has stopped visiting downtown or asking Naadey to visit him, although on occasion he will grudgingly give her some money to buy food for the children. The young wife objects to his associating with Naadey at all (partly because he told her he had no wife before they got married), and wants all of his resources to go to her own two children, aged one and three. Naadey is finding life increasingly difficult, despite putting in more time fish-selling than ever before. She cannot afford to buy meat or eggs to eat, and their diet consists largely of a starchy cassava product (*gari*) with little nutritional value. She particularly worries about the future of her sons, 'as for my daughters, they can always trade, but my sons, what can they do without a good education? I cannot pay the school fees.'

Men usually dominate among service workers except in South Africa, as shown in Table 2 in this chapter and Table 7 of the Appendix. Many services developed under colonial rule, where it was a distinct advantage for a domestic servant, for instance, to speak the colonialist's language. Since boys were more often educated than girls, and since it was often not acceptable for women to work in the houses of unattached white men (since most wives were left in Europe), domestic service came to be dominated by men in many places.

In the post-independence era this trend has sometimes been reversed, leaving low-status domestic work to men. South Africa is an exception where women strongly dominate domestic work, which absorbs more female wage laborers there (37 percent) than any other field. In 1980 their average work week was 61 hours in length, and their average wage, 11 cents an hour (Lapchick and Urdang, 1980).

Matilda Smith is a domestic servant for a white family in Johannesburg. She is in her mid-thirties, a small sturdy woman whose experiences have left her bitter. She lives in a tiny, flimsily constructed, torrid room on top of a modern high-rise, one of a row of cells occupied by the servants employed by the white residents. It is furnished with whatever odds and ends she can find; she cannot afford to buy furniture. Her pay is $30 a month, plus room and board. Any meager savings must go to her mother who lives in an African 'location' with Matilda's two children and her younger sister, also a servant. Matilda's job is to care for the three small children of her employers. Servants are not allowed to have their families with them in white areas, so she only sees her own two children on her day off. If by chance a family member is caught visiting by the police in their periodic raids, stiff fines are imposed on both employees and employers. She is on call twenty-four hours a day, six days a week, is fed poorly ('kaffir food'), and treated disrespectfully by her employers. One of her children is the son of a former employer, who raped her several times; her pregnancy resulted in her dismissal. She would prefer not to do domestic work, but finds her employment opportunities severely limited. She dislikes the low pay, the humiliation, and the boredom, but her training and experience, as well as the laws limiting black pay and job opportunities, give her few alternatives.

When Matilda is not too tired to think, she wonders what will come of all this misery. She was only with her husband two years before he lost his job as a mechanic and got caught picking pockets. She has hardly seen him since he got out of jail. Her daughter, now sixteen, quit school several years before finishing the maximum number of years allowed to South African blacks. She has become a prostitute. On the rare occasions when Matilda sees her, they have arguments while Matilda tries to get her to change her ways. In her mature years, Matilda has become a devout Christian, a member of a fundamentalist sect popular in the location. On her day off, she goes to church and talks to the minister about her daughter. Her son, now eight, has been doing better at his studies than her daughter did, but Matilda worries that the lack of opportunities will discourage him and that he will begin running around with one of the young gangs in the location. Then she worries that her mother will be arrested and they will lose their house (two rooms with no indoor plumbing or electricity). This could happen in any case, since they have no legal right to it, no longer having a male head of household who has worked in Johannesburg the requisite number of years. In this event, her mother and children would be sent to live on the reserves, where her mother has never lived and knows no one. The family is a third-generation urban one, far removed from farming skills. But beneath everything Matilda feels the corrosion of her self-respect. She holds her employer's eighteen-month old daughter and says, 'I love this child, though she'll grow up and treat me just like her mother does. Now she is innocent' (adapted from Cole, 1967).

Migration to towns

In many southern African countries and in the Congo, restrictions were placed by colonial governments on women coming to town. The idea was (and still is in South Africa) that Africans are by nature bush dwellers, that only male labor was needed for the mines and other industries, and that African men should return to their rural homes after completing their work contracts. The provision of urban employment for men but not women, even in places where restrictions were not imposed on female urban migration, led to severely unbalanced sex ratios in some cities, especially in the period between the two World Wars. Table 3 shows that even well after the Second World War, the imbalance prevailed; it was particularly characteristic of central, east and southern African towns populated mainly by migrants, such as Nairobi and Cape Town, and mining towns like Lubumbashi (Zaire) and Johannesburg.

In Table 3, Maseru shows the results of intensive labor migration of men to South Africa, for which Lesotho serves as a labor reservoir just as the official South African reserves do. The European presence, as in Abidjan, exacerbated the surplus of men, as did the successful South African effort to restrict the influx of women to Cape Town. However, in most places such policies failed; in South Africa they succeeded only because of severe apartheid policies which resettled Africans outside of town in segregated areas such as Soweto, from which Africans required passes to leave.

As a final comment on Table 3, we should note that the populations of African towns have increased geometrically through natural increase and migration since these censuses were conducted. In some cases, this has helped to remedy the unbalanced sex ratios. For example, in Kenya and Tanzania, women's migration to towns has increased during the postwar years, and female migrants are more often coming independently, for economic and educational reasons, rather than as dependents of males (Shields, 1980: 17-27). In other cases, however, the differential employment opportunities for men and women still leave an imbalance. Population imbalances and differential employment opportunities in turn encourage the employment of women in services such as the provision of prepared foods and prostitution. The case of Wambui Murithi illustrates how prostitution can be an advantageous strategy for some women.

Wambui Murithi is an elderly Nairobi woman in her seventies, who was a prostitute in her youth. In 1922, when she was still in her home area, she married a part-Indian, part-Kikuyu man after her circum-

TABLE 3 Population and sex ratios of African cities, 1955-1976

City	Country	Year	Total population	Proportion of men: women
Abidjan	Ivory Coast	1955	120 051	100 : 72
Accra	Ghana	1970	564 194	100 : 97
Bamako	Mali	1960	125 300	100 : 99
Cape Town	South Africa	1970	1 107 763	100 : 100
	Bantus only	1970	108 827	100 : 52
Dakar[1]	Senegal	1955	230 887	100 : 89
Dar-es-Salaam	Tanzania	1967	272 821	100 : 81
Fort Lamy	Chad	1962	88 162	100 : 91
Khartoum	Sudan	1955/6	69 006	100 : 75
Lusaka	Zambia	1969	184 895	100 : 91
Maseru[2]	Lesotho	1966	171 226	100 : 127
Mombasa	Kenya	1969	247 073	100 : 72
Nairobi	Kenya	1969	509 286	100 : 68
Tananarive	Malagasy Republic	1960	247 917	100 : 102.4
Yaoundé	Cameroon	1976	291 071	100 : 88

Notes:
[1] African population only
[2] District

cision. After a few years, she left him because of repeated beatings and returned to her parents for several years. In the late 1920s, she went to Nairobi along with a friend who had also recently divorced an Indian man. In Nairobi, Murithi added English to her vocabulary (she already knew Swahili) by attending night classes given for Christian converts by the Church Missionary Society.

She and her friend rented a room downtown and began street-walking. Streetwalking, known locally as *watembezi*, offered more adventure and higher profits than the form of prostitution practiced in Nairobi's African location; she had a clientele composed of Europeans, Indians, and better off Africans. Her profits allowed her to begin assuming some family obligations. By 1930, Murithi was regularly paying the hut tax for both her father's wives and also the hut tax for her brothers on occasion. She built a stone house for her parents on their farm in about 1933. She made the marriage payment for two of her brothers' wives. Between 1933 and 1936, her sister was widowed, being left with three children. After her sister returned to their parents' land, Murithi promised to support her and the children. She paid for their education, and eventually made the marriage payments for her nephews.

In 1937/38, Murithi built a six-room house in Nairobi's African location. She moved into one room and rented out the others, mainly to teenage Kikuyu girls who were beginning to dominate *watembezi* prostitution in Nairobi. By this time, Murithi had given up that form of prostitution but maintained close relations with several men who had been her lovers over the years. She never had any children, probably due to gonorrhea. She helped socialize her teenage tenants into the norms of Nairobi prostitution during the Second World War, and recalled warning them not to accept gifts in kind from soldiers, since they then would be liable to arrest for receiving stolen goods. Between 1937 and 1946, Murithi's earnings from prostitution were only slightly more than those from rent.

At the end of the war, she bought her parents two cows. In 1948, when restrictions on African coffee production were lifted, she bought coffee trees for her parents' farm. One of her reasons for subsidizing the family farm was to give her sister's children a place to live. In the 1950s both of Murithi's parents died, but her brother and sister still work the family farm, where she visits them. She now lives on the income from her Nairobi house, which she currently shares with the seventeen-year-old grandson of her sister, who is in Nairobi looking for work (adapted from Luise White, private communication, January 1981).

Both Naadey the trader and Wambui Murithi are or were employed in what is often called the 'informal sector'. This term usually refers to the labor-intensive, non-wage employment which is most Third World countries absorbs over half the population of both sexes, but especially the women. The characteristics of the 'informal sector' are usually described as underemployment, labor intensity, low productivity, and lack of capital formation. Analysts using the term often measure economic progress according to how far the population of a country has been absorbed into capital-intensive, large-scale enterprises—the 'formal sector'—and deplore the continued existence of the 'informal sector'. However, there is increasing evidence that small-scale enterprises are efficient and can lead to capital formation, especially if they receive help in the form of the types of loans and credit from the government that the 'formal sector' enterprises routinely obtain (ILO, 1978; Liedholm and Chuta, 1976). In a situation where management skills are scarce and transport and supply problems persistent, small-scale enterprises often have the advantage over larger ones. Here it can be seen that Naadey's enterprise contributed to human capital in paying for education and Murithi's to education and agriculture, where she invested her profits. It is especially important, then, in the African context to measure both the paid and unpaid labor of women, and to appreciate the fact that there is a continuous gradation of enterprises in terms of size, and an interpenetration of wage earners and self-employed which makes the arbitrary classification of the terms 'informal' and 'formal' sectors of questionable value. Nowhere is this more evident than in considering the role of women in manufacturing.

Male dominance in urban occupations is most overwhelmingly evident among the production and manufacturing workers in Table 2, although, as pointed out in the Appendix, women do somewhat better in this area in certain West African countries than they do elsewhere. There are several reasons for male dominance here. First, because of the bias in the statistics toward wage workers in large-scale enterprises, many small industries conducted by women do not get counted. Second, men were considered by the colonialists to be more suited than women for work involving the use of machines, because of the European sexual division of labor. Thus, vocational schools were established most often only for boys, if they were established at all, or male workers only were recruited for wage labor, whether agricultural or industrial. Third, these policies occasionally reinforced an indigenous sexual division of labor which did not encourage women to obtain formal education or to work for wages outside the home. This was particularly true in Islamic areas where women were secluded (not a common practice in sub-Saharan Africa). Home production was particularly important for those women, since outside work was forbidden. Fourth, women craft-workers in pre-colonial Africa made soap, pottery, medicines, cloth, baskets, and other things. In some areas putting-out systems similar to those in early industrial England were operated by women. However, women's products incurred competition from European manufactured items and often lost out. European items had more status as imports and often were of more uniform quality. Their importation was encouraged and protected by the colonial governments, who were not only looking for raw materials, but also for markets for manufactured goods. Local African businesses, whether male- or female-owned, often suffered from lack of credit, tariff protection, and the other resources of the large foreign firms. They often failed. But whereas the men were often offered education and alternative employment, the women were not. It is no wonder, then, that in Accra (Ghana), Lusaka (Zambia, Kisangani (Zaire,) Kampala (Uganda), Ibadan and many other cities women are turning in large numbers to small-scale trading in local commodities (Schuster, 1979; Pons, 1969; Southall and Gutkind, 1957; Lloyd et al. 1967).

Before discussing the role of education in influencing women's employment, a comment is needed on women's urban agricultural activities. Agricultural work is, of course, not common in an urban situation for either sex. One reason it appears in the statistics is that fishing and related activities are still pursued in coastal or riverine towns. Women's work in this regard is probably under-recorded because men more often own the land or land rights. One of the significant changes for many women who come to town is that they may lose their rights to agricultural land. Migrant women often accompany their husbands to town. In many African societies a woman's access to farmland depends on her continued relations with her family of origin, or with the family of her husband. Even indigenous women city-dwellers are often in a similar situation; their lands were either lost or sold in the immense growth of towns during the colonial period, the proceeds going mainly to male lineage members. Women are nevertheless expected to feed their families. If they cannot grow the food, they must earn money to buy it or become dependent on their husbands for that money.

The impact of formal education

According to Table 2, more women are home-makers than anything else.

This, of course, is the census-takers' catchall for women who do not do other things, and masks a lot of self-employed women. However, it does reflect the fact that in the urban situation women's industrial and agricultural opportunities are severely limited. Nor are there many professional, technical, administrative, managerial, or clerical opportunities for them. Their lack of education contributes substantially to this situation, as Table 8 in the Appendix shows. The Appendix also discusses some of the differences between African nations with respect to women's education.

There are several stages in the development of formal education for African women. In the colonial era, in the mid-1950s in Dakar and Abidjan, for instance, there was a large disparity between boys' and girls' literacy levels, because the colonialists were not usually concerned about providing education for girls. This situation is reflected in the statistics for older age groups in most ex-colonies: in Yaoundé in 1976, some 38.5 percent of the men aged 65 and over had gone to school of some sort, compared to only 8.2 percent of the women aged 65 and over. (All education statistics are delivered from the sources listed on page 50.) It is common to find complete illiteracy among women over 65 in some areas.

In the 1960s there was a push for education in most of the newly independent countries, and primary and/or middle school education was often made compulsory. Facilities were expanded drastically to accommodate the influx of students of both sexes, and in some cases, the access of boys and girls to primary school was equalized. In Accra in 1970 more girls were in primary school than boys (because there were more girls in the population). Children in urban areas, of course, have had more access to schooling than those in rural areas because development spending has usually been concentrated there.

The third stage is reflected in higher percentages of females than males having primary school as their highest level of education—in Accra, Maseru, Tananarive, and Yaoundé, for instance, because more schools have been provided, but more boys have gone on to middle and secondary school. The educational system is steeply pyramidal for everyone, with very few secondary schools compared to middle schools, but even fewer secondary places for girls than for boys. Many secondary schools are private and/or costly, and enrollment is not compulsory. A few elite women, however, were able to complete secondary school or university and combined high education levels with an indigenous tradition favorable to influential female roles. The case of Funmilayo Anikulapo Kuti, a Yoruba women, is outstanding in this respect.

Funmilayo Anikulapo Kuti was a lifelong resident of Abeokuta, a large older town in southwestern Nigeria. Her grandparents were taken by Portuguese slave dealers to Sierra Leone, having been captured by the British antislavery patrols. They subsequently returned to Abeokuta. Her mother and father were both born in Abeokuta of Christian convert parents.

Kuti was christened Frances Funmilayo, but studying in England she dropped the Frances altogether. In England she studied general education, French, and domestic science, and in 1922 returned to

Nigeria and began to teach at the Abeokuta Grammar School. It was there she met her husband, the Rev. Ransome-Kuti, and they were married in 1925. From 1925 to 1931 Kuti and her husband resided in Ijebu-Ode near Abeokuta where Kuti became the principal of a girls' school and began literacy classes for adult women. Upon her return to Abeokuta in 1931 she founded a nursery school and became its head-mistress. In 1942 she organized a club of educated women known as the Abeokuta Ladies' Club, which subsequently undertook to aid the market women who complained that their goods were being confis-cated by the government to aid in the war effort. It was now that Kuti truly became involved with the market women, and by 1946 the Ladies' Club had become the Abeokuta Women's Union, which with Kuti at its head spearheaded the protests of the market women that were to culiminate in the abolition of female taxation (for a time), the resignation of the Alake (king) of Abeokuta, and the total reorganiza-tion of the Native Authority System in Abeokuta. These were tremendous victories for the women and Kuti became an international figure, travelling in eastern Europe, China and Israel.

By 1950 the Abeokuta Women's Union changed its name to the Nigerian Women's Union and was documented as having about 80 000 members. It began to inaugurate branches in other parts of Nigeria, and in Abeokuta operated a weaving corporation, ran a maternity and child welfare clinic, and conducted literacy classes for adult women.

In 1980 Kuti died; the news was front-page headlines throughout Nigeria. She had spent her life in active pursuit of basic human equality of the sexes, recognition of the rights of ordinary people to have their basic needs met, and the creation of a Nigeria where justice reigned (adapted from Cheryl Johnson, private communication, June 1982).

In general, however, it was not so easy for women to translate educational credentials into an actual job. Accompanying the provision of primary schooling came a steady inflation in the amount of education required for a job, and sometimes a lowering of the quality of the educa-tion provided. In addition, the generally worsening economic situation of the 1970s meant that wage employment was not available for many primary or middle school leavers, and especially not for girls, who had to compete with the better-educated boys. Even in Kenya, where in 1976 some 89 percent of the secretarial workers were female, only approxi-mately 16 percent of the wage labor force was female, and 77 percent of self-employed women in the modern sector were in trade, restaurants, and hotels (Republic of Kenya, 1978: 43, 45, 46). The primary refuge for the unemployed is self-employment in small, sometimes illegal, enter-prises. Self-employment offers the advantage to young women of being able to watch their children while they are working. Even in areas where self-employment of women was not formerly common, it is becoming more so out of economic necessity.

The provision of formal education, then, has not so far remedied the economic inequalities between men and women, because that educa-tion has been provided unequally. Furthermore, it may be damaging women's opportunities for self-employment where these are well developed. For instance, a girl who spends her time at school will not put in the same number of hours as an apprentice seamstress, market trader, or potter. Formal education could in theory teach skills valuable for self-employment (such as accounting, carpentry, car repair), but too often it does not. Instead, girls may be taught home economics, which may concentrate on convincing girls that Western ways of housekeeping, table-setting, and child care are superior to indigenous ones.

Formal education may also arouse expectations in girls that they will obtain a clerical job and a lifestyle similar to that depicted in the movies. Thus they may no longer be interested in pursuing self-employment as a trader, for instance, because trading is too low in socioeconomic status for them. And because trading itself is less lucrative than previously, it is less attractive. In the end, many women will have to compromise and take up some sort of self-employment because other opportunities do not exist, are not open to them, or are not compatible with child rearing. Inexpensive day care is hard to come by for many urban women, and they are less likely than rural women to have coresident relatives who will help.

The problem of child care is particularly acute for the women who have obtained jobs as secretaries or typists. Their wages do not usually allow payment for good quality day care, governments or businesses seldom provide it, yet their long hours require it. They often rely on the help of a poor relative, usually a young girl, living with them. They usually have fewer children than poorer women — four or five instead of six or seven, still a substantial burden. Some governments provide or require benefits such as day care, maternity leave, and hospital care; this has only caused some employers to become even more reluctant to hire women.

There have been complaints from clerically employed women in many countries that men regard them as legitimate prey for sexual exploits. Sexual harassment may even cause some to leave their jobs for self-employment, which at least offers more control over their environment. Where self-employment is not attractive, some workers find they can supplement their pay with occasional prostitution or long-term liaisons with office superiors. In countries where the inflation of the 1970s has been particularly severe, real wages have fallen, causing people to supplement their earnings by part-time self-employment.

The higher the stage of technological development, the more clerical jobs are given over to women (Boserup, 1970). This process has both good and bad aspects for women. In Africa, as in developed countries, very little is being done to avoid the sex-stereotyping of women into secretarial-clerical roles which may prevent their advance into other economic positions. Other positions which are becoming typically female in Africa include nursing and lower-level teaching positions.

The type of education offered is partly responsible for this trend: the denial of technological education to women is particularly important, and appears not only in Africa but also in most Third World countries (Tadesse, 1982). The case of Mary Chinubu is pertinent as a typical woman clerical worker.

Mary Chinubu is a young woman of twenty-two working as a clerk-typist in Lusaka. She grew up in a village with her parents and siblings; when she showed promise as a student she was sent to live with her older brother (a half-brother by her father's first wife), who had become a successful businessman in a small way selling auto parts. She finished her middle schooling while living in Lusaka with her brother and his wife, and helping to care for their three children. She then was fortunate to get a place at a secondary boarding school; her brother paid the fees, although it strained the budget. After a year or so she started slacking off in her work; at age sixteen she was developing an interest in boys, whom she would meet secretly to go to the cinema. After a time she got pregnant and was forced to leave school; her brother was furious and reluctantly allowed her to return to his home. He was even more upset when she named one of her teachers as the father of the child. Under pressure from their mother, her brother agreed to keep the baby, a girl, while Mary went to a commercial school to get secretarial training and, with her brother's help, she got a job clerking for a mining firm.

After several years of work Mary took a flat which she shared with another woman in similar circumstances. She could afford it only because she had become, under much pressure, the mistress of an older man who was one of her bosses. She was more attracted to some of the younger men she and her friend occasionally met in bars, but they could not provide for her as lavishly. Also she wanted to keep her job. Her sister-in-law remonstrated with her, saying that already at age twenty she had ruined her life. Mary gave in to the pressure when her affair with the boss waned, partly because she had fallen in love with a younger man she had met at work who had promised to marry her.

She married the twenty-eight year old rising young engineer and everything went well for six months. Then her husband's sister came to her and told her that he had another wife, whom he had married in his village some time before; they had a child. Mary was unhappy that he had not told her this (although she had not told him about her daughter). But more important, she had suspicions that he was being unfaithful. He had quit taking her out with him in the evenings several months after their marriage. Furthermore, he was increasingly leaving the household expenses to her, even though he earned far more than she did. Eleven months after their marriage she had a child, a boy this time. By then they were quarrelling a lot and he was spending most evenings out, giving no explanation for his absence. After another six months of deteriorating relations, he ceased paying any household expenses altogether, and she moved out, taking the child and her belongings with her.

Now Mary has returned to her former way of life. Through thick and thin she hung onto her job; by supplementing her pay with donations from boyfriends she can afford day care for her son. She seldom sees her daughter, although she occasionally contributes to her support but she wishes great things for her son. She plans to send him to school, and expects him to be smarter than his father, and the support of her old age when he is a success. She does not plan to remarry, although she would if it provided financial security. However, she is skeptical that it would. She likes the freedom of being single and controlling her own finances. 'I wouldn't like to begin giving my salary to a man while my parents and family suffer . . . I would not like to live under a hawk's eye every day . . . men are very jealous' (adapted from Schuster, 1979).

Conclusions

For all of these reasons, most urban women find that they cannot grow what they need in town, so they must buy it, meaning that they must work outside the home. Wage work opportunities are severely limited, however, because of discrimination in education and hiring and the economic situation, so that women must be self-employed in a shrinking number of occupations. The skills imparted by home economics courses, baking cakes or bread, for instance, can help them to make a living selling prepared foods, one area where competition from foreign firms has not been a major factor, but selling prepared foods is not a lucrative occupation for most people. The result is that urban women are generally far more dependent on their husbands for support than are rural women, while they are also more likely to be living with them. Their husbands may resent this increased dependence and incessant demands from their wives. As described in Chapter 4 on the family, men formerly were not expected to provide as much support as is now necessary. Urban living brings new demands and expectations in terms of standard of living—boys must go to school, rent must be paid, entertainment is costly. The husbands may demand that the women work harder, since the women's earnings are usually needed. Spouses do not usually pool their incomes, so that a woman without an income is in an invidious position with no say in household decisions. Her very dependence may make her hesitate to seek her way out of an intolerable marriage, but she may be forced to if the man stops providing adequate support.

In earlier times and in rural areas economic pressures on marriage were alleviated by substantial contributions from women for household expenses. Spouses often pooled their labor in communal enterprises. Even now in South Africa, some urban African men are subsidized by rural women sending them food, despite the desperate poverty of the reserves. In Ghana children suffer as their mothers cannot earn enough through trade to feed them properly. Women, then, must still bear much responsibility for the economic well-being of their families, while they have few resources to enable them to fulfill it. Even after working hard to fulfill their responsibilities, they may find themselves partially or wholly abandoned in the increased mobility that marks many towns. My friend Nsuwa is a good example.

Nsuwa is an old woman living in central Accra who is partially blind and totally dependent on her two daughters who live with her for support. Their children run errands for her, and they share their food with her. Her two surviving sons live elsewhere, one abroad and one in the suburb of another town. Although both are educated and doing well, she rarely receives anything from them. She surmises that they put their obligations to their own children first. She feels poorly used since in her youth she worked hard at trading to pay for their secondary schooling. 'They were my investment', she says, 'but I never expected this would come of it. My daughters help me and their father with food, even though they themselves are poor. My sons never come here,'and only send money maybe once a year. It's not enough; I often go hungry but I don't like to deprive my grandchildren of food'.

Because more women than men are poor, the already high birth rate for sub-Saharan Africa will remain high. Women look to their children for social security and help in their labor-intensive activities. Only when their standard of living rises considerably will they limit their fertility, particularly if they go into more skilled occupations that are not labor-intensive. As long as the women's sector remains mostly poor, the cycle will be perpetuated of high fertility→low education→low skills→low income→high fertility. If development planners and executors are serious about the long-term economic health of Africa, they will incorporate women from the areas concerned in development planning. Non-elite women need equitable well-paid employment and appropriate education to develop marketable skills inside and outside the home. Many development efforts have failed because of their negative impact on women, or because they do not address women's needs. We will return to the imperatives of development planning in the last chapter.

We can conclude, then, that women's socioeconomic status can be very different from that of the men related to them. These differences must be considered in our attempts to understand social and economic processes and develop new ways to look at class formation. In economic terms, it is productive to look at money flows in separate men's and women's spheres, whose interactions can change over time. In the realm of society and politics, it is worthwhile analyzing change in the relative strength, functions, and power of male and female networks. These methods can help us to develop more refined ways of analyzing women and class formation.

Statistical sources for Tables 2 and 3

Cameroon, Statistics and National Accounts Department, *Census 1976,* **Vol. I**, Tome 2, 105-19.

Chad, Bureau de la Statistique, *Recensement de Fort Lamy*, 1962, 27-30, 1.

Ghana, Census Office, *1960 Census*, Special Report A, 71, 115; *1970 Census,* **Vol. III**, 199, 202-3.

Ivory Coast, Direction de la Statistique et des Etudes Economiques et Démographiques, *Recensement d'Abidjan, 1955*, 39, 41-3.

Kenya, Statistics Division, *Census 1969,* **Vol. 1**, 78; Central Bureau of Statistics, Ministry of Finance and Planning, *Women in Kenya* (July 1978).

Lesotho, Bureau of Statistics, *Population Census, 1966,* **Vol. 1**, 173.

Malagasy Republic, Institut National de la Statistique et de la Recherche Economique, *Recensements Urbains 1960*, 26, 145, 162, 171.

Mali, Service de la Statistique, *Bamako Recensement 1958-1960*, 13-14, 20, 24-5; Bureau Centrale de Recensement, *Recensement Général de la Population, Dec. 1976,* **Vol. 2**, 205-7.

Senegal, Service de la Statistique et de la Mécanographie, *Recensement de Dakar 1955,* **Vol. 2**, 7, 25.

South Africa, Department of Statistics, *Census 1970* (Metropolitan Area, Cape Town), **Vol 23**, 372, 411, 424.

Sudan, Statistics Department, *Census 1955/56*, Town Planners Supplement, **Vol. 1**, 111-14, 170-1.

Tanzania, Economic Affairs and Development Planning Ministry, *Census 1967,* **Vol. 2**, 92, 107-8, 154-6.

Zambia, Ministry of Education, *Annual Report, 1974;* K. T. Hansen, 'When Sex Becomes a Critical Variable, Married Women and Extradomestic Work in Lusaka', paper presented at African Studies Association Conference (Nov. 1979), 6.

PART TWO
African women in society and culture

4   Women in the changing African family

Luise White

The adult primitive woman is above all a wife, whose life is centered in her home and family . . . a woman passes at marriage from under the authority of her father to that of her husband . . . the husband's authority as such is not challenged. Neither the wife nor anyone else disputes that important decisions with regard to the home, the up-bringing of the children, the betrothing of daughters and sons, and so forth, rest with him and him alone (Evans-Pritchard, 1965: 46, 51).

The [Kikuyu] customary law of marriage provides that a man may have as many wives as he can support . . . The custom also provides that all women must be under the protection of men, and that in order to avoid prostitution [although no word exists for 'prostitution' in the Kikuyu language] all women must be married . . . It is held that if a man can control and manage effectively the affairs of a large family, this is an excellent testimonial of his capacity to look after the interests of the tribe . . . (Kenyatta, 1937: 167-9).

The . . . myth that must be banished is that polygyny has anything to do with the concupiscence of the male. Polygyny is a state into which most African men enter with a certain trepidation. If you think one wife can henpeck a husband, you should see what three wives in league can do. If co-wives live up to the ideals of their roles, even just barely, no man exists but is under greater strain and control . . . The man who has a strong senior wife is a fortunate individual, because she will run the household and will straighten out the fusses among the co-wives. He will not have to bother. If he does not have such a wife, two thirds of his energy goes into administration (Bohannon and Curtin 1971: 108).

What is the role of women in African families? Are adult women merely passive breeders, under the jurisdiction of their husbands, as the first quotation announces, or are women in fact creatures of such intense sexuality that only the institution of marriage and the firm hand of a husband can control them, as the second quotation asserts? Or perhaps African women actually run their families from behind the scenes, as the third quotation suggests, and Africa husbands just take the credit for the smooth workings of daily life?

These three views—all written by men, all in this century—describe

African wives in varying degrees of passivity and dependence, and they define a married woman's place in her family in terms of her relationship to her husband. In the quotations above, there is no hint that a woman's relationship to her natal kin, her children, her co-wives, or to the crops she cultivates, might order and govern her days: the authors share a very Western notion that families can, and indeed should, be studied through marriage. Perhaps the most important thing we can learn from these quotations is the common point of mystification they share: that the organization of African family life depends not on economics or ecology, or indeed anything outside the homestead, but on the capabilities and qualities of individual men and women. In this essay I hope to show that women's role in the family has changed not according to the personal traits of individuals, but as a result of the family's changing relation to natural resources, the state, and society.

The family in Africa before 1900

Prior to the European domination of Africa, the family was not an unchanging unit of loyalty, protection, and production dwelling in a timeless, static space that had never undergone radical social change. African families had their own local trials and tribulations, and the disruption caused by famine, epidemic and drought, the slave trade, and the extreme political dislocation that some parts of Africa experienced in the nineteenth century amended customary law. For example, the international slave trade drastically reduced the male population of Angola in the eighteenth century, and this increased the number of wives available to each remaining man, so that the size of polygynous households increased dramatically (Thornton, 1980: 417-27). Ideologies and methods to control these wives may have been elaborated as well. At the turn of the century in South, East, and East-Central Africa ecological and political crises first and foremost altered the institution of marriage: it was paid for differently, if at all; it occurred later or earlier, or among people who would not otherwise have married (or met), who sometimes changed their forms of inheritance within a generation (White, 1983; Wright, 1975: 808). Other aspects of African family life were simply pronounced expendable. Thus leviratic marriage—in which a widow was taken as a wife by the brother of the deceased—became an occasional and luxurious institution in the warlord-torn Nyasa-Tanganyika corridor at the end of the nineteenth century (Wright, 1975: 808-10).

But these breakdowns in kinship ties and distortions of customary law were the exceptions in pre-colonial times, not the rule. The fact that African families regrouped under their old customs once conditions returned to normal, testifies to the vitality and elasticity of African family institutions: they could be expanded in times of prosperity, such as in Angola, and ignored in times of crisis, such as in the Nyasa-Tanganyika corridor.

What generalizations can we then make about women in the pre-colonial African family? Not many, because for the most part, pre-colonial families have been studied and subsumed under the very substantial rubric of kinship systems. As one scholar reported, 'I had learned during my seven years of anthropological training . . . that kinship was equivalent to society in primitive tribes and that it was a way of life' (Chagnon, 1968: 4-5). While kinship systems certainly include women, they do not have very much to do with women. Indeed, from one perspective, kinship systems—and families themselves—classify the ways men arrange for men's access to resources, including women. Women are necessarily deliverers of men into the world, and are sometimes the custodians of the property destined for their sons, but systems of marriage (how to choose a mate), of residence (where to live and work), and of descent and inheritance (how to establish heirs and transmit property) never provide for autonomous links between women of different generations. Instead, 'patriliny creates ties between the "father" and his wife's sons; matriliny . . . between the mother's brother and her children' (Meillassoux, 1981: 23). Thus peoples reproduce themselves by insuring that they have enough women to replenish their numbers: in some societies, many of which are patrilineal, women are exchanged for other women; in others, many of which are matrilineal, women remain in their homelands and men come to form families with them. In such systems, and in the academic ruminations on them, one woman is very much the functional equivalent of another: they are interchangeable. There are even institutions that express this explicitly; sororate marriage, for example, requires that a runaway wife, or one who dies without children, be replaced by her sister.

If we take this equivalency as our starting point, however, it is possible to see in the worldwide distribution of kinship systems something about women's role in pre-colonial African family life. In general, people who practiced intensive hoe agriculture tended to be matrilineal. In densely forested regions (the West African forest zone, the Zaire River basin to South-East Africa, or the East African coast), men usually cleared a piece of land which was then farmed entirely by women. The natural fertility of the soil decreased in a very short time, so after several years that parcel of land was allowed to lie fallow while men cleared new land. There was thus a constant need for women's agricultural labor and an annual need for men's farm work (Boserup, 1970: 16-19; Meillassoux, 1981: 26-7). Because in these societies women monopolized the skills necessary to feed their families, descent was organized around and through women. These societies imported men to marry women, and did not exchange 'their' women for outsiders, who might not have the requisite farming skills.

In some of the societies that practiced intensive cultivation, especially of tubers such as yams or manioc (cassava), which do not store well, men hunted or fished and thus occasionally contributed to the family's subsistence (Meillassoux, 1981: 26). Many of these peoples traced descent bilaterally, through both mothers and fathers. In practice, however, many bilateral societies have tended to behave as though they were patrilineal either when the scales tip to favor the practical economic significance of the father's work, or when the society comes under the influence of patrilineal ideologies that diminish the status (but not the material proceeds) of women's work (Leach, 1973: 56-8; Robertson, 1976: 122-33). For example, the Igbo of eastern Nigeria cultivate tubers. They are patrilineal, and have been for hundreds of years. But within their patrilineality is a hierarchy of tuber production based on the diminution of women's work. The hero of *Things Fall Apart,* Chinua Achebe's novel of the last years of Igbo autonomy, reflects on his natal family: 'His mother and sisters worked hard enough, but they grew women's crop, like coco-yams (taro), beans and cassava. Yam, the king of crops, was a man's crop' (Achebe, 1959: 25).

This is not to say that patrilineal kinship results from historical deformations of matrilineality. African pastoralists, like their Biblical counterparts, have been patrilineal for millenia. Among livestock-keeping peoples, men both own and herd the resources that either through consumption or exchange support their families. Women milk livestock, and have limited rights over the stock their sons shall inherit, but they themselves never own the disposable property that is their society's wealth. At best, they are allowed to look after and allocate live-stock; they cannot decide what to do with it. Among the pastoral Masai of East Africa, women milk livestock, raise children, and cook; their identification with sedentary, house-bound work is so strong that they are responsible for building the family's dwelling (Llewelyn-Davies, 1979: 210-12), a male task in many other societies. Women's productive role in agricultural and pastoral systems is described more fully in Chapters 1 and 2 above.

The fact that peoples who combine agriculture (particularly the cultivation of cereals) and pastoralism are overwhelmingly patrilineal cannot be explained in any clear-cut way. But because livestock-keeping has always been the prerogative of the wealthy, it may be that patrilineal descent systems emerged where pastoralism was the ideology (see Kettel, 1981) rather than a constant or even frequent reality for all. We have already seen that African kinship customs were elastic, and patrilineal kinship may be one of the most elastic and contingent customs of all. The social roles of women in both matrilineal and patrilineal systems were circumscribed, not by the imperatives of female biology but by (literally) man-made cultural norms (see Guyer, 1981). We must now look at some of the factors that affected women's roles in pre-colonial family life.

The pre-colonial patrilineal family tended to be polygynous, as the quotations on page 53 show. The marriage of several women by one man was evidence of his wealth (however much the wives' work would make them virtually self-sustaining). wives were usually acquired through the payment of bridewealth, usually reckoned in livestock, from the husband to the woman's father. Thus the men who owned the most livestock, were often considered the wealthiest, for they had the greatest opportunities for acquiring many wives (who in turn could provide them with agricultural produce), either for themselves or their sons, whose loyalty they could guarantee with the promise of livestock when they were about to marry. This probably served as an excellent mechanism to keep families residing together.

In most of pre-colonial Africa men married at relatively late ages, around thirty or even older, to women who were usually more than a dozen years their junior (for example, see White, 1979; 1983). However, once men from the wealthier families married, they married additional wives at a relatively rapid rate. In pre-colonial times, a man would marry and within two years take a second wife, and a third the year after that (Kenyatta, 1937: 169; Acheve, 1959; 1969; Emecheta, 1979: 30-6). This meant that in practice the co-wives were almost the same age (exceptions usually resulted from leviratic marriage), and that they became mothers at about the same time, and could literally share the tasks and experiences of family life. Few if any women of the pre-colonial era had the experience of being the sole wife for five or ten years and then being joined by a younger second wife.

High levels of fertility were greatly desired in pre-colonial Africa, by ٭both men and women. Fertility was important because of the high rates of infant and child mortality, because of the economic importance of children's labor contributions, and because of the many advantages and services available to those who were members of large extended families. Parents often relied on their children for support in their old age. Scholars believe that some rituals and customs reflect this emphasis on fertility; the custom of woman – woman marriage, for example, allowed a barren woman to 'marry' another woman who would then bear children for her partrilineage (see, for example, Oboler 1980).

In its traditional form, however, polygyny served to limit total fertility to a certain extent, because of the presence of co-wives with whom a man was expected to spend relatively equal amounts of time. Another such limitation was the common requirement of sexual abstinence for from one to three years after the birth of a child; this custom served to protect the health of both the infant and the mother.

If one change brought about by colonial rule was the physical separation of African men from their families, another was to lower the age of first marriage for men, but to delay the onset of polygynous marriage, and thus to increase the length of time between the acquisition of the first and second wives. In addition, the spread of modern medicine has significantly lowered the death rate, and this, together with the growing lack of observance of the postpartum sexual taboo and the decline in polygyny, has led to a marked increase in fertility levels in most African countries. Although an urban family in Africa now has about five children on the average, rural family sizes are larger, and there is as yet very little evidence of the fertility decline that accompanied industrialization in Western European societies. This means that the majority of African women spend a good part of their adult lives bearing children.

Women in the colonial African family: scholarship and stereotypes

In recent years, American historians have presented a portrait of the family as the institution that controls the emotional and intimate lives of its members. They have shown us that families are the site of all the social conflict taking place in the wider society, and that families at once enforce repressive gender roles and are nearly torn inside out by them (Ehrenreich and English, 1979: 101ff.; Ryan, 1981).

At the same time, African historians and anthropologists have tended to concentrate on how women have lost status and material benefits within the family in the last seventy-five years (Robertson, 1976: 111-33; Etienne, 1980: 214-33; Okeyo, 1980b). Thus some of the more sensitive and analytical studies of African life published in recent years have simply ignored questions about emotional relationships, while capably documenting changes in labor time and leisure time (examples dealing with Kenya alone include Parkin, 1972; Strobel, 1979; Kitching, 1980). Other studies, less sensitive and analytical, have labeled poor women in rural Africa 'unstable' (LeVine, 1979: 386) and urban women 'fatalistic' (Pellow, 1977: 61-3) or, at worst, unable 'to experience love' (Schuster, 1979: 103). According to such studies, any problems women might have within the family are personal; they are due to the qualities of different individuals. Such studies repeat the same assumptions that dominate the quotations with which I began this essay—that women are either so weak and easily deluded that they need men's help, or that they are too strong for their own good. Until quite recently, many scholars presented West African women as strong-willed and economically independent (Boserup, 1970: 85-105; Little, 1973) and rural women in East and Central Africa as passive and stoic, requiring men's innovation and motivation to generate village wealth (Richards, 1939: 404; Mitchell, 1961: 320-1).

With such stereotypes, how do we learn about women's role in African families as they were transformed by colonial rule? We learn by looking not at individual family members, but at the structure and the experience of colonization.

Colonialism, labor, and family life

In order to build the apparatus of the new colonial states and produce exports, African colonies at the turn of the century had enormous labor requirements. In order to induce able-bodied African males to leave their homes (where many had been producing export crops for years) and go to work in European-owned enterprises, taxation was introduced in most of Africa by 1903. Men had to work in order to get the money to pay taxes. The first tax was usually levied on huts, which amounted to a tax on wives, so that polygynous men had the greatest tax burdens. In areas growing cash crops, some men simply sold part of their own or their wives' produce to pay their taxes (for example, Arrighi, 1970: 230), but other men sent their sons into wage labor to pay the family's tax obligations (for example, EAP, NLC 1912-13). In order to get more men into the nascent labor force, between 1906 and 1910 a tax on males over sixteen was introduced in many colonies. Not only did this increase the number of young men leaving their rural homelands to go to work, but it gave them the wherewithall to begin acquiring bridewealth, a process that kept them working for most of the year for several years (Hay, 1972: 172-3; Kitching, 1980: 217). As young men gained independent and relatively early access to bridewealth, the African family lost some of the control it once had over all its members.

Marriage itself was not disrupted by the introduction of wage labor. In Kenya, for example, the total number of marriages seems to have increased in the first quarter of this century, because there were more men with greater access to bridewealth than there had been before (EAP, NLC, 1912-13; Fazan, 1932). Unlike pre-colonial marriages, however, these marriages seem to have remained monogamous for many years: men would sometimes take ten years or more to acquire a second wife, as the cost of living rose more rapidly than did men's wages (White, 1979: 8-15). This delayed onset of polygynous marriage seems commonplace in much of sub-Saharan Africa in this century; it also seems to put co-wives in more competitive situations. The equation that the more wives a man has, the more grain and tubers he can cultivate (Boserup, 1970: 38-51) has been outmoded by the harsh realities of colonization—it is only true if land and wives are plentiful and easily acquired. In South Africa, for example, where the purchasing power of industrial wages paid to Africans has been in steady decline since 1910 (Legassick, 1977: 184ff.), the incidence of polygynous marriage among those peoples who supply labor to the mines has declined by about 40 percent of its 1912 levels (see Goody, 1973: 182). Colonial and post-colonial polygynous marriage should be seen as a reflection of men's access to wealth, not the utility of women in rural agriculture.

Most studies for other parts of Africa suggest that the rate of polygyny either has dropped or will drop with urbanization, since polygyny is relatively more expensive and less functional in the modern economy. There are significant differences in the rate of polygyny from one African country to another, and even from one region to another. In the 1950s one scholar estimated that about a third of all married African men had more than one wife. (Dorjahn, 1959: 102). More recent estimates for the main West and East African countries suggest that even in African areas where polygyny is widespread, only about 36 percent of the men have more than one wife. (Welch and Glick, 1981). Polygyny is lower in urban than in rural areas; for example, the rate for the Ivory Coast in the early 1960s was 29 percent in rural areas, and 14 percent in Abidjan (Clignet and Sween, 1969: 134).

As men came to the new colonial cities, ports, railheads, and plantations, to work, a tradition of male labor migration was born, as described in Chapter 1. Policies governing wages, housing and vagrancy tried to guarantee that single men would have neither the interest nor the funds to stay in town any longer than their labor contracts allowed, so that at their termination they would hurry home, only to return when the next tax payment was due. Wages paid to Africans were minimal, based on the idea that a worker's family could provide the carbohydrates his wages were insufficient to purchase. The twin factors of depressed wages and male migration allowed for a regular supply of cheap and unskilled labor going from countryside to town and back again. The result was that men began to be absent from family life in rural Africa, and that the new colonial towns rapidly filled up with large, temporary populations of underpaid single men.

Rural women in their families, c. 1900-1980

Colonization and labor migration placed an intolerable burden on the African women left behind. They had to increase (or at least maintain) agricultural production, feeding themselves and their children, and sometimes their absent sons and spouses, while providing cash crops for export or market sale. Between food and cash-crop production, the amount of time women spent cultivating increased dramatically, and they still had to perform their traditional tasks of child care and cooking (see for example, Skinner, 1965: 70; Vail and White, 1977: 249ff.; Hay, 1976, and Chapter 1 above). Indeed, the only area in which women's workload did not increase was in the day-in, day-out role of wife. In Botswana by the early 1930s, for example, it was exceedingly rare for married couples to live together for more than two months at a time (Schapera, 1971: 165); in the years that followed in East and Central Africa, 40 to 60 percent of all males were away from their villages at any given time (Richards, 1939: 404-5; Harris, 1959: 51). In Upper Volta, about 20 percent of male Mossi migrants did not return home to join their families for the rainy season planting in the 1950s (Skinner, 1965: 68).

Rural women nevertheless adjusted to these situations, sometimes with ingenuity and innovation, sometimes at incalculable cost to themselves. They adjusted by utilizing, and occasionally modifying, all the sources of support available to them: customary law, natal kin, marital kin (including children), and the software of the colonial effort, missions and women's self-help organizations (see Hay, 1976: 98ff.; and Chapter 5 below). The degree to which African women were able to control their own position in their families was affected by whether or not their natal families were engaged primarily in cash-crop cultivation or labor migration and food-crop cultivation.

Where labor migration was the norm, some women had new opportunities to trade in foodstuffs year-round. In East and Central Africa, local employers found it cheaper to encourage peasant women to sell cooked food to their work-force, and this provided a new source of cash for women who would otherwise have had to scrape by with farming (Hay, 1976: 92ff.; Chauncey, 1981: 136-42). The paucity of rural enterprises, however, meant that this was not a viable alternative for most women. In some areas where labor migration was seasonal, women were able to sell cooked food to men travelling to find work (Skinner, 1965: 67).

In areas where labor migration led to rural impoverishment, it had the effect of making married women closer to their natal families. This had long been true in matrilineal societies, but only began to apply to patrilineal peoples during the colonial era, as women married into patrilineages that were too impoverished to look after them fully. As early as the 1920s, East African prostitutes of Masai, Ganda, Nyamwezi, Kikuyu, and Kamba origin (all patrilineal peoples) were willingly supporting and educating the children of their widowed sisters, and sometimes providing the bridewealth for their brothers as well (White, 1983). In western Kenya, on the other hand, married women lived in their absent husbands' households, subordinate to their mothers-in-law. Nevertheless, Kenya Luo women entering the produce trade were most frequently subsidized by their brothers and sisters (Okeyo, 1979: 339).

If labor migration strengthened African women's relations with their siblings, in many areas it made their relations with their in-laws especially brittle. Looking once more at western Kenya—by the 1940s 'a society of women, children, and old men' (Hay, 1976: 102)—pauperized Gusii women returned to their parents' homes after disastrous marriages, generally those in which an absent husband's wage was not enough to make up for a mother-in-law's labor demands and animosity (LeVine, 1979: 49ff.). Many young Gusii women who stayed in their marriages were said to suffer from the kind of jealousy that makes 'you so angry with someone that you wish that person were dead', often brought about when a woman sees 'her sisters-in-law, eating better than she does and having better clothes' (LeVine, 1979: 177). These women await money from their spouses' salaries before they can even plant staple crops. The intertwined events of abandonment and impoverishment frequently left young wives angry and anguished. Their fears often took the active form of patronizing local witches, and the passive form of secrecy and increasing privatization about what had been in pre-colonial times the joyous events of a pregnancy or a bountiful harvest (LeVine, 1979: 115ff.; Hay, 1976: 107).

In western Kenya, women have access to land only within their husbands' households, so that many twentieth-century marriages there may have remained intact precisely because wives had no other way to support themselves or their children (Potash, 1978: 387; Hay, 1982). But the conditions of labor migration and marital stability were not identical in colonial Africa. In Upper Volta, for example, Mossi women in former times frequently resigned themselves to unhappy marriages; by the 1950s, however, dissatisfied wives were said to run off with migrants heading south (Skinner, 1965: 74). Indeed, many Mossi women seem to have been able to enforce new marital norms out of the conditions of labor migration: wives who accompanied their husbands to the towns of Ghana and the Ivory Coast sometimes returned home—either alone or with a co-wife—to curtail their husbands' unpopular actions, as if they were going on strike (Schildkrout, 1978: 108). On the other hand, among the Igbo of Nigeria, young mothers tended to stay in marriages, however unhappy or poor, unless they were driven out (Emecheta, 1979: 126ff.). This was probably because women without male children were unable to inherit anything when their husbands died (Uchendu, 1965: 50).

Since there are few statistics on divorce in pre-colonial societies, it is difficult to make actual comparisons between present and past. But it is not necessarily the case that divorce today is more frequent than in the past; in some rural African societies, especially matrilineal ones, divorce used to be quite frequent.

One way for women to strengthen their position in their marital families was to function as men: woman-to-woman marriage is an example of how a patriarchal aspect of customary law could be manipulated to the advantage of individual women in recent years. Originally, the very widespread custom of woman-marriage enabled dead men to have descendants: a barren widow (or a widow with daughters only) could marry another woman who would cohabit with men of her late husband's lineage or age-grade to provide offspring for the dead man. Some widows with children have been able to use woman-marriage as a way to avoid leviratic marriages (Oboler, 1980: 69ff). In western Kenya, there is evidence that previously unmarried women with independent thoughts and income (generally obtained in illicit occupations in the new colonial towns) used their wealth to marry wives and found lineages, either in their own names or those of fathers or brothers (Hay, 1982). But it was in the palm-oil producing areas of West Africa that women-marriage was the most widespread and sophisticated. Where women could own palm trees, wealthy women often married wives to acquire a cheap labor force whose heirs they could also control (Bohannon, 1968: 99). Where women could not own palm trees, such as among the Igbo, they traded, and married women traders sometimes married 'one wife after another' as their businesses expanded and they needed more help (Uchendu, 1965: 7). In both these cases, we see women using customary law to bond a small labor force to their own enterprises, and to strengthen and underwrite their otherwise tenuous position as household head and employer.

The small and fragile forms of autonomy described above are generally not available to women whose families' primary source of wealth comes from the production of cash crops, especially coffee, tea, cocoa, and cotton. These crops were introduced by the colonizers as men's crops, and ever since have sporadically brought riches to their producers: in this way, cash cropping seems to have reinforced patrilineal control. The result has been the increased diminution of women's work in this century (Boserup, 1970: 53-63), and a tendency toward the use of women as pawns in the acquisition and redistribution of paternal capital in the twin forms of inheritance and bridewealth.

For example, where customary law would benefit a woman and her descendants, it has been partially rewritten. Among matrilineal cocoa farmers in southern Ghana, where a sister's son would normally inherit a man's very profitable farm, some fathers have recently insisted that their children marry their sisters' children (cross-cousin marriage), while others have simply given land irrevocably to their own sons (Hill, 1963: 124-36). In the patrilineal coffee-producing Bukoba District of northwest Tanzania, the boom of the 1920s enabled Haya fathers to command a cash brideprice equivalent to nearly $100 for their daughters, who were most often married to the highest bidders. When the crash of 1929 reduced the world price of coffee by a staggering 99 percent, husbands ordered their wives home and divorced, and their bridewealth returned (formerly an easy thing among the Haya). Obviously, the fathers were equally in debt and could not come up with the refund. Their daughters, however, had already been taught 'that they had a cash value' and, whether of their own accord or not, they journeyed to the major cities of East Africa and became highly competitive prostitutes. They were said to send money home regularly, and when they returned years later, they were hailed as 'the economic saviours of their families' (Sundkler, 1945: 254-8; see also White, 1983).

On the whole, labor migration and rural poverty have increased women's workload and anxieties, but have also increased the options and social relations available to them, and placed many of the latter under the women's control. In African families of rural wealth, however, women have become appendages of their fathers and/or husbands much more than their poorer counterparts have. This becomes especially clear if we look at poor and wealthy women farming adjacent land in the same society.

The Kikuyu occupy the central highlands of Kenya; Kiambu is the lower end of the highlands, with elevations between three and five thousand feet. The land is very fertile, and the district's proximity to Nairobi has enabled most of the menfolk to seek work there. Even in the nineteenth century, the powerful and wealthy clans used more land than others, and as has happened elsewhere, the land consolidation that preceded independence concentrated the available land in the hands of the few. Indeed, more than half the Kikuyu in Kiambu had less than two acres in 1962 (Kershaw, 1975-76: 182-6).

In pre-colonial times, Kikuyu women had their own gardens which fed their families; men had their own gardens which women worked, the produce from which was either stored or sold. Kikuyu men were said to have made all major decisions about social, political, and legal affairs, and all decisions about what to plant in their own gardens (Kenyatta, 1937: 167ff.; Kershaw, 1975-76: 178-80).

Almost one hundred years later, the situation for the poorest families in Kiambu was reversed. Among the landless (half of whom had the insecure use of some land from their clans) and the virtually landless, food crops were generally all that families grew, and they preferred to cultivate those foodstuffs that required the least labor, so that the wife could work for wages whenever possible. Women's wages (usually earned from seasonal harvesting on European-owned farms) were used to purchase additional staples. The men worked, but in unskilled jobs with very poor pay: men earned enough to pay their taxes, and to maintain themselves in Nairobi with weekly food contributions from their wives. It is the women's work that 'makes the difference between abject poverty and subsistence'. The husband's absence means that the poor Kiambu wife is the major decision-maker on virtually all matters. Indeed, the landless Kikuyu husband's 'burdens have not lightened with the passing of the traditional period, his decision-making role has been reduced, and his dependency on his wife has increased'. Thus women have obtained new power, which some husbands resent and regard as illegitimate, since it originates in their poverty.

Kiambu Kikuyu with sizeable parcels of land—between two and

seven acres—grow mainly cash crops, which men control. While some of the husbands and wives also work as professionals (teachers, clerks, and civil servants, for example), relations between husbands and wives seem to be very traditional: men take responsibility for all major decisions, and women control their own gardens. For these people, there is a strong continuity between the pre-colonial era and the present day.

The wealthiest Kikuyu of Kiambu, those who own seven acres or more, have earned their wealth through cash crops. Much of the production of cash and food crops is performed by hired labor. The wives of such households have lost much of their economic independence and are at best regarded as 'farm managers' by their spouses: they have influence but no authority. Outside the home, they have responsible positions in church groups and women's organizations, but on their farms, they have been 'reduced ... to a position of second in command' (Kershaw, 1975-76: 186-91).

Obviously, it is not rural wealth in and of itself that subjugates women, but when rural wealth develops in contexts imbued with notions about male superiority and male privilege, the subjugation of women seems to follow.

Urban women in their families, c. 1900-1980

We have already seen that a great many African men originally came to towns somewhat involuntarily, to work. With the exception of those runaway wives who sought refuge and happiness with urban migrants, women came to towns to work as well, but usually voluntarily. In the words of a Meru woman who became a prostitute in Nairobi in about 1925, 'at home, what could I do? Grow crops for my husband or my father. In Nairobi I could earn my own money, for myself' (quoted in White, 1983).

But most African towns—especially those founded in the early colonial era—had anywhere from four to twenty times more men than women (Bujra, 1975: 217-20; Van Onselen, 1982: I, 104; White, 1983). They were also characterized by substandard, insanitary, and overcrowded housing for Africans, at high rents; job insecurity even for those in long-term employment; and virtually no demand for female wage labor (Stichter, 1976: 51). These factors have been discussed in Chapter 3 on urban employment. What were women to do? To earn money, they became independent suppliers of those domestic services that made town life tolerable to men living in cramped quarters on low wages. They sold sex, companionship, bath water, beer, food (greatly in demand by men with no previous cooking experience), and sometimes a dinner for two. They enabled African men to return to their jobs somewhat replenished.

Thus four main roles emerged for urban women in modern Africa: as housewives, sellers of cooked food, prostitutes, and brewers of illegal liquor (most African home brews were illegal in the towns and impossible to regulate in the countryside). Housewives were numerically a tiny category, because few men earned enough to support dependent wives and because privacy was at a premium (Parkin, 1969: 60; Chauncey, 1981: 138). These roles could of course overlap, and many West African women combined housewifery and food trade, while others combined prostitution and brewing for varying periods of time. But what is most important about these latter roles is that the illegality of prostitution and brewing brought women into close and cooperative relations with their colleagues and neighbors, rather than their kin, while the selling of cooked food increased women's dependence on their urban families.

Given the numerical dominance of men in the African towns and the scarcity of legal work for women, prostitution represented a rational nomic choice (Ardener, 1961: 93-4; Bujra, 1975: 213ff.; Dirasse, 1978: 99ff.). Although prostitutes frequently supported segments of their rural kin and often sent children home to be raised there (Cohen, 1969: 66; Little, 1973: 83-90; White, 1983), their ties with their relatives within the town were limited. Prostitutes' livelihoods depended on their living alone or with sympathetic and cooperative room-mates, and the relationships that provided financial and emotional support were based on neighborliness and friendship rather than on ethnicity and kinship. Neighbors would routinely pay the bail for a jailed prostitute (White, 1983), and friends would take money home for a colleague (Little, 1973: 89) and look after another woman's child while she walked the streets (White, 1983). Many prostitutes formed professional organizations, as discussed in Chapter 5. Similarly, brewers banded together to schedule liquor sales for different days, to warn each other of police raids, and when the warning system failed, to help others prepare for expensive and lengthy trials (Nelson, 1979: 83-93). Thus, work created relationships that kinship and gender did not. And work paid off for prostitutes and brewers: in the rigidly segregated townships of colonized East and South Africa, between 20 and 50 percent of African property owners were single adult women (Southall, 1961: 223; Bujra, 1975:225ff.; Abrahams, 1970; White, 1983).

Women's trade in foodstuffs, on the other hand, seems to increase women's relations with the families into which they have married, since the food preparation and sale is often managed within extended family groups. The women who trade in cooked food—supplemented perhaps by cigarettes and matches or bars of soap—are both producers and vendors. Because they produce their commodities within their own homes, their trade increases their dependence on those family members who can perform the same tasks, those of the same gender as themselves. Such trade can take place even where women are confined to the home by Islamic custom (see Hill, 1969). In these areas, young female children anywhere from five to fourteen often shop for ingredients, help prepare the food, and hawk the product or tend the stall (Cohen, 1969: 65-7; Emecheta, 1979). Thus, daughters extend the role of housewife out of the house and into the streets, where a profit can be made from the sale of women's work. This is perhaps best illustrated by the Muslim Hausa housewives who live in the strangers' quarters of the Yoruba city of Ibadan, in western Nigeria. These women are strictly secluded even by

Muslim standards, to distinguish them from the divorced women who, without stigma or censure, become prostitutes until they marry and become secluded wives again.

Hausa men must give their wives household money daily, and men claim their wives 'steal' from that, or use some of their marriage payment, to set themselves up as cooked food traders. The Hausa menu is so varied that women can profit greatly by cooking one speciality in bulk and purchasing all their other food needs from other women doing the same, since the husband's money pays for the family's food and the earnings from trade are a woman's own.

What is truly impressive about this trade is that the wives do not leave their houses to purchase ingredients or to sell food: instead they use female child labor. They either use their own daughters, or foster the daughters of their siblings, or as a last resort, hire local young girls. Women whose daughters are either too young or too old to help them trade prefer to rely on fostering, as it links them to their natal families and provides them with a fairly regular supply of child labor (Cohen, 1969: 64-7).

Even in non-Muslim areas, this dependence on biological or fictive daughters takes its toll. Daughters are frequently denied education because it interferes with their mothers' profits (Schildkrout, 1978: 149; Emecheta, 1979: 176), and mothers may be isolated within the nuclear family whether or not they are secluded by Islamic custom. The Igbo heroine of Buchi Emecheta's *The Joys of Motherhood* supported herself, her husband, and six children in Lagos through petty trade, with considerable help from her daughters. She lived in the city for over twenty years, and only considered one woman her friend (Emecheta, 1979: 176).

Other changes in African family structures and marriage relationships have had a profound effect on women. These are more common among families in urban areas and those in which husband and wife are highly than in rural and lower-income families, however.

The nuclear household seems to be gaining greater autonomy from the extended family, especially in its day-to-day living patterns, although extended family ties remain important in many ways, for example in financial arrangements and inheritance. As in other parts of the world, the decision to marry has become more an expression of personal preference than an alliance between kinship groups, and the parents' role in choosing a spouse has declined. Although young men still play the more active role in choosing mates, this is one area in which young women have gained some independence. Geographical mobility and urban heterogeneity have meant that marriage partners are more likely to come from outside the rural homelands, a fact which may also weaken extended family links.

Among higher-income groups in urban areas, husband and wife are more likely to reside in the same house than they were in many rural societies, where women often remained with their own natal families (in matrilineal societies), or lived in the husband's village but in a separate hut with their children. In Ghana, for example, an area of traditional female independence, about two-thirds of all married women were living with their husbands in 1960, and joint households were even more the norm in rural than in urban areas (Smock, 1977a; 1977b). Still, one-third of the wives headed their own households, and the percentage of female-headed households is even higher in the areas of male labor migration in Southern Africa (See Chapter 2).

Among high-income urban families, a woman's status has come increasingly to depend more on her husband's success than on her own economic activities or those of her extended family. For example, high-income women in Ghana have lost what was a very substantial say in household matters when they married men of equal or greater wealth (Smock, 1977). Educated urban men tend to marry women with slightly less education or status than themselves, and thus educated women must compete to marry the few elite men with high earning power. If they succeed, they become dependent on their husbands for a high standard of living. The shortage of such men, and their tendency to take mistresses or second wives to the neglect of the first wife and her children, leaves many urban women in a state of emotional and sometimes financial insecurity (Harrell-Bond, 1975; Schuster, 1979).

Some scholars have argued that many urban women with some education look to an idealized version of the Western nuclear family as a model for family life. Thus they often want more monogamous, 'companionate' marriages, fewer children, and more privacy from other relatives (Caldwell, 1968: 65-6; Whiting, 1977). Some African men, however, are not used to spending much leisure time with women and children, and may prefer to spend their time with other friends and business associates, out 'on the town', or with their own parents and siblings. Often, they remain ambivalent about the new demands of the 'nuclear family'.

Educated women generally object to polygyny, since it means that they must share their husband's limited economic resources. Some educated men also disapprove of the practice (Caldwell, 1968: 55). Many urban men, however, are reluctant to give up traditional privileges. If unable to afford actual polygyny in urban areas, they still tend to have mistresses or 'outside wives', seeing this as a similar way to produce a large number of children and increase their prestige. Polygyny, actual or potential, open or secret, remains an important factor influencing the character of African family life.

Extended kin continue to place financial and emotional demands on the fragile conjugal unit, often, for example, visiting for long periods of time during which they expect to be fed and entertained. This practice greatly increases the workload of the wife, who may already be employed full time. The husband's extended kin often make more demands than do the wife's kin. Even among customarily matrilineal ethnic groups, such as the Akan elite families studied by Christine Oppong in Ghana, wives now live with their husbands and have thus tended to become separated from their own matrikin (or become dissatisfied with the minimal level of economic security available from them), while at the same time, their security in the nuclear family is undermined by competing demands from the husband's matrikin. In this situation, many women wished for a more 'closed' nuclear unit, in which kin demands were limited, and for more 'joint' participation in household work and child care; at the same time, many wished to preserve the traditional 'segregation' in relation to personal control over financial resources (Oppong, 1974).

Conclusions

Colonialism and labor migration took adult African men away from their families for years at a time, and made African women functional heads of households in some areas. They made most decisions, dealt with kin, and raised their children. Men suffered real hardships while in wage labor, and they suffered their privations away from their homes, and they must have imagined their wives to have led idyllic lives during their absence. The tensions this produced in African households cannot ever be quantified, but many writers have commented on increased rates of violence against women and increased drunkenness (see for example, LeVine, 1979: 63, 225ff.; Schuster, 1979: 96-103; Dikobe, 1973). These developments can perhaps be attributed to the frustrating and painful experiences African men have had finding out that their patriarchal ideology of African family life is being threatened. It is an ideology only the very rich can afford.

Throughout the colonial period and after, women endured a great deal of social and economic exploitation. Whereas the rapid rate of polygynous marriage had in pre-colonial times ameliorated some of women's burdens by making co-wives peers, the economics of colonialism and wage labor meant that those men who could afford second wives usually married them years after they had first wed. The changing economic situation and changing expectations about marriage brought jealousy and conflict into a situation already stretched to its limits by finances and the vastly increased labor requirements of African cultivation. Wives thus competed for their husbands' affection (presumably also stretched to its limits by long absences) instead of providing support for one another. Under the new economic order that has governed sub-Saharan Africa in this century, husbands, wives, and in-laws all had the potential to become adversaries overnight.

5 Women's voluntary associations

Audrey Wipper

This chapter describes some bases of associating among African women today outside their immediate domestic or family group. To provide some background, several types of traditional groups will be discussed. The main aim, however, is to examine several types of present-day women's associations. Among the groups to be discussed are (1) rural cooperatives and self-help groups, (2) occupational associations, (3) urban business enterprises, and (4) social welfare, church and entertainment groups.

We will concentrate on indigenous collectives, many of which have their roots in traditional groups, and will exclude such Western-sponsored groups as the YWCA, the Girl Guides, the Red Cross, the University Women's Association, and trades unions. One main difference between traditional and present-day associations is that in the former, membership was largely ascribed; women automatically became members of a particular group because of birth, age, sex or adoption into a kin or territorial unit. In contrast, membership in today's associations is largely voluntary; a person chooses to join a particular group. A voluntary association is thus an organized, corporate group, in which a person chooses membership. Examples are drawn from various African countries but because of the author's work in Kenya, examples from there predominate.

Voluntary associations are important for a variety of reasons. Traditionally, women came together to promote their common economic, political, and social interests. Colonialism and urbanization, however, undermined many of these associations, leaving women in a much less powerful position than men (Ardener, 1973; Boserup, 1970: 53-60; Van Allen, 1972, 1976). In the modern context these associations help women adjust to urban life. They regulate and promote trade, extend credit, teach new social and occupational skills, and provide monetary and psychological support (Little, 1973: 49-60). Furthermore, the persistence, variety, and number of these associations illustrate the reality of female bonding, and suggest that if anthropologists such as Lionel Tiger are to be consistent, they must argue that women, as well as men, are biologically programmed for bonding (Tiger, 1969).

Some traditional groups

In traditional African societies, the bases of women's associations included kinship (membership in lineages), age (age-sets), sex (society-wide puberty rites, secret societies, and women's interest groups), and village-level dance or work groups. Because of the limitations of space I will comment on only three kinds of groups that have particular interest for the modern era: work groups, women's interest groups, and secret societies. Traditional dance groups wil be briefly discussed in the last section on Muslim women's associations.

African women have traditionally engaged in cooperative efforts for the efficient cultivation and harvesting of their crops (Boserup, 1970). Since women do most of the day-to-day farming, it was less onerous and more sociable for neighboring women to get together on the time-consuming tasks. Work groups of perhaps a dozen women would farm one member's farm one day and move on the next day to another member's. These groups often served wider political and social functions providing women with organizational and affiliative bases for non-agricultural pursuits (Lambert, 1956:67; Stamp, 1975-76).

Among the Kikuyu, *ngwatio* was the custom whereby women cultivated each other's farms. This cooperative spirit was carried over into other aspects of their lives. *Matega* was the custom in which women would bring enough firewood to a woman who had just given birth to last until she was capable of collecting it again herself. The other women in the new mother's compound would provide food for the assisting group.

Women's interest groups

In some traditional societies women had considerable autonomy in such areas as farming, trading, markets, and female rites of passage. In these areas, women's groups made and enforced rules and regulations. We will look at how the Igbo women of Nigeria and Kom women of Cameroon protected their interests, wielding effective sanctions not only over their own membership but over the entire community. Interestingly, their sanctioning procedures were transformed into political weapons that led to riots and rebellions against colonial rule.

'Sitting on' or 'Making War'

In pre-colonial Igboland the women's base of political power lay in their own gatherings, of which there were many kinds, performing a wide range of social, economic and political functions. The gatherings which performed the major role in women's self-rule and which articulated their interests as opposed to those of men were the village-wide meetings of all adult women based on common residence (wives of the lineage, *inyemedi*) which under colonialism came to be called *mikiri* or *mitiri* (from 'meeting') (Van Allen, 1972: 169-70). *Mikiri* played an important role in women's daily self-rule, serving as a forum where they could air complaints about people breaking the rules. Women were used to protecting their own interests as farmers, traders, wives, and mothers, and if their requests for compliance with the rules were ignored, the offender was first warned and asked to mend his/her ways. If compliance was not forthcoming, then other tactics such as strikes, boycotts, force, and 'making war' were used.

When carrying out the sanctioning device known as 'sitting on' or 'making war' on someone, the women dressed in the same attire: their heads were bound with ferns symbolizing war, and their faces were smeared with ashes; they wore short loincloths, and carried sticks wreathed with young palm fronds. The sticks supposedly invoked the power of the female ancestors. They gathered at the offender's compound, usually at night, where they danced, sang derisive songs outlining their complaints, banged on the offender's hut with their pestles, covered it with mud, and in extreme cases, destroyed it and 'roughed him up'. This raucous behavior was kept up until the man repented and promised to mind his ways. 'Making war' was the strongest sanction women had for punishing wrongdoers and for enforcing compliance with their rules and judgements. It was regarded by the community as a legitimate institution.

Anlu

Like the Igbo, Kom women of Cameroon had spheres of activity that fell under their jurisdiction. They, too, had a punishment that bore a strong similarity to 'sitting on' a man. *Anlu* was employed to punish men who committed certain offenses such as beating or insulting a parent, beating a pregnant woman, incest, causing the pregnancy of a nursing mother within two years of a previous birth, abusing old women, or seizing a person's genitals in a fight. An offended woman would summon other women with a high-pitched call. Upon hearing the call, other women would echo it, leave whatever they were doing and go to her aid. A crowd would gather quickly, followed by a wild dance during which the offended woman would tell the gathering about the offense. The accused would state his case to the head woman of the compound who would discuss the matter with the older women and they would decide on a course of action. If they decided he was guilty, they might accept his apologies and payment of a goat and fowl, and this would settle the case. If he were an habitual offender, however, a more drastic sanction was meted out.

On a set day, the women, dressed in pieces of men's clothing, painted their faces, covered themselves in leafy vines and paraded to the offender's home around 5 a.m. There they danced, sang obscene and mocking songs, and defiled his compound by defecating and urinating in the water storage vessels. 'Vulgar parts' of the body were exhibited (Ardener, 1973: 428). If the man was present, he was pelted with stones or a type of wild fruit called 'garden eggs'. Then the women shed their vines and garden eggs in his compound leaving some of each on the threshold as the *anlu* sign that its use had been banned. Sometimes they would prohibit the offender from visiting other compounds as well as forbid people to visit him. If he fled to another compound or even to another village, *anlu* activity continued.

An offender could seldom endure this kind of treatment for more than two months. When he capitulated he put the *anlu* vines around his neck and went to the women to plead for their pardon. If his pleas and the offered compensatory goods were accepted, the women took him naked to a stream and bathed him in a purification ritual. If his cooking pots had been contaminated with garden eggs (contact with this fruit was believed to cause one to become sick and thin), they too were washed in the stream. Then the man was led back to his compound, rubbed with powdered camwood and palm oil, and given food. After this, the incident was never mentioned again.

Anlu was greatly feared, for there was no appeal against its rulings. If pardon was refused, the culprit was forced to leave the country. Since the invoking of *anlu* was such a serious affair it was used sparingly. One informant about 35 years of age, said he had seen it used only four times in his lifetime (Ritzenthaler, 1960: 152).

Women's organizations were not only important in protecting women's interests but they provided a milieu in which women could develop skills essential to participation in the wider political sphere. In these groups women learned to cooperate towards attaining common goals, and through discussion acquired a knowledge of, and means to protect, their rights (Clark, 1980: 367). Women in such a milieu were hence more likely to evaluate male action, and, if they disagreed with it, to reject it than women acting alone.

Both 'sitting on a man' and *anlu* became vehicles for political protest during the colonial period. The Women's War or Aba Riots in 1929 among the Igbo, and the Anlu Uprising in 1958 among the Kom, are both described more fully in Chapter 9. These two rebellions illustrate the strength of women's traditional collective actions when they felt their rights had been jeopardized and trodden upon.

Secret societies

Secret societies are another type of traditional group; some of them are still functioning. They exist under various names in West Africa, especially in Sierra Leone, the Ivory Coast, Guinea and Liberia. Here we will look at the functions of the Sande society among the Kpelle of Liberia. Though there are similar societies throughout much of Africa, Sande is regarded as characteristic of West Africa.[1] The parallel male secret society is known as Poro.

The functions of female secret societies are several: the education of young girls, the creation of cohesion among women, the provision of cross-cutting mechanisms to balance secular political power, and the strengthening of patterns of stratification in the larger society. In particular, these societies provide vehicles through which older, aristocratic women control younger women's sexual and labor services, thereby consolidating and increasing both their own power and social status and that of their lineage and age group.

Every Kpelle girl from the age of six to sixteen is encouraged, if not forced, to join Sande, though occasionally girls sent to distant government or mission schools will avoid initiation. For different periods of time, ranging from several days to several years, initiates live in secluded bush schools, isolated from their everyday activities. During this time they undergo clitoridectomies, labiadectomies, and scarification. They are instructed in household and family tasks, farming, medicine, dancing and singing, acquiring knowledge and skills that fit them to be wives and mothers.

The girls learn that absolute obedience to their leaders is expected of them both in the bush school and later in life. The breaking of the rules of obedience and respect may bring threats of infertility, even death. The initiates are expected to obey the husbands their leaders give them, but they know that their ultimate loyalty lies with their leaders who could order them to poison husbands who had violated higher tribal authority. Initiates swear to keep the cultural secrets. When their training is over, they return to their families.

The Sande society is graded. The initiates have the lowest status, but they enjoy more prestige than the few Kpelle women who are not members of Sande. Generally the older women are, the more status they have in Sande.

These societies foster unity among women and loyalty to tribal institutions. The elders of secret societies make important decisions for the community in secret and wear masks when publicly announcing their decisions in order to appear unanimous. 'The common bonds [of such secret societies] unite men with men, and women with women, as fellow members over a wide area, and to an extent which transcends all barriers of family, class, tribe and religion' (Little, 1949: 202).

Sande leaders use their connections with land-owning lineages and their control over their initiates' productive and reproductive capacities to solidify the existing patterns of stratification and power. This is accomplished in several ways. Sande leaders are closely linked to the elite land-owning lineages. Only certain older women from these lineages who obtain religious and secular office get an opportunity to learn the society's most important secrets. These older women use their positions as leaders in the secret societies to expose the ancestry of newcomers who are challenging the elites' power and to select and approve secular leaders. In the name of social unity, these older members call upon those beneath them for duty and self-sacrifice. Hence secret societies exist primarily not to eliminate factional lineage interests, but to preserve their differences and to protect the aristocratic lineages from threats to their position by aspiring newcomers (Bledsoe, 1980: 70).

In Liberia today, the protection of powerful patrons is still necessary in order to ward off unjustified taxes, fines, lawsuits and the like (Little, 1966: 66-7; Hoffer, 1972: 161). The secret society is an institution in which low-status people can attach themselves to powerful lineages through their daughters in the hope of protection and upward mobility. Parents sometimes compete with each other to enroll their daughters in bush schools run by powerful women, a tactic resembling clientship.

Leaders of the secret societies profit from their initiates in several ways. Parents pay entrance and exit fees as well as providing food and other favors during their daughters' training period. In Sierra Leone, the leaders also benefit from the initiates' labor on their farms (Hoffer, 1972). Young Sande dancers turn over the money they collect from spectators to the older leaders.

The power of Sande leaders over the initiates' sexual services can be used to acquire the support of young men or those from outside lineages whom the leaders wish to control. The husbands-elect often vie with each other for the best singers and dancers or the most beautiful girls and bestow quantities of goods on secret society leaders hoping to be successful in their quest (Bledsoe, 1980: 74). The girls are carefully allocated to young men, powerful men, and rival families. In this way, aristocrats gain followers and allies and fortify their control over potentially dissident individuals and families.

Furthermore, it is the older women from the land-owning lineages in Sande who are the most important midwives. Women prefer to patronize midwives of powerful lineages and those who occupy important leadership positions in the Sande society because they believe these women possess the most powerful medicine which will protect their own life and their baby's life. Women are highly dependent on the midwives' knowledge of obstetrics and gynecology and this knowledge is jealously guarded. Midwives are well paid for their services. They wield considerable power and sometimes resort to threat and blackmail having extracted private secrets from a woman during childbirth.

One scholar concludes that women who become powerful secular or secret society leaders 'achieve their status mainly by playing the "male" game of trading rights in the women they control for political support' (Bledsoe, 1980: 78).

Rural cooperatives and self-help projects

From traditional work groups and the spirit of helping each other have evolved many of today's independent cooperatives where the members carry out projects and business ventures. These cooperative endeavors permit them to engage in undertakings far larger than their own limited resources would permit. Kikuyu women in Kenya often pool efforts to build better housing, for example, and a roof of iron sheets is considered an improvement over the traditional thatch. Such work groups are known as *mabati,* referring to the iron sheets used for roofing.

In the rural community of Mitero in the Kikuyu Highlands the women are committed, full-time agriculturalists (Stamp, 1975-6: 19-43). An expanding population has reduced the amount of land farmed per family to two acres or less, with the result that adult men migrate to the towns or large farms to secure wage employment and are away a good part of the year. The women, who number around one thousand, engage in subsistence agriculture; corn (usually called maize in Africa), beans, and potatoes are the main crops grown for consumption. Coffee, the chief cash crop, is cultivated on a family basis on a scale ranging from a few hundred bushes to plots of several acres.

In 1975-1976 there were ten women's groups in Mitero. The women pool their meager resources in order to buy farms and businesses, with the resulting profit being divided equally among the contributors according to the number of shares held. Any profit is reinvested, used for their children's school fees (traditionally the father's obligation), or used to purchase manure, fertilizers, water tanks, or cows. These groups sometimes buy collectively and thus more cheaply for their members and assist them with loans. Poor women can join, since work gangs hire themselves out for farm work and the women use part of their earnings to buy shares in these cooperative ventures.

One of these contemporary groups, the Riakarime Women's Group, includes twenty-two women and was founded for the purpose of co-operative farming, the traditional practice of *ngwatio*. The women found that they could not manage singlehandedly because one woman did not have sufficient money to employ laborers. They decided to cultivate for each other, to build houses for themselves, and to work for wages. They purchased manure, fertilizer, and water tanks jointly for their own use, and bought farms and shares in other businesses. As of 1976, they had purchased shares in four companies (Stamp, 1975-76: 41).

What is striking about these women is their entrepreneurial spirit, their drive to succeed against insuperable odds. They obviously realize that, if husbands cannot be counted on to help improve their standard of living and to educate their children, then they must do it themselves. Many appear addicted to 'Protestant ethic' values that command a life of unrelenting toil, savings and investing for the future. Though faced with pressing needs and a chronic shortage of money, they still reinvest their small earnings (Wachtel, 1975-76; Stamp, 1975-76). Growing coffee is seen as an investment that provides security, 'like putting your money in a bank,' as one women put it.

Corn mill societies

Governments often have a role in helping to organize women's associations. Corn mill societies in Cameroon were at first government-initiated projects. Rural development officers, remembering the effects the Women's Institutes in rural England had on the people's standard of living, decided to try to organize African women into societies that would meet monthly and help to raise the living standards of rural Africans (O'Kelly, 1973: 108-21). In an attempt to reduce the heavy work-load of the women and to attract women to these societies, the Department of Education bought fifteen corn mills in the 1950s and made them available on loan to several villages. Corn mill societies were formed whose members paid a monthly fee for the use of the mill. By the end of the first year, thirty villages had repaid their loans and more mills were purchased for distribution to newly formed societies. The mill societies spread until they totalled 200 with a membership of some 18 000.

From the social gatherings that took place around the corn mills came the idea of holding classes in cooking, soap-making, child care, hygiene, and nutrition. The women then set about making bricks and cutting bamboo in order to construct a meeting hall. As the societies' strength increased, the women began to handle long-standing problems. They bought barbed wire on loan and put up fences to protect their gardens from stray cattle. The loan was repaid by putting more land under cultivation. Department of Agriculture assistants introduced a new and better strain of corn, which yielded an abundant harvest. The women began to understand the need for contour farming. Poultry schemes were begun, village plots reforested, and water storage facilities built. The societies' most ambitious scheme was the establishment of a cooperative store to allow women to import articles unavailable locally. Five thousand women raised the initial capital and several stores were soon in operation.

Harambee self-help projects

Kenya's *Harambee* projects, in contrast to the government-initiated corn mill societies and to the independent women's work groups, illustrate grass-roots efforts that are later followed by government support. The Kenyan government has successfully cultivated local development by emphasizing that it helps those who help themselves. *Harambee* (Swahili for 'pull together') puts the accent on people coming together in their communities and carrying out projects without waiting for the government to do something. The rural populace decides what new programs and projects it wants, and only after these projects are underway will the government step in with aid. Schools, dispensaries, and roads have been built in this way. The people build a school and the government later staffs it. Although these projects are not exclusively women's projects, they are discussed here because women provide the bulk of labor and funds. In the Northern Division of Machakos District, the administrators pointed out that women constituted 80-90 percent of the unskilled labor involved in self-help projects (Mutiso, n.d.: 42-3). The manual labor ranges from making bricks to white-washing completed classrooms.

The traditional spirit of independence and self-help is largely responsible for the success of *harambee* projects. The following figures provide an idea of what this mobilization entails. From 1965 to 1970, *harambee* projects worth 3 197 966 shillings were carried out in the northern division of Machakos District. Of this sum the central government contributed only 44 061 shillings and the local government 8 301 shillings. The bulk of the money, more than 98 percent of the total, came from the rural people (Mutiso, n.d.: 41-2). It is clear that these projects constitute an important contribution to economic and social development.

The persistence of traditional forms of cooperative work in Kenya and the proliferation of new cooperative forms appears to be in marked contrast to the situation in the 'labor reserve' areas of Southern Africa. There agriculture is not flourishing and rural women depend on their husbands' wage from migrant labor for subsistence. Cooperative work arrangements and village development efforts, while sometimes attempted, produce little enthusiasm and are not very successful (Mueller, 1977: 156-9).

A serious problem encountered by the self-help groups in Kenya is their utilization by some individuals for personal advancement. The more successful the projects are, the more desirable they are for this purpose. Politicians have used *harambee* projects as campaign platforms. As the role of Third World women became recognized, politically aspiring women found it advantageous to be able to 'speak for' so many thousand rural women at international meetings, academic seminars, or political caucuses. The following examples are both drawn from Kenya.

Mbai sya Eitu ('clans of girls') groups were originally organized among the Kamba by the local member of parliament (MP) for electoral purposes in 1961. They were active in vote-getting in the 1963 and 1969 elections and raised the revenue for many *harambee* projects.

The Swynnerton Plan, produced in 1953 to combat the growing threat of the 'Mau Mau' rebellion, was designed quickly to expand African economic development. With British aid, a rapid increase in African cash cropping took place over the next few years. Coffee production in particular was emphasized (Rosberg and Nottingham, 1966: 304). The land, however, had to be terraced before coffee could be planted. Communal labor was used under the aegis of the chiefs and sub-chiefs. The villages were organized into the traditional *mwethya* work groups which went from farm to farm, terracing. Since more women than men were in the *mwethya,* the informal leaders were mostly women, and these were younger women and not the grandmothers who had traditionally occupied the public roles. Later, most of these women turned up in the *Mbai sya Eitu.* Thus it was through the experience of terracing that Kamba women learned of the status to be gained through public matters. The mobilization of women into modern politics had begun (Mutiso, n.d.: 7-8).

The MP's electoral strategy was simply to control the votes of the biggest clans and thereby assure himself of victory in the 1963 and 1969 elections. The women were sent to organize their clans of origin into matrilocal clan organization led by a woman, and in this way voting could be controlled. It was this practice that gave rise to the *Mbai sya Eitu,* in which we see traditional organizations playing modern political roles (Mutiso, n.d.: 16-17).

The largest women's association in Kenya and the only one with a network of rural clubs is *Maendeleo ya Wanawake* ('progress for women'). It was organized by a small group of European women in the early 1950s under the auspices of the colonial government's Department of Community Development and Rehabilitation and is another example of an organization patterned after the Women's Institutes of rural England. Its objectives were to promote the advancement of African women and to raise African living standards through self-help. *Maendeleo's* activities ranged from instruction in farming methods to child care. Day care centers were opened, and new ideas about diet and hygiene were presented. Traditional handicrafts were encouraged, including basketwork, pottery, palm leaf and woodwork. Traditional dancing and singing were cultivated and competitions in various skills instituted. Homecraft centers were built, financed by central government funds with some help from district councils. Literacy classes were held and a monthly newspaper started that was translated into four languages: Swahili, Kikuyu, Luo and Kamba. And for the first time women participated in team sports (Wipper, 1975).

In its early years the leaders of *Maendeleo* were militant, dedicated women who continually campaigned for women's rights and prodded the government for more financial support. These women, a 'thorn in the government's side', called attention to the discrepancy between the government's verbal support for *Maendeleo* and its meager financial support. In the 1970s, however, the movement's leadership changed, and a number of the new leaders at the national level were related to Kenya's political elite. With fathers, brothers, and husbands occupying some of the most powerful positions in the country, they had too much self-interest involved to query, let alone oppose, government practices. Charity balls, first nights, embassy receptions, donations to charities (when *Maendeleo's* own impoverished rural endeavors were floundering), and jaunts to UN agencies to talk about the problems of Third World women, suggest that the national executive was out of touch with rural women, and developing a lifestyle far closer to that of the European elite than to the rural people. Tired of unfulfilled promises and fed up with what they saw as hypocrisy, the rural members were alienated in many ways from both the government and its own national executive (Wipper, 1975: 99-119).

Occupational associations

Under the colonial system, education and training were primarily available to men, as were the new jobs in industry and government. As described in Chapter 3, there were few formal positions for illiterate women in the urban areas. Consequently many women became petty traders, prostitutes, and beer-brewers, the latter two occupations being illegal in many places.

Prostitutes' associations

The preponderance of single men in the urban areas, described in Chapters 1 and 3 above, provided a ready market for female sexual and domestic services in towns. Prostitutes were often estranged from their relatives in the countryside. Faced with considerable competition from other women, they were in insecure social and economic positions. These women had exchanged family and other traditional forms of security for personal liberty (Little, 1966: 122). As a result of migrating to urban centers, they had to depend on their own limited resources for survival. In West Africa, prostitutes' associations act as mutual aid organizations providing the protective functions that were formerly performed within the rural kinship structure.

The most prestigious of these organizations is one composed of the very successful 'courtesans' who sell their companionship and sexual services to successful business men, high-level civil servants, and professionals. In Zaire such women set up professional associations with a president, vice-president, treasurer, and other officials, for the purpose of providing aid to members in difficulty, and organizing festivals and funerals (Balandier, 1956). Similar professional unions exist in Nigeria and Ghana (Boserup, 1970: 100). Of Igbo women it is said that 'prostitution is merely a new calling like any other; they become prostitutes as reasonably and as self-righteously as they would have become typists or telephone girls' (Leith-Ross, 1939: 267-8). In the West African countries of Dahomey, Senegal, and Togoland these women are known as *femmes libres*[2] and some fraternize with an elite clientele, sometimes deputizing at presidential balls and other diplomatic affairs, and are highly rewarded for their company (Little, 1972: 287).

The associations formed by successful prostitutes and courtesans aim at high standards in deportment and dress, discourage 'unprofitable' business contacts, and help the members advertise their best features, functioning like finishing schools for upwardly mobile prostitutes. In Brazzaville, these associations provide musical and other kinds of public entertainment, where the experienced members teach the newcomers about elegance and deportment. Societies such as *La Rose, Violette et Elegance,* and *Dollar* try to maintain their good reputation by limiting their membership to carefully selected young women. A mutual aid fund is maintained to help the members financially. Should they die, their funeral expenses will be paid by the association. The members also function as a substitute family for the deceased. Should a member die, her fellow prostitutes go into mourning for six months, during which time they do not wear their fine clothes or jewelry. At the end of the mourning period they hold an all-night celebration (Balandier, 1956: 145-8).

Such voluntary associations can be seen as assisting the socially mobile prostitutes and courtesans who do well financially and have no difficulty in retirement. They may own a house or two, or have saved enough money to open a hotel or start a business, or they may be wealthy traders. Irrespective of how they earned their money, they are usually able to assume a relatively prestigious and respectable position in society (Little, 1972: 287).

The associations formed by the ordinary prostitutes, the street-walkers and bar girls, emphasize the bread-and-butter issues and no prostitute is allowed to charge a customer less than the price fixed by the president of her society (Rouch and Bernus, 1959: 237). The associations protect streetwalkers who are preyed upon by criminal gangs, and intervene on their behalf when prostitutes are arrested by the police. For these lower-class women, many of whom are unmarried or have left their husbands and have lost complete contact with their kin in the countryside, these associations provide not only monetary but psychological support.

Market associations

Trading is the main occupation of urban women in West Africa. Its popularity rests on the fact that women can combine it with domestic duties, it is lighter and more pleasant than farm work, and the market, the focal point of much social activity, is a congenial place to be. Eighty percent of all traders are women in southern Ghana and among the Yoruba, 50 percent in eastern Nigeria, and 60 percent in the Dakar region of Senegal. The majority operate in the internal market system, trading in food and portable imported goods. They participate at the lower levels of trade where profits are small, while the higher and more profitable levels are dominated by men and large European firms.

Women traders have established associations which perform a variety of functions. They assist their members in starting or in expanding a business by lending them the needed capital. They train women, new to the urban milieu, in business methods, and they put traders in contact with potential customers. At times they have become politically influential; this aspect is described in Chapter 9. Another important function of these associations, similar to those of prostitutes, is the enforcing of rules concerning prices and competition. In Lagos market, for example, each commodity has its own section—cloth, fish, vegetables, and so on—and the women sit according to the commodity they sell. Each section has its own association, or *egbe*, which discourages competition among women dealing with that particular article. The unity among the women, who spend many hours together each day gossiping and eating, is so strong that is said no trader would think of disobeying her *egbe*. However, should one undercut the others in price, she would be ostracized by her fellows who might report her offense to the leader of the *egbe* and if need be to the *iyalode*, the 'queen of the markets'. The queen is recognized as a chief and is second only to the *oba* or king at official functions. The *egbe* makes certain that commodities designated as the exclusive concern of women traders are not sold by men (Little, 1973:50).

Sometimes, in the absence of a formal association, there are informal arrangements among the vendors as to who is allowed to sell what in a particular area. In a Kampala market, the sellers refer to each other by kinship names such as sister or daughter. This pseudo-kinship system, loosely organized, apparently works to prevent too many women from selling *matoke* (cooking bananas) all within the same spot. The object is to disperse sellers and to prevent too intense competition (Southall and Gutkind, 1957: 138).

Some market associations buy in bulk for their members, thus acquiring the goods more cheaply than a single vendor could. Other associations make sure there is an adequate supply of the commodities that their members sell. A few associations have even gone into the production of goods for themselves. In southern Nigeria these societies have run such projects as a bakery, a laundry, and a calabash factory (Little, 1973: 51).

There are many variations of these mutual societies. In Abidjan, market women join associations which are designated to deal with particular occasions requiring money. For instance, if a trader had a daughter of marriageable age, she would join a marriage association to cover the costs of the wedding. If a baby is expected, a woman might join a birth association to help defray the financial obligations involved. The specific association joined reflects the economic position of its members, for the required contribution varies from twenty-five cents to ten to fifteen dollars (Lewis, 1976: 147). Many efforts at forming mutual aid societies failed shortly after their creation.[3]

A final type of mutual aid society is the rotating-credit association. Its prime function is to provide its membership with capital. For example, among the Society of Friends (*Nanamei Akpee*) in Ghana, the members agree to make regular contributions to a fund which becomes the property of each contributor in turn. It provides its members with a lump sum, more than they could save on their own, given the constant demands upon them for money. The system is fairly flexible and if one member urgently needs some money, she may be permitted to jump the queue and receive the collection before she is entitled to do so (Little 1973:52).[4]

Beer-brewers' associations

It should be borne in mind that while the occupations of trading, prostitution, and beer-brewing are carried on by separate groups of women, there is much overlapping with women who engage in long-distance trading or who operate bars, often selling their sexual services. Not infrequently women engage in all three activities. Hence market traders' and prostitutes' societies may also serve beer-brewers. In Nairobi, beer-brewers formed cooperative societies that spread the risks over a wide base and divided up the labor and the profits. One such association, called *Tazamu Lako* or 'Mind Your Own Business' had a membership of 150 women. Premises for brewing were rented and the women were divided into three two-week shifts. Each shift shared in the brewing and in the profits.

What was more common among the illegal beer-brewers who lived in a very poor squatter settlement on the outskirts of Nairobi, was the formation of residential and friendship networks of cooperation and mutual assistance. Constant police raids were a fact of life in this community and made it almost impossible for formal associations with high visibility to operate. Police made official raids during their on-duty hours and then returned in their off-duty hours to harrass the beer-brewers in the hope of collecting bribes. By brewing and selling individually, the women minimized both the risk of discovery and the loss when discovered.

The brewers' neighbors and friends cooperated in the labor involved and in protection against the police. The moment the police van left the main road to enter the village, the news spread like wildfire. Children ran though the village singing a riddle song which warned the inhabitants, or a passerby would murmur *tikwega* (not good) or *miriam* (the police van). The beer-brewer would immediately lock up her house and run to stand on the road. Neighbors would hide brewing equipment and the beer itself (Nelson, 1979).

Urban business enterprises

Women's involvement in the modern economies of their countries is still generally weak, especially in the business sector. Yet in the last fifteen years urban women in Kenya, like the rural women in Mitero, have formed associations in which they pool their meager funds in order to invest in some business enterprise. Through such collective endeavors, sometimes built on traditional organizational bases, poor women are able to carve out a small stake for themselves in the modern economy.

In Nakuru, a medium-size town in Kenya, women's corporate activity is composed of formal and informal groups which mobilize resources and channel them into various kinds of businesses (Wachtel, 1975; 1975-76). Membership criteria vary and may include ethnicity, religious affiliation, neighborhood, and place of work or occupation. One group, for example, was recruited from a traditional dance group which entertained visiting dignitaries. In the following section we will briefly describe two of these business ventures.

Kangei na Nyakinyua ('Mothers and Children') Consumers' Cooperative Society[5]

In mid-1969 an emergency meeting was called to discuss the plight of a destitute woman who had given birth in the Nakuru railway station. The gathering of around fifty women from different ethnic groups took up a collection for the woman, then discussed the need for women's unity in the face of urban insecurity. The group decided to collect money to buy a large building to rent out; the money earned from it would provide some income for unemployed women.

The membership grew to 250, but the women had several setbacks before they found a large building on Nakuru's main commercial street. They had accumulated about $7 000 from the sale of shares and they gave that for an option on the property. Some influential men decided that they would bid against them, and the women almost lost their $7 000. In a spontaneous expression of solidarity, around 1 000 women (many more non-members than members) marched to State House and secured the intervention of President Jomo Kenyatta. The women concentrated on developing this property and have acquired a few smaller plots on which they hope eventually to build. The membership increased further to 400.

Although *Kangei na Nyakinyua* had its start in welfare activity, the economic side came to dominate as it evolved. The original welfare fund was misued so it had to be reorganized, but considerable money has been dispensed in helping women, not necessarily members.

Ikobe Farmers' Cooperative Society

Nakuru's first large-scale economic enterprise was started in 1964 by a core of market women with the support of the rural women with whom they traded. The society's goal was to buy a large farm. Each member paid a registration fee of 20 shillings on joining and purchased individual shares of 500 shillings. Money was raised by work groups hired out to local farms. A woman could apply all or part of her wage towards buying shares.

After the women demonstrated their seriousness by accumulating funds, they successfully negotiated a loan and purchased a 511-acre farm which grows wheat, barley, and pyrethrum, and grazes 300 sheep. The society employs a farm manager and hired labor to run the farm. Profits are applied towards repayment of the loan, and money over and above that has been set aside for the purchase of another farm. Though other women's groups in Nakuru had attempted to buy a farm, this was the only group that succeeded. Land ownership, especially a farm, represents the ultimate security in the opinion of most town dwellers.

Urban insecurity and corporate activity

The cost of urban living is high. For the average family there is never enough money to meet all the demands. Group ventures, if properly managed, can be a satisfactory solution. Savings increase, emergency loans can be made against paid-up shares, and through participating a woman can become part of an enterprise far beyond her own resources and capabilities.

These advantages cannot be gained, however, without considerable risk. The attrition rate of these enterprises is high. The goals of many projects are unrealistic and the projects are sometimes poorly organized. Unsophisticated in the ways of business, women suffer from severe handicaps that are only partially alleviated by their collective efforts: they usually lack literacy and bookkeeping skills and are unaware of such formal requirements as registering a company. Lacking capital and business know-how, they are easy prey for unscrupulous managers who abscond with the groups' money (Wachtel, 1975). And while their entrepreneurial spirit, boldness, and willingness to sacrifice present rewards for investment in the future is laudable, if many projects are doomed to failure at the outset, it may be that the energy and money of poor people might better be used elsewhere. Since this is the very spirit that governments usually wish to cultivate, however, it might behove them to assist the women by providing the needed expertise to assure more success in these cooperative efforts. For example, a particularly successful cloth-dyeing cooperative in Mali depended greatly on the involvement of both the Malian government and international agencies (Caughman, 1981).

Social welfare, church, and entertainment associations

We will now look at some voluntary associations among Protestant and Muslim women in East and West Africa. These groups are mainly concerned with fund-raising, social welfare projects, and entertainment. The church associations in Sierra Leone support traditional Christian values, and while the Muslim associations in Kenya worked towards eradicating some forms of discrimination against women, women's issues were only one concern among many that they worked on. None of these groups made women's issues its sole focus.

Protestant church associations in Sierra Leone

Creole women of Freetown, the capital of Sierra Leone, have a number of Protestant church associations similar to the women's associations in the parent churches: the Mothers' Union, Women's Guild, prayer groups, and so on; these associations are autonomous bodies within each church (Steady, 1976: 220-37). Women work to preserve Christian values and to support their particular church by means of fund-raising endeavors such as teas, bazaars, and luncheon sales. The proceeds go towards the maintenance of the church or the purchase of some special item, such as a stained glass window or a silver chalice. The members of the Ladies Working Band (Anglican) undertake to keep the church and its premises clean and to decorate it for religious ceremonies. In keeping with Christian teaching on philanthropy, part of their funds are donated to charities, and members visit hospitals, orphanages, and homes for the handicapped to present gifts and to sing on special occasions.

These groups provide women with avenues for religious leadership and still support the status quo in which men occupy most prestigious and official church roles. Leadership of women's groups commands considerable respect outside the churches and this accounts largely for their importance among women. Being a leader not only makes a woman an 'exceptionally good Christian', it adds to her status in the community at large (Steady, 1976: 228-9)

Muslim women's associations in Kenya

Associations for Muslim women in Mombasa have evolved over the past fifty years from *lelemama* dance groups to contemporary associations concerned with current problems facing women (Strobel, 1976). This evolution signifies important value and role changes for women in the Arab-Swahili community as these associations mobilized women in pursuit of values deemed important by the community.

The *Ibinaal Watan* and *Banu Saade* were only two of many associations that danced the *lelemama*, a dance brought from Zanzibar in the late nineteenth century. The popularity of these groups was greatest during the 1920s and 1930s, although there are still a few dance groups in existence. *Lelamama* groups competed with each other, the idea being for one group to outspend and outperform another. These competitions involved enormous expenditures and were eventually banned by the government. The associations had sets of titles that reflected the social hierarchy of the Arab-Swahili and colonial communities. A woman rose in rank, securing more prestigious titles, by spending lavishly. Thus the associations enforced status distinctions in a society concerned with hierarchy.

Lelemama provided entertainment at weddings. Several hundred women attended, displayed their new clothes, and cheered the dancers on. The dancers sang songs, some of which shamed or ridiculed members of the community for various offenses, or challenged rival *lelemama* groups by impugning their dancing abilities. (The use of song as an instrument of social criticism, revenge, and the enforcing of norms, already mentioned above in the discussion of *Anlu* and 'sitting on a man', is discussed further in Chapter 7 below.) The members of these associations helped each other out, by giving money and helping to prepare the food, especially during weddings and funerals.

By the 1950s, these dance associations had begun to decline, and fewer young women were interested. Rising prices prevented the members from continuing with the lavish celebrations. Alarmed at their expenditures, the government had limited the competition between rival groups, and hence a major reason for dancing had been removed. At the same time, a new consciousness was evolving about the status of coastal women. Arab leaders and the colonial government strongly encouraged secular education for Muslim girls. Debates raged about the seclusion of women, sex equality and the great expenditures for weddings and funerals. Questions were asked as to whether Muslim women should go to the movies or be allowed in mosques for communal prayers. New political and social issues had arisen which *lelemama* failed to address, and these issues contributed to the emergence of new associations like the Muslim Women's Institute (MWI) and the Muslim Women's Cultural Association (MWCA), formed in 1957 and 1958 respectively.

These new associations concerned themselves with issues of social welfare and education by establishing adult classes in literacy, sewing, child welfare, and religion, and by fund-raising for philanthropic causes. The MWCA has concentrated on the building and running of a nursery school since 1960. The MWI has had a more varied program, which has included relief funds for Zanzibari refugees and Lamu fire victims, aid to mosques, religious classes for children, and scholarships for students abroad. The MWI and the MWCA have tried to equip their members with an array of skills needed in a broader, more open society. Hence their concern for literacy, education, health and hygiene, poise in public gatherings, and economic independence through sewing and handicrafts. The members also participated in the campaign for female voting rights, visiting women in their homes to explain the importance of voting, and they condemned the forced marriages of Zanzibari girls.

The concern for modern education is shared by the Muslim women's associations in Freetown as well. The All-Muslim Women's Association, the Amalgamated Muslim Women's Movement, and *Tariku Fil Islam* raise funds to provide secondary school scholarships for Muslim girls, in addition to giving religious instruction to their members and providing mutual aid services. The fact that many Muslim women in Freetown have always had a great deal of mobility and earning power as traders may have contributed to an independent outlook and a wish to secure modern education for their daughters (Steady, 1976: 223)

Conclusions

The many women's groups amply demonstrate that present-day African women, as in the past, have the ability to take collective action to solve their various problems. Work groups are used today as they were in the past to lighten the farm chores of individual women. They have also been put to new uses such as working together for wages. With the money they earn, poor women can buy shares in businesses and farms, thus acquiring a stake in the modern economy. Other types of rural self-help groups have made important contributions to development projects.

New groups such as occupational associations have arisen with women's migration to urban areas and engagement in work other than farming. These groups provide financial and psychological support and training, and establish standards. In urban areas these associations take on a number of functions traditionally performed by the rural family. Church groups and Muslim women's associations perform social welfare functions, support particular religious organizations, and provide an avenue for women's leadership.

An area where women have lost considerable power and significant political roles is in the deterioration of such institutions as *mikiri* and *Anlu* which specifically protected women's interests, and provided them with considerable self-government. This loss in autonomy and power has often been regained with independence. Present-day African politicians are often only too aware of the power of women's corporate action. An ever-present danger is that women's groups will be diverted from serving women's interests to serving the interests of male politicians.

Notes

1 This account of secret societies relies heavily on Bledsoe (1980): 64-80.
2 Although the term *femmes libres* applies generally to West African prostitutes, it also has a specific legal meaning. In Zaire these women qualified for residence in the township in their own right, and they carried their own identity books (Little, 1972: 285).
3 For discussion of some weaknesses of market associations, see Lewis (1976). Her account suggests that some writers have presented a somewhat idealized picture of these associations.
4 For more information on rotating credit associations, see Geertz, 1966 420-2, and Ardener, 1964: 201-29.
5 *Kangei na Nyakinyua* literally refers to two stages of motherhood, before and after the children's circumcision. The ties between mother and children are emphasized here.

6 Women in religion and in secular ideology

Margaret Strobel

In the beginning of things the man Gikuyu, the founder of the tribe found that the Mogai (the Divider of the Universe) had provided him with a beautiful wife whom Gikuyu named Moombi (creator or moulder). [Gikuyu had no male heirs, which situation Mogai rectified by providing nine strangers who marry Gikuyu's nine daughters, setting up nine matrilineages.] It is said that while holding superior position in the community, the women became domineering and ruthless. Through sexual jealousy, many men were put to death for committing adultery or other minor offenses. The men were indignant at the way in which the women treated them, and planned to revolt. It was decided that the best time for a successful revolt would be the time when the majority of women, especially their leaders, were in pregnancy. [The men impregnated the women, the revolt succeeds. Polygyny replaced polyandry.] The women frankly told the men that if they dared to eliminate the names which stood as a recognition that women were the original founders of the clan system, the women would refuse to bear any more children [hence the men agreed to let the nine main clans retain the names of the daughters of Gikuyu] (Kikuyu creation myth, excerpted from Kenyatta, 1938: 5-10).

. In the beginning God created the heavens and the earth . . . So God created man in his own image . . . and the rib which the Lord God had taken from the man he made into a woman. [Eve eats the fruit of the tree of knowledge, expressly forbidden by God. In punishment they are cast out of Eden and God says to Eve], 'I will greatly multiply your pain in childbearing . . . yet your desire shall be for your husband, and he shall rule over you.' (The Bible, excerpts from *Genesis* 1 and 2.)

. God made us male and female, and in her wretchedness He filled women with weakness in body and weakness in thought. In His bounty He filled men with goodness in strength, great intelligence, and good thoughts, and for this reason He ordained men to be the ones to oversee women in their affairs, to take care of them. As He told us in the Koran: Men shall oversee women (a Muslim leader in 1930: Al-Amin bin Aly Mazrui, 1955: 1).

I am afraid that the young women who are today shouting for 'liberation' are handling wrong arguments and are causing unnecessary breakups of marriages and murders in a country where there are no discriminations between the sexes. Again, our educated women, as usual, are aping arguments and activities of some ugly, disgruntled, lonely and derailed American and English women. Our values are definitely very different from their values. I can remember that there used to be a time when African women were very *real* women, and their menfolk were proud of them (a university lecturer on the occasion of International Women's Year, 1975: Ochieng', 1975: iv).

Gender difference, ideology and religion

Sexual differences are a fact of biology, but what significance societies attach to sexual differences is a human cultural creation. These differences in value and behavior assigned to women and men are embodied in gender roles. Thus, gender is a cultural construct; sex is a biological condition. Various ideas, values, and beliefs about women and men are expressed through an ideology, that is, a coherent set of values and beliefs held by members of a particular society. Though coherent, an ideology may contain conflicting elements; for example, Western literature and thought have viewed women as both madonnas and as whores. Nonetheless, the ideology forms the basis of what members of a society think is true and natural. The connection between gender and sex makes the ideology of gender seem all the more a fact of nature rather than a result of human culture. Furthermore, the apparent natural basis for attitudes about women reinforces the ethnocentrism of people, who find it hard to believe that alternative conceptions of gender roles or of women are valid.

The quotations above are part of the ideology of gender and of women as expressed in religious and secular writings. The Kikuyu myth exemplifies traditional religions of African societies. The second and third quotations are part of the Islamic and Christian beliefs shared by many Africans, although, of course, each society blended its own indigenous traditions with the Islamic or Christian ones. The Kikuyu and Christian examples express the primacy of patrilineal descent. Although respect is accorded women as givers of life in these myths, females are also associated with negative characteristics in all three religious selections: in the Muslim statement they are weak and in need of supervision; in the Bible Eve introduces evil into Paradise; in the Kikuyu myth women are unjust in running society and must be replaced. The fourth extract represents a secular ideology: a description of history and the present in which a golden age of harmony between men and women has been disturbed. In this view, women are causing disharmony by listening too closely to another foreign ideology: feminism.

An analysis of religious and secular beliefs provides an excellent insight into a society's attitudes about gender differences and women, although neither can, of course, be reduced to beliefs about gender. In addition, we must remember that neither religious beliefs nor secular ideology have created gender. Rather, they are an expression of the ideas concerning gender that have evolved out of the economic, political, and social organization of a particular society, and, as the other chapters in this book have shown, gender differentiation is a basic feature of the social organization of African societies, in the past as well as today.

Religion in Africa

Roughly 50 percent of the African population follows traditional religious practices, some 25 percent are Muslims who follow the way of Islam, and the remaining 25 percent are Christians, including Catholics, Protestants, and members of African independent churches (Middleton, 1981: 410, 412). In reality, each category includes wide variations, and these religious systems and beliefs have interpenetrated. Traditional circumcision has become integrated into Christian and Islamic rituals. Prayers to Muhammad that He intercede now preface puberty rites for girls that have no basis in Islam. In particular, Christians and Muslims have infused their beliefs with elements drawn from traditional African religions. Thus, the beliefs and activities described under traditional practices can be found in Muslim and Christian communities as well.

African traditional religions

Traditional religious activities are focused on protecting the well-being of the lineage or society; dealing with routinely difficult or anomalous situations such as jealousy between co-wives or marriage partners, foreign invasions, or disease; and marking important changes of status such as birth, puberty, marriage, and death through rites of passage. In societies that did not have highly developed political structures or states, religious authorities often performed political functions. Religious specialists would be called upon to adjudicate between complainants through divination, filling the role of judge in a kingdom or nation-state. Sometimes religious heads became the leaders of anti-colonial rebellions in the absence of a chief to lead the resistance, as in the case of the priestess Muhumusa described later. Thus it is not always simple to differentiate the religious from the political, or from the secular generally (see Chapter 9, below; Jules-Rosette, 1979: 12).

Various religious roles are open to women. They may be ritual specialists for activities that pertain to women's affairs or concern fertility. For example, the *omu* among the Igbo of Nigeria controlled medicines and performed sacrifices to ensure the safety and success of the marketplace, where women were active traders (Okonjo, 1976: 49). Among the Lovedu in South Africa, the queen was responsible for bringing rain when needed and for guaranteeing the fertility of both the soil and the population (Lebeuf, 1971: 97). The link between agricultural and human fertility is clear: since women give birth, they are thought to have special capacities related to fertility generally. Moreover, most African women are active farmers, hence the link is not merely symbolic.

Often women act as mediums and members of spirit possession cults. These cults are found throughout African religious groups and are not just limited to the traditional sphere. They include people who feel themselves to be possessed by an external spirit who comes under control only by the individual joining with other afflicted persons. Some anthropologists have explained women's predominance in spirit cults as an aspect of the 'war between the sexes'. In male dominated societies, they argue, where women are excluded from political and religious positions of authority, spirit possession compensates for their otherwise low status (Lewis, 1971: 79-80). While possessed, women are allowed to utter the unutterable, to be placated, and to receive gifts for the spirit, thus alleviating their misfortunes. Other scholars explain spirit possession by emphasizing the real physiological basis for some of the problems, particularly those relating to reproduction, the stressful situations to which possession is a response, and the creation of a community of women outside their shared domestic role (Spring, 1978; Sibisi, 1977; Middleton-Keirn, 1978). The following example drawn from the lake regions of East Africa illustrates both the basis of the cults in women's experience and the way in which female mediums could exercise uncommon influence.

Among the peoples of Uganda, Burundi, Rwanda, and northeastern Tanzania, spirit cults were common. Many of these societies were and are hierarchically structured. Chiefs representing one group rule over others, and females are subordinate to the males of their own group. Women frequently participated in these cults and were conspicuous among the mediums. Often the cults dealt with female problems such as childbirth and agriculture, sterility, or marital problems. For the female mediums, their ritual role allowed greater physical mobility than was usual among women and made possible the accumulation of wealth through initiation fees in amounts beyond those of ordinary women. In some kingdoms female leaders functioned at the highest level of political authority. In Kitara, part of present-day Uganda, the female medium of Ndahura, the spirit of smallpox, controlled her own territory and wealth and played an important role in the ceremony acknowledging the new *mukama*, or king. To the south, the priestess Muhumusa, who claimed to be the wife of a nineteenth-century Rwandan king, led an anti-European attack in 1911 as the personification of Nyabingi, a female deity of the area (Berger, 1976). For most women, however, this level of influence was beyond their reach. Average women benefitted from relief from low status and everyday problems or from increased influence and respect locally or within the lineage through their role as spirit mediums.

In present day South Africa women participate in spirit cults. As a result of apartheid they are forced to live separately from their families and suffer a multitude of daily problems. For those who have jobs, wages are low. They live in fear that family members may be arrested and detained for opposition to apartheid. The reminders of their lack of citizenship in their own country are always present. In addition, they are subordinate to their husbands. Under these circumstances, women turn to spirit cults as relief from the tensions of daily living and to create a community of sister sufferers (Middleton-Keirn, 1978). In this way they collectively deal with the special problems they face as a result of gender roles assigned to them under apartheid. Analyzing the Zulu in particular, one scholar sees in spirit possession the response of these people to conquest by alien whites, the separation of families and mixing of ethnic groups that are part of the migrant labor system, and the general insecurity of lives that marked the twentieth century. Spirit possession is a manifestation of mental disturbance; diviners diagnose and treat the disturbance (Sibisi, 1977).

Even more than spirit cults, perhaps the most prevalent religious experience for females both as participants and as leaders has involved rites of passage that mark transitions from one socially significant stage in life to another. All societies mark birth and death, the most basic human experiences. Puberty, marriage, and childbirth not only are significant human experiences but also provide the opportunity for societies to express through ritual the ideology regarding gender. At puberty and marriage, females and males are taught what is proper behavior for their gender, in particular sexual mores and marital roles. Childbirth, particularly the birth of the first child, often brings the acceptance of a female as a full, adult member of the community and acknowledges her value in the role of mother.

Puberty rites vary widely across Africa, and traditional rites have changed over time with the introduction of new rituals from other societies, the coming of Christianity and Islam, and changing attitudes on the part of urban or educated Africans. The example described here is particular to the Bemba, a matrilineal group in Zambia studied in the 1930s (Richards, 1956), but the structure and content of the rites are common to many societies. *Chisungu* is the name given to the rites performed for an individual or a small number of girls prior to marriage. A brief ritual is performed at the onset of menstruation, but the larger *chisungu* awaits the family collecting the necessary food and items. The *chisungu* rituals are led by the *nacimbusa*, a woman of talent and reputation whose special relationship with the initiate (the *nacisungu*) lasts through the birth of her first child.

During the month-long ritual the initiates are instructed in secret rites. Clay figures and drawings in red, white, and black colors illustrate the lessons: work hard, don't have intercourse too often, don't deceive your husband. Instruction entails learning the proper attitudes toward her gender role rather than domestic duties as such.

Acknowledging and reinforcing the community of women is a crucial function of *chisungu*. The young girls are initiated into a group of women beyond that of their immediate family. Many of the elements of the ritual in fact express the hierarchy of relations among females in the group, which suggests the importance of *chisungu* for adult women participants in addition to the initiates.

Finally, *chisungu* expresses the tensions between the importance of the matrilineal principle and the fact of female subordination. Matrilineality offers women the support of female kin, which strengthens their position within the conjugal unit. Yet men dominate in various ways: they can beat their wives, they receive the first and best food, they initiate sexual intercourse. The ritual expresses this contradiction between the 'masterful man and the submissive son-in-law, between the secure young married woman backed by her own relatives and the submissive kneeling wife' (Richards, 1956: 10).

As with spirit possession, life cycle rituals are not limited to the sphere of traditional religion. Circumcision rites of boys became Muslim ceremonies, as in the case of the *jando* rituals in Eastern Africa. Female puberty rites were not challenged, rather they coexisted alongside Islamic rituals. In Mombasa, on the Kenya coast, slaves brought female rituals, and their descendents have continued to perform them. Now, after several generations of performance in an urban, patrilineal, Muslim environment, the functions of the rites have changed and the rituals are introduced by prayers to Muhammad, but the Muslim hierarchy has not attempted to forbid them. Criticism of the rituals from elites relate to their slave origins rather than their non-Muslim character (Strobel, 1979: Ch. 8). However, as we will see later, life cycle rituals sometimes sparked conflict between Christian missions and their local followers.

Christianity and independent churches

The spread of Christianity was integral to the extension of European influence in Africa, although missionaries were often at odds with colonial governments over the treatment of 'the native'. The first arrivals were Portuguese priests, who were encouraged by the positive reception of the faith by Alfonso, the 'king' of the Kongo in the early sixteenth century. They were later augmented by Protestant missionaries from the various colonizing powers and the United States, who came particularly in the nineteenth century with the establishment of formal colonial rule. Converts found various attractions in Christianity. For some, the failure of traditional spirits to protect them from the disruptions of war and disease led to a crisis of faith, which they resolved by adopting a more universal and cosmopolitan religion. Others fled to mission stations in order to escape slave traders and slave owners. There they recreated kin ties and a new community to replace the lost lineage and home (Wright, 1975; Alpers, forthcoming). Access to mission education and the new source of power in the colonial situation drew some to join the mission. Christian marriage practices appealed to Yoruba women in western Nigeria, who saw advantages in the right of a Christian woman to share her husband's property. Not all aspects of Christian marriage were followed or were valued, however. Men routinely avoided monogamy by taking mistresses; and Yoruba women, used to active and independent business careers, chafed under the dependence embodied in the ideal of the Christian wife (Mann, 1982).

Gender differences penetrated this process of the spread of Christianity just as they did the other changes associated with colonialism. Christian missionaries brought with them to Africa strong beliefs in the 'separate spheres' of male and female activity. (Africans also separated male and female activities but the content of the spheres was different.) For nineteenth-century Victorians, the role of women was that of mother and wife, to preserve the home as a haven from the difficult world of capitalist competition in which men operated. Politics belonged to the world of men, as did the running of the church itself. Moreover, Victorian sexuality posited that the normal female felt little sexual arousal and that sexual activity that did not result in conception was a dangerous waste of precious energy. Needless to say, such an ideology found much to criticize and question in African societies where, for example, women were active traders as well as homemakers, or where the conception of a child was an essential proof of fertility prior to marriage, or where women played an important role in decision-making for the entire group.

In the course of the development of Christianity in Africa, various groups split off. In some cases they objected to European control of church governance. In others, they sought to preserve such practices as polygyny that missionaries opposed. These new religions represented a synthesis of Christianity and traditional religions (Sundkler, 1961). The Harrist movement is one example of a syncretist religion, and one in which women played a key role. In the early twentieth century a Liberian, William Wade Harris, began converting masses of people to Christianity. He advocated giving up indigenous gods and reformed some practices with regard to women, but did not renounce polygyny. As his movement spread, women became leaders. In southwestern Ghana Maame Harris 'Grace' Tani joined with Papa Kwesi 'John' Nackabah to form a branch of the Harrist movement. Their roles balanced one another. Tani, a traditional priestess, conducted healing rituals primarily directed at alleviating women's problems; Nackabah's role was to preach (Breidenbach, 1979). In the Ivory Coast another woman, Marie Lalou, was inspired by a dream to found a cult in the Harris tradition. Previously outcast because of her inability to conceive children and the death of her two husbands, Marie Lalou founded a cult that criticized indigenous practices towards women. As this cult became institutionalized, however, political control devolved to men, while women retained positions of ceremonial leadership (Walker, 1979). Thus, while missionaries and leaders of independent churches criticized some traditional customs regarding women, they maintained a clear sense of gender roles, both within the church and in society at large (Jules-Rosette, 1979: 84-5).

Islam

Islam spread to Africa before Christianity, moving into North Africa and along the East African coast in the centuries following the life of the Prophet Muhammad in Saudi Arabia in the seventh century A.D. Often Muslim traders brought Islam to an area, or a ruler was converted, thereby gaining access to the highly developed administrative skills and literacy of Muslim advisors. In the colonial period, Islam became attractive for another reason. Many persons, whose faith in the power of indigenous religion to prevent European invasion was challenged by the successful extension of colonialism, turned to Islam as a universal religion, like Christianity, but one which was not the religion of the oppressor. Thus some areas, such as southeast Tanzania after the unsuccessful Maji Maji rebellion in 1906, experienced mass conversion to Islam.

Like Christianity, Islam contains an ideology of gender and embodies assumptions about women. Wherever it spread, Islamic beliefs and practices intermingled with local custom, exhibiting perhaps a greater acceptance of indigenous culture than did Christianity, as long as certain basic precepts were followed. The most significant elements of this ideology of gender include the extension of basic legal rights in marriage, divorce, and property; the practice of purdah, or the seclusion and veiling of women; and the exclusion of women from formal office in the governing structures of the religious community.

Muslim law ensured basic rights, if not equality, for women. An adult woman had to consent to her marriage. Once married, a woman was entitled to be maintained at the level to which she was accustomed. She could obtain a divorce from the Muslim judge for breach of this maintenance, among other grounds. Finally, she could own and inherit property in her own name. Each of these rights was limited compared with those of men: a man could marry up to four women, a woman could marry only one man; a man need not present grounds to divorce his wife, a woman had specific grounds that qualified; a man inherited twice the share of a woman unless otherwise specified in the will. Furthermore, in the absence of significant power and influence, a woman's rights could be abrogated or ignored or manipulated by her male kin. Nonetheless, when upheld, these rights represented an advance for some African women from societies where women were legal minors, unable to own property (Strobel, 1979: 54-76).

Purdah separates women from men who might be marriage partners. Spatially this is accomplished by segregating male and female areas within the home (since visitors and some kin are potential mates) or in public. Women are encouraged to remain at home or, if they go out, to travel veiled. One Muslim scholar has argued that the rationale for purdah is rooted in the Islamic ideology of female sexuality. In contrast to the Victorians who saw females as asexual, Islam sees women as very sexual creatures who, if not restrained, will distract men from the proper and loftier pursuit of religion. Control of female sexuality follows: proof of virginity upon marriage is required, and its absence is an affront to family honor. (Men are to be chaste also, but it is harder to find evidence of male sexual misadventures: Mernissi, 1975.)

The rigor with which purdah is observed varies. In rural areas where women must work outside the house, they are secluded less thoroughly than they are in urban centers. The same woman may wear her veil in her home village but remove it if she is visiting relatives in Nairobi. Older women, well past the age of sexual attractiveness and childbearing, may go to a market that their younger sisters avoid. Lower class women are less bound by the propriety demanded by purdah than are upper class women. Finally, with increased secular education and the adoption of Western practices, some women wear the veil little or have discarded it altogether.

Purdah is not necessarily experienced as restrictive by Muslim women. In rural areas of the Kenya coast of East Africa, women work in fields without wearing a *buibui*, the required covering (Bunger, 1973: 97). Hausa women in northern Nigeria are active traders, working out of their houses with children as intermediaries (Hill, 1969). Moreover, at the turn of the century both Swahili and Hausa women of low status eagerly adopted purdah as a way of elevating their status. Hausa ex-slaves, for example, began to demand that their husbands gather wood and water, tasks that might expose the women to inappropriate encounters with men (Smith, 1981: 22). Nonetheless, where seclusion was strictly followed, it could inhibit a woman actively pursuing her own economic interests and force her dependence on male representatives (Strobel, 1979: 58-63, 73-6).

Conflict between religious practices

Although Christianity and Islam have absorbed traditional practices and vice versa, it would be misleading to imply that there have been no conflicts between the missionaries' views of female sexuality and associated practices on the part of indigenous people. Such conflicts are illustrated in the following examples of the Masasi mission station and the various missions in the Kikuyu area.

Missionaries in Masasi, southern Tanzania, responded differently to boys' and girls' initiation ceremonies. Briefly, in the second and third decades of this century the Universities Mission to Central Africa (UMCA) in Masasi successfully developed a Christian ritual to replace the indigenous boys' rites. Attempts at a similar substitution for female rituals failed; women consistently evaded the mission's directive not to participate in 'heathen' rituals. The explanation for the failure goes beyond the missionaries' sexual mores, although this was part of the problem, to structural features of the church and Masasi society. The decision to adapt local puberty rituals to a Christian form came at a time when the UMCA was also developing African clergy in intermediate positions of authority. The young African men who became teachers and clergy took over the running of the Christian boys' rites. They helped develop its content, they supervised the rituals, they received payments from the initiates' parents. Religiously, the symbolic content of the Christian ceremony was rich and meaningful. In contrast, virtually all aspects of the successful adaptation of the boys' rites were lacking for the females'. Women were not consulted in devising the content of the female rituals, which were symbolically impoverished. Moreover, an important part of the girls' puberty initiation was the elongation of their labia through massage and their instruction in sexual movements designed to heighten sexual pleasure. Such items were considered inappropriate to the Christian ritual. In addition, the patriarchal structure of the mission admitted no role for female leadership comparable to the male African clergy. In fact, there was often implicit conflict between the patriarchal assumptions of the mission and the matrilineal principles of its converts. Thus the interaction of African and mission ideology and practice exacerbated gender differences in the resulting Africanized church (Ranger, 1972).

The complexity of the conflict between missionaries and their African followers on the one hand and supporters of indigenous customs on the other is vividly illuminated in the Kikuyu clitoridectomy controversy of the late 1920s and early 1930s (Murray, 1974). Clitoridectomy, or the removal of the clitoris, also known as 'female circumcision', was a key component of Kikuyu female puberty rites, as was circumcision for boys.[1] As Jomo Kenyatta, later the first President of Kenya, wrote in his 1938 anthropological study *Facing Mount Kenya*, 'No proper Gikuyu

[Kikuyu] would dream of marrying a girl who has not been circumcised, and vice versa. It is taboo for a Gikuyu man or woman to have sexual relations with someone who has not undergone this operation' (Kenyatta, 1937: 127). It was the cutting itself, rather than educational instruction, that formed the core of Kikuyu puberty rites.

The controversy developed in the decade of the 1920s, as white settlers consolidated their political power within Kenya and their farms encroached on Kikuyu lands. Experiencing the brunt of colonial intrusion into Kenya, some Kikuyu groups began to develop their own resistance organization, the Kikuyu Central Association (KCA), which in particular expressed concern over the land question. By 1920 the various missionary groups operating among the Kikuyu all opposed clitoridectomy. All but the Anglican Church Missionary Society (CMS) explicitly forbade it; the CMS taught against it but did not forbid church members to have it performed. In 1925 and 1926 the colonial government issued circulars intended to give official weight to the attack on clitoridectomy: the operation was to be less extensive and was to be timed so as not to interfere with the white settlers' need for labor on their coffee farms. To many Kikuyu it appeared to be a settler/government/missionary conspiracy to attack an important aspect of Kikuyu culture.

The KCA organized to defend the custom; the missions focused international attention on the custom and in some cases organized against the KCA specifically. Thus the issue of the alleged harm done to females through this custom became intertwined with the Kikuyu's complaints against white settlers taking their land. The antagonists, settlers/missions/government vs the KCA, were playing for bigger stakes than the health and comfort of women. The clitoridectomy question represented an early part of the anti-colonial struggle, which developed later into demands for schools independent of the missions, and finally for independence for the nation of Kenya. At this stage, however, the key expression of the anti-colonial impulse was the KCA counter-attack on cultural imperialism through defense of indigenous culture. Within white colonial circles, liberals such as MacGregor Ross, Leonard Woolf, and Norman Leys argued against suppressing local custom; those most adamant in their concern for the girls' health appeared to be insensitive to the integrity of African culture. Ideologically and politically, the issue pits the oppression of women against the oppression of colonialized Africans, among whom are women. And, however correct it may be to criticize clitoridectomy on humanitarian and hygienic grounds, in this historical context the criticism became part of consolidating the exploitative system of colonialism within Kenya. There appears to be a significant decline in the practice among the Kikuyu themselves; only about 40 percent of Kikuyu schoolgirls were excised in 1974, whereas nearly all of their mothers had been (Murray, 1974).

Conflict within religious groups

Not only did conflicts arise between Christian missionaries and traditional religious leaders, tensions at times emerged within a religious community over the role accorded to women. Islam provides several examples of this tension. First, women have been excluded from authoritative political and religious roles within the community because of purdah and the belief that men must 'oversee women', as the third quotation at the beginning of this chapter states. This exclusion from formal power has resulted in women's active participation in unorthodox spirit cults, known as *zar* in the Horn of Africa, *bori* among the Hausa, or *pepo* for the Swahili—all Muslim communities (Lewis, 1971; Smith, 1981; Strobel, 1979). Similarly, women play a greater role in some *tariqas*, usually translated as 'brotherhoods', which are groups organized around charismatic leaders, often with greater mystical and emotional focus than orthodox Islam contains. For example, the Qadiriyya in the 1930s in Bagamoyo and Tabora, Tanganyika, involved women in mosque activities (Strobel, 1979: 77-8).

Second, in some cases the coming of Islam undercut women's ritual roles. Among the Pokomo, who live inland from the northern Swahili coast and have become Muslim in the past century, conflict arose between Muslim leaders and women over who would bury babies who died at birth. In demanding that the babies be washed and buried by Muslim custom, the local Muslim authority was intruding on the women's prerogative and duty in local custom to bury under the house any child who died within thirty days of birth. A compromise was arrived at in which the women collectively delivered the baby to the Muslim official, who performed a Muslim ceremony (Bunger, 1973: 96).

Finally, where men utilize Islam to claim their control and superiority over women, women sometimes reassert pre-Islamic rituals to maintain their autonomy. Such a dynamic occurred in Upper Volta in the late 1960s. Men had given up an earlier form of dancing associated with the Dioula warrior ethos. Women wished to continue their dancing. When the male Muslim leader declared it inappropriate behavior for Muslims, the women countered by arguing that earlier religious authorities did not forbid the dancing. In so doing they appealed to a pre-Islamic religious authority to legitimate their actions, which local people themselves acknowledged to be linked to a struggle over domestic authority (Quimby, 1979: 217).

Thus, even where the official structures and authorities of religion seek to restrict their roles, women pursue various strategies to assert alternative views. In some cases they may participate in less orthodox aspects of religious practice; elsewhere they may reaffirm their rights according to earlier traditional religious custom.

The transmission of religious ideologies regarding women

Ideas about the characteristics of and relationship between men and women are represented in various ways, sometimes symbolically, sometimes didactically. The idea of female inferiority can be conveyed through taboos. Certain foods, usually those high in protein, are reserved for men to eat: for example, Mbum women in Chad did not eat chicken, eggs, or game meat; Luo women in western Kenya were forbidden chicken, eggs, milk, sheep, rabbit, and other game (O'Laughlin, 1974; Hay, 1976). In addition to seriously affecting women's health, such food taboos express a male/female hierarchy. Other taboos surround sexuality and purity. Muslims must purify themselves after sexual intercourse and before performing religious rituals such as prayer. Although sexual intercourse is seen as polluting for both sexes, females are at a biological disadvantage. Menstrual blood is polluting; a menstruating female therefore does not perform such religious duties as praying or fasting during the month of Ramadhan. A man may avoid some pollution by avoiding a menstruating woman, but a woman cannot escape pollution; it is part of her nature.

Less subtly, the ideology of female subordination may be overtly stated or taught. Often female obedience is a lesson learned in female puberty rites. Or, didactic literature directed to young women may preach wifely obedience. An example is the poem *The Advice of Mwana Kupona Upon the Wifely Duty*, composed in the 1850s on the northern Swahili coast and transmitted orally until it was collected in the 1930s. An aristocratic woman, Mwana Kupona advised:

She who obeys her husband, hers are honour and charm; wherever she shall go, her charm is published abroad.

Be gay with him that he be amused; do not oppose his authority. If he bring you ill God will defend you.

(Werner and Hichens, 1934: verses 96, 36)

As colonialism proceeded, secular voices joined religious ones in shaping people's values.

Secular ideology

Increasingly in the colonial period, the source of authority became Western life-styles, articulated through Western education and the media, but the content of that gender ideology maintained the idea of female subordination. Often imbedded in female domesticity, this new expression of gender ideology can be seen in some of the voluntary associations in West African towns in the 1950s which taught women the proper (that is, Western upper or middle class) way to dress or conduct dinner parties (Little, 1966: 160). American and European cinema emitted powerful messages about romance, sexuality, and male-female relationships. Such films were a source of controversy in the *Mombasa Times* in the 1950s, in which educated Muslim men debated whether or not Muslim women should be allowed to go to the movies. As one advocate of films stated:

the cinema has revolutionised, at least in us men, our conception of love. I submit that to live with this new type of husband, a new type of wife is required . . . Either the cinema is a good thing or it is bad. But it cannot be good to me and bad to Fatma. Yes, Clark Gable might 'impress' her. But since no one objects if Ava Gardner impresses me, I fail to see the potency of the argument!

Feminist film critics today see Gable-Gardner films as reinforcing stereotypes of female subordination and seduction, male strength and domination. Yet for Mombasa's educated Muslim men, such films were one more example of 'sex equality, the West's "deadliest misfortune" ', as one man labeled the issue generally (Strobel, 1979: 118-23).

The contemporary picture of women in most secular media—films, magazines, newspapers, television, popular theater—represents an ambivalent portrait. Town women in Zambia, according to one scholar, are seen as both 'folk devils' and 'folk heroes'. In the first guise they are a threat to social values; in the second they act as a role model (Schuster, 1979). Women in the media are sexier than before. Women's magazines such as *Viva* from Kenya or *Africa Woman* are filled with the appropriate commodities and fashions for maintaining the sexy image. (Some discussion of women's equality is broached as well, and *Viva* has run articles on clitoridectomy, but the predominant image is fashion.)

While town women can be an attractive model to some, their sexuality acts as a pole for negative images as well. Modern Yoruba drama, performed by male touring companies in western Nigeria, incorporates five predominant roles: the prostitute, the co-wife, the witch, the half human/half animal, and the transvestite. None of these roles are flattering, and the characterization represents the conflict between independent Yoruba women and otherwise dominant men (Hoch-Smith, 1978).

The association of female equality and independence with fashion and sexiness has unfortunate consequences for feminism as an ideology that challenges the ideology of female subordination. Generally, feminists argue that society and women alike will benefit from the equality of women with men. Some go further and state that gender difference inevitably leads to inequality, that 'complementarity' ultimately masks inequality. Some feminists see a woman's right to control her own sexuality and reproduction as central to female equality. Thus while the issue of women's rights to go into bars, get drunk, and lead sexually uninhibited lives is not peripheral to feminism, it is neither the form of sexual equality that most feminists would advocate nor the issue that most see as pressing. Yet the issue of sexual independence—'loose women'—becomes linked in popular thought with the whole issue of equality between the sexes.

With the development of African nationalism came a systematic critique of cultural imperialism and pride in African traditions, reminiscent of the Kikuyu clitoridectomy controversy of the 1920s and 1930s. However, the critique of cultural imperialism easily lapses into a scapegoating attack on urban women, focusing on their dress, sexuality, greed, and parasitical nature. Government ministers join the man on the street in attacking immoral fashions such as mini-skirts, urban prostitutes, and women who stepped away from the African tradition of homemaker (Wipper, 1972; Schuster, 1979: 165-79). An editorial in the *Malawi News* in 1968 regarding mini-skirts illustrates this trend:

The move by the Government to ban mini-skirts and dresses has come at the most appropriate time. Mini-skirts and dresses are a diabolic fashion which must disappear from the country once and for all. Foreign women such as the one seen on Sunday by the President, Ngwazi Dr Kamuzu Banda, indecently dressed, are setting bad examples to our young girls and we will not tolerate anyone who wants to spoil our nation by importing these diabolic fashions (Wipper, 1972: 332).

Fashion has been seen as a foreign import; feminism has taken on the same taint. In the 1970s some African women began articulating ideas similar to those of Western feminists, although the evolution of an African feminism has followed a rocky road at the international and local levels. The 1975 International Women's Year activities in Mexico City spurred interest in many nations. Those same meetings witnessed angry confrontations. Third World women criticized European and American feminists for their perceived preoccupation with issues of sexuality and their avoidance of issues of imperialism and development. Moreover, African female scholars and government officials, witnessing a wave of Western feminist researchers, accused the latter of misrepresenting and misunderstanding the African reality and of disproportionately obtaining research funds unavailable to African women themselves—that is, of cultural imperialism.

The struggle to challenge the ideology of female subordination is a long and difficult one. Some progress has been made; see Chapter 10 of this book. In the 1970s the official support of inequality has lessened: President Samora Machel of Mozambique declared in 1973 that 'the liberation of women is a fundamental necessity for the revolution' (Machel, n.d.) and President Jomo Kenyatta proclaimed the same year that 'equality is women's right' in Kenya (*East African Standard*, Oct. 23, 1973). Still, the content of what constitutes equal treatment is debated. Hence in parliamentary debates over a marriage bill in Kenya, one member of parliament, Kimunai Soi, stated that it was 'very African to teach women manners' by beating them and bemoaned, 'If this legislation is passed, even slapping your wife is ruled out' (*Los Angeles Times*, July 27, 1979: part 1, p. 10). Male prerogative dies slowly.

To summarize, various factors impede the general acceptance of an ideology of male and female equality in place of an ideology of female subordination. At the most abstract level, people feel that their beliefs in gender difference and inequality are natural rather than created or variable. In addition, men benefit in real ways from a system of gender differences that reinforce female subordination. As President Julius Nyerere of Tanzania noted, African women work harder than African men (Nyerere, 1968: 109). Challenges to custom, even when 'progressive', are experienced as cultural imperialism; conversely, defense of customs, even 'reactionary' practices, can be interpreted as politically progressive. Finally, the ideology of female subordination is rooted in economic and political structures of inequality; to challenge the ideology effectively, those economic and political structures must be changed.

Note

1 Clitoridectomy is the more limited form of the operation. Infibulation

involves the removal of the clitoris, the cutting of the labia, and the sewing together of the vulva, leaving a small hole for the drainage of urine and menses. One study has estimated that 66 million women have been excised or infibulated in Africa (Hosken, 1979). A World Health Organization conference held in 1979 called for educational campaigns to abolish these practices. For an overview of the subject, see Hosken, 1979; for an Egyptian woman's view, see Nawal el Saadawi, 1981.

7   Women in African literature

Deirdre LaPin

Recently some attention has been given to the place of women—as writers and as subjects—in African literature. Commentaries stimulated by the new feminist wave have sought to answer such questions as: 'What image of women is projected in traditional literature?' 'In what measure has this image been altered or maintained in the writing of the colonial period and after independence?' 'Can women writers be said to offer insights into the feminine condition which male writers have overlooked?' Literature reflects society, the questions imply, and women's experience of society is different from men's. Indeed. But the women's voice has not lain dormant to be suddenly unleashed by the world of print. It has spoken for centuries in an unbroken chain of verbal creations, some of which were gradually transmuted into the written word.

Because in traditional Africa woman reigned supreme as the giver and sustainer of life, she met the most urgent requirements of the family unit and underscored her concern in creations of verbal art. She soothed her newborn with rocking tunes, composed verses to praise a son, sang bride's laments at her daughter's marriage, instructed children through traditional tales. In this way she became a medium for the words of tradition. By recreating ancient images on behalf of her loved ones, she moved them to a sense of well-being and promoted harmony in her domestic domain.

This classic and inescapable image of wife-mother rests at the core of the feminine literary persona. Whether as an object for the writer's imagination or as a writer herself, the African woman evolves from the past bearing an unmistakable domestic stamp. It is one best described as 'sweetness'. In many African language equivalents, 'sweet' connotes a cluster of ideas that embrace notions of happiness, harmony, pleasantness, grace, and charm. The application is broad, for 'sweet' refers less to the various qualities inherent in things than to the particular human response these qualities elicit. To say, 'This is sweet', is to claim that a thing affects men and women in a positive, deeply personal, and wholly satisfying way. Sweet things thrive best in the nurturing intimacy of the household, where they feed directly on the pulse of human life. Good food is 'sweet'; so, too, a visit from a friend, a private moment with a lover, a soft affecting voice, a well-executed story or song.

Even so, the sweetness of the woman's voice has occasionally turned strident. Mocking verses, work songs, political ballads, satirical festival tunes, and songs for women's societies have given ample expression to the aches particular to the female sex. Using sweetness as a touchstone in their presentation of feminine experience, modern authors often harness the woman's image to an ideal collective harmony. But it, too, occasionally goes wrong. Nigerian playwright Zulu Sofola entitled her domestic comedy *The Sweet Trap* (1977), using 'sweet' sardonically to describe four middle-class households dominated by husbands who create discord by ruling with an iron hand. Still, many of these expressions fall into the literary preserve called irony, which, for all its appearance of challenging the norm, casts words into a context where they hover ambiguously between sincerity and mockery; irony leaves the ideal sweetness intact.

And intact it remains. Nearly three dozen women are currently recognized as authors across the African continent, and they have been joined by male writers in giving serious treatment to women-centered themes. In many of these works the women's condition serves as a barometer for measuring social health. Writers draw this equation in countless ways. A mother stands for traditional African society straining to uphold its standards against the corroding influence of the West. A wife reduced to servitude represents the cruelty of badly managed polygamy. A prostitute exhibits the aberrant individualism fostered by social exploitation. Behind the wrongs that women suffer looms the specter of social disruption. Often female protagonists deploy their energy, doing battle to restore life's sweetness, either head-on in the manner of Ousmane Sembene's revolutionaries or in the probing style of Bessie Head's psychological changelings.

The women's voice, then, tells the story of a sweet feminine image evolving in response to social change. Here, we shall trace this image from its roots in traditional oral forms, through transitional expressions that bridge speech and writing, and conclude with the searching debate that engages modern voices in a reassessment of women's roles.

Women and the spoken arts

African audiences, as a general rule, think of oral performances as 'beautiful' or 'good' to the degree in which they persuade listeners of social truths. A good artist, one who is both affecting and clear, needs to have a thorough command of traditional themes, characters, and images; moreover, she (or he) must know how to combine them according to accepted canons of composition. At the same time the artist must be sensitive to the make-up and interests of the audience; for successful performances can shape individual minds, bring them into line with prevailing attitudes, and by their lessons prevent social disorder.

In the past, though somewhat less regularly in the present, prose forms such as legends and tales equipped young people with a basic education. Bamana-born Madame Aoua Kéita, once such a listener, recounts vivid memories of stories told during village evenings in her autobiography, *Femme d'Afrique:*

> Very often they involved good and bad children, courageous men and lackeys, liars and truth-tellers, miracle-workers and misers, domestic animals endowed with speech, ceremonies held by wild beasts, and so on. These tales always ended with the triumph of the good or courageous characters over the rest. They always ended with admonitory warnings in which goodness, generosity, courage, and straightfor-

wardness were in all cases strongly emphasized (Kéita, 1975: 16; my translation).

They were not idle lessons for the young Aoua, who later led a woman's resistance movement that called for the independence of French Equatorial Africa. She drew her followers from among the women she cared for as a midwife but took her moral strength from the stories she had heard years before.

These story images made a tangible impression on juvenile minds across the continent, attracting boys and girls equally. At times, however, the performance of certain kinds of stories might be reserved for one sex or the other. Women performers could be linked, for example, with young people's fictional tales, while more practical, serious accounts might be associated with men. But across cultures—and even within them—these divisions remain in reality quite fluid.

More important to Aoua than the sex of the teller was no doubt the courage and determination of certain women who peopled the tales. Heroines who restore balance, or sweetness, to society are a regular feature of many traditions. The Yoruba tell about Moremi, the Nguni about Nongqase (Dhlomo, 1935). Both made great personal sacrifices to save their people from foreign incursion. Yet the power these heroines wield is rarely political. Absent, too, is the bullish, warring spirit typical of such masculine heroes as Chaka or Sundiata. Rather, the heroine's power seems to emanate from a superior moral conscience aided by an extraordinary intelligence and zeal.

A fine example of this uniquely feminine style of heroism appears in a traditional saga created over seventeen days by a Xhosa storyteller and diviner Mrs Mazithathu Zenani. Her epic explores three generations of characters, each with a woman at the center (Scheub, 1977). In it the girl Mityi, chief protagonist, fuses these parts into a single narrative thread.

The story opens with the young orphan Mityi being threatened by a hostile grandmother. Eventually she wins the protection of a magnificent ox, a symbolic transformation of her dead mother's spirit. In time the girl escapes into the veld, taking with her the ox's magical, all-providing horns. One night she uses them to build a fine homestead. The people of a nearby village conclude that the act is a miracle and that the homestead must be God's residence. They are in disarray because their chief has died without a male heir, and they set out for the homestead to seek God's advice. Mityi cleverly assures them that God lives in the homestead; he is away, and she will deliver the message. A few days later, when they return, she announces that God has advised them to make his daughter Mityi their chief. It is unusual for a woman to take such a title, but they accept her because it is God's will. Mityi's horns supply the people with homes, cattle, social institutions—in short, a whole way of life. She becomes the founder of Xhosa civilization and, in a final act, she establishes a male chieftaincy by passing power slowly to her shy and awkward husband.

Myths across the continent credit women with the founding of civilizations long before men established their present administrative supremacy. A similar Kikuyu myth is recounted at the beginning of Chapter 6, above. Later on, when men took charge, it was still women—

the force behind social order—who intervened when things went wrong to put them right again. The Oǹdó Yoruba create a story about one such heroine, who willingly endures trials and hardship in order to mend a family broken by her father's rash pledge. A king has sired twelve sons, and fearing financial ruin from the brideprice he will pay for their future wives, he declares that if his thirteenth child is a girl, he will sacrifice the brothers to her personal spirit (*ori*). Their mother bears a girl and helps her sons escape into the forest. When, some years later, the heroine learns the story of her birth, she resolves to reunite the family. She undertakes a treacherous journey into the forest and narrowly escapes the murderous intentions of her brothers who have made a blood oath to kill any woman who comes their way. In time she sets up a household for the young men. But again their domestic happiness ends when she unwittingly casts their lives into jeopardy by plucking the twelve flowers containing their souls. Her seven-year ordeal of silence saves them, and the joyful band is reunited, this time at home. Once again woman is the agent of harmony in a domestic world disrupted by a failure of masculine insight (LaPin, 1977: II, 9-48).

Whereas such heroines are superordinary by definition, the vast majority of female protagonists are more recognizably human. Story plots often turn on conflicts between co-wives, marital infidelities, courtship, childrearing—anything in short that touches on everyday feminine experience in a traditional setting. 'Don't be jealous in your husband's house', the performer will admonish. 'Treat your co-wife's children as if they were your own'; 'Don't marry a man against the advice of your parents'. Women, the stories suggest, are more likely to achieve happiness if they follow the guidelines tradition hands down.

If one purpose of narrative is to lay down canons of social behavior, such a message is most readily accepted when the story characters strike the listener as plausible. Routine perceptions of women enter oral tradition and harden into normative images that shape expectations of feminine behavior. Hausa tradition, for example, contains few positive characterizations of women (Skinner, 1969: xv-xvii). The tales, owing perhaps to a Muslim bias, are replete with female figures who pose a danger to the community. Yet when these stories of nefarious females are compared with variants from nearby cultures, we often find the women's places taken up by mischief-making men.

One such Hausa tale depicts a girl who insists upon marrying a young man against the wishes of her parents. When they object, she asks the boy for a knife to kill her mother. The boy refuses, but the girl ultimately obtains the knife and does kill her mother. Together the boy and girl escape into the bush, where she dies—presumably punished by a divine force. As the boy is guarding the body, an eagle comes and asks to feast on the flesh. The boy refuses. The eagle then gives him some magic feathers to revive the girl, with the warning, 'Do not put your trust in women'. The girl revives, and ultimately betrays the boy, compounding her evil by passing the feathers on to her new slave lover (Tremearne, 1913: 326-33). The Yoruba version of the tale focuses on the themes of jealousy and betrayal between two male friends rather than on the evil nature of women (performance by James Ola, recorded by the author in

May 1982).

As carriers of oral tradition, women do more than simply parti-cipate in the transmission of their image; in some measure they exercise their prerogatives as oral artists to control audience attitudes toward their sex. They embellish, enliven, and invent elements to bring fresh light on characters and themes. Mrs Mazithathu Zanani, who created Mityi's adventure, is a feminist storyteller who, by peopling her narra-tives with large numbers of 'rudderless' men, tips the balance in favor of women (Scheub, 1977: 69). In a similar vein, a powerful Yoruba market trader, Alice Oyedola, once gave a feminist interpretation to a female character from a story a man in her village had told weeks before. The man's account presented an elder so staggered by the beauty of a young, passive woman that he began a relentless campaign to win the girl. She remained indifferent and too dim-witted to take interest in the passion she had inspired. Eventually, the man's desire waned and the girl's life returned to normal. Alice Oyedola's version developed the same plot, but she portrayed the girl as a shrewd, independent trader who had made a handsome profit at a young age. In this account, she refused the elder's proposal outright, choosing a business-woman's freedom to the dull life of an elder's 'parlor' wife.

Feminine personalities also come alive in skilled impersonations by women performers. A gifted storyteller learns to assume the roles of her characters by achieving subtle changes in her voice, posture, or the expression on her face. In a performance about two rival co-wives, for example, a Yoruba storyteller will deftly shift back and forth between the humble, solicitous junior wife and her arrogant, imperious senior. One speaks with downcast eyes and a tremulous voice, the other in a booming, strident tone. At a passionate moment the dramatized 'face' of the senior wife may contort into an angry rictus of hate, while the body of the storyteller swells with the force of her anger.

Poetic genres usually require additional training and study, thus granting women more opportunity to achieve status as oral performers. Poetry is specialized. Bound up with occupational or special interest groups, it marks life transitions and important events; it defines biological and social roles. At Limba memorial ceremonies in Sierra Leone women instruct and entertain with a variety of dancing songs (Finnegan, 1970: 98). At Hausa marriage dances young girls were famed for singing verses filled with sexual innuendo, to the accompaniment of erotic mime. Sarcastic 'reed' songs permit Khoisan women to criticize the errant ways of others (Hahn, 1881, in Finnegan, 1970: 98). The wives of Fon chiefs practiced group performances in praise of their husbands (Herskovits, 1938: II, 322), while female eulogists among the Hausa were specially trained in the praises of kings (Smith, 1957: 27). Even in modern times, fresh poetic expressions embellish new contexts. Zinc roofing parties, school sporting events, and political rallies are natural occasions for the celebration and commentary that flow from the sweet words of women's songs.

Sometimes a woman will distinguish herself in one of these poetic genres and gain fame for her expertise. Anyone who spends time in an African village is likely to hear such remarks as 'Fatima is an excellent singer of wedding songs', or 'Mama Tunde chants praise poetry (*oriki*) more sweetly than anyone else'. In some communities these stars are elevated to a near-professional status. Among the Ila and Tonga of Zambia, for example, *impango* song performances are the work of a semi-professional hand. At one time every woman was expected to develop a personal repertoire of these songs, but it was understood that only a few singers were also gifted composers. Typically a woman would first air her ideas with her friends, and then they would all together call on an expert *impango* artist and sing their oral 'rough draft'. For several days this expert would privately embellish and prune. Her 'editing' done, she would call the group back and organize several after-dinner rehearsals. Once it was learned, the song would revert to its original owner. Thereafter, whenever she forgot an important line, her friends were able to assist her (Jones, 1943: 11-12, in Finnegan, 1970: 269-70).

An *impango* composer might receive a sixpence or a bit of tobacco for her service, but in the western Sudan women working as professional praise-singers and historians command a higher price. *Maroka*, or praise singers among the Hausa, include women performers who specialize in poetry honoring women. Malinke, Bamana, and Wolof griot traditions embrace a variety of women artists. Elsewhere, women may practice these arts professionally by virtue of occupation or status. Cult priestesses, herbalists, diviners, and midwives become performers whenever their role requires training in a body of verse.

In general, however, women are unspecialized, domestic poets. Their songs and verses are learned and reproduced informally at home as part of daily life. Any time women congregate around a grinding stone, delight in a new child, welcome a new wife into the household, or gather children beside an evening fire, they may embellish the event with the spontaneous sweetness of song. Poetic forms most frequently associated with women center naturally on the household. Lullabies, praise poems, courting songs, bride's laments, and dirges are examples of oral genres that validate and give meaning to important moments in the human life-cycle. From infancy a child is soothed with his praise name when he cries, nursed to the cadence of incantations, bounced to catchy tunes during play on his mother's lap. In the Dogon country of Mali a rhythmic lullaby entertains a child whose busy mother has left him tied to a minder's back. There, his little oval bottom sits perched, like a chicken egg:

Where has the little one's mother gone?
Gone to draw water
Not yet back from drawing water
Gone to pound baobab leaves
Not yet back from pounding leaves
Gone to prepare a meal
Not yet back from preparing the meal
On the cliff, on the cliff, hangs a chicken egg!
(Griaule, 1938: 226; my translation)

In some parts of Africa the transmission of praises for family members is a feminine duty. Praise poems are society's way of giving a person definition. Verses link the subject to an ancestral history and at the same time draw attention to distinguishing traits. Here, in a Dinka praise poem from the Sudan, a bride exhibits a joyful absorption in the child she has made. She sings for herself as much as for the child, for he has granted her a new status, that of 'Mother-of-one':

O son, you will have a warrior's name and be a leader of men.
And your sons, and your son's sons, will remember you long after
    you have slipped into darkness. . . .
O my child, now indeed I am happy.
Now indeed I am a wife—
No more a bride, but a Mother-of-one.
[My man's] soul is safe in your keeping, my child, and it was I, I who
    have made you.

(Brooks, 1974: 234-5)

Poetry is also an integral part of courtship. Forty years ago among the Luo of Kenya, girls of marriageable age still courted their young men in groups by visiting the youths' meeting houses at night. En route to the rendezvous, their insistent, bird-like voices could be heard across the fields as they sang special love songs called *oigo*. On arrival the singing continued to the accompaniment of men's reed flutes. The songs, which the girls composed out of traditional motifs, anticipate marriage by making subtle references to physical love. The following example takes as its central image a bell, 'probably', explained Mr Owuor who collected the songs, 'a ceremonial bell hanging on the reed walls of the grain store, which the young would be forbidden to touch' (Owuor, 1967: 51). Yet in a second sense the bell becomes a sexual image, an avenue for procreation and harvest among men and women:

The *ree* for Ameli, daughter of Omolo,
She is the Achichi who goads the encircling crowd . . .
Shaking the bell
The one who dares to shake the bell,
It's the naughty one who longs to tickle the bell;
Tickling the bell.
I dare you to tickle the bell,
The forbidden bell . . .

(Owuor, 1967: 53)

Marriage follows courtship in the life cycle, and harvest time is a preferred moment in many African communities for taking marriage partners. The romantic spirit, brought on by the expectation of leisure and plenty, spills into the entire region. Among the Kikuyu of Kenya the sweet voice gives way to jovial satire as men and women assemble in the fields to assail one another in turn with mocking verses filled with erotic abuse (Ngugi, 1977: 148). In Mali the Dogon enliven the fonio harvest with a similar jocular exchange. Women tease men about the painful ordeal of circumcision, and ridicule male sexual desire (Calame-Griaule, 1965: 303-5).

Death closes the life cycle, and at funeral ceremonies women are the most frequent singers (Finnegan, 1970: 148). At Akan burials, women soloists chant dirges to mourn and eulogize the dead. Every woman is expected to achieve competence in this literary mode as part of her social upbringing. Here, a mourner laments the loss of her mother by portraying a home robbed of sweetness through the absence of her nurturing presence:

O mother, I am struggling; all is not well as it appears. . . .
The god *opem* has failed; the gourd of charms has won.
O mother, there is no branch above which I could grasp.
Mother, if you would send me something, I would like parched corn
So that I could eat it raw if there were no fire to cook it.

(Nketia, 1969: 196)

Finally, women may become spokespeople for their own sex by selecting examples of literary materials and shaping their interpretations to fit feminine-centered themes. Verses sung privately by women during domestic chores often communicate their most intimate feelings indirectly to a casual passerby. An Ngas woman living at the foot of Nigeria's Bauchi Plateau, for example, sang a grinding song lamenting her husband who had abandoned her, and mentioning the young soldiers in the area to whom she had turned for consolation (recorded by Bankole Bello at Amper, May 1974).

Transition: traditional heroines in print

The heroines of tradition, reshaped for generations by the bodies and minds of successive performers, in time became material for the medium of print. A continuity of spirit informed the transition. Often, these writers viewed their task as that of an oral artist recreating old images in a written mode. And yet, because the new medium encouraged individuality of expression, authors learned to experiment with traditional forms and themes. In his episodic novel *The Brave African Huntress* (1958) Amos Tutuola transformed the romantic Yoruba saga of the girl rescuing her twelve brothers into a highly charged adventure story about Adebisi, who saves her four brothers who vanished on a hunting trip. By discovering the cause of their disappearance, she will preserve others from the same fate. More important, as her father's only remaining child, she must prove her mettle so that 'hunters will not die out in the family' (p. 14). Adebisi's bellicose spirit contrasts boldly with the patient suffering of the traditional heroine who inspired her. The 'huntress' confronts the monsters of the forest world with lusty, masculine drive. She drinks alcohol, enjoys the male prerogative of administrative power, and, like certain men, abuses both. In her zeal for dangerous living, this super-woman is only minimally community-conscious. Rather, she is a metaphor for the self-willed female who exercises her personality to the furthest limits. The outrageous product of a fancy gone riot, she delights; but as a man-woman she adds little to the literary exploration of sweetness—that distinctly feminine source of fulfilment.

Meanwhile, the women writers of this transitional period had very different reasons for attaching their heroines to traditional plots. Old tales furnished a natural starting point for re-thinking the woman's role. Flora Nwapa's novels *Efuru* (1966) and *Idu* (1970), for example, retain the flavor of Igbo imagery by putting it literally into English. Her lively dialogues recall the dramatized interactions of characters in oral tales. Her real attention, however, is centered on characters and themes, and most especially on non-conforming heroines who seek happiness despite their failure to bear children or behave in prescribed feminine ways. Nwapa the storyteller leaps beyond the old saws about a woman's proper conduct and anticipates the feminist literature of the next decade.

During this period Ghana's women authors Efua Sutherland and Ama Ata Aidoo undertook the same earnest appraisal of feminine potential in a masculine-oriented world. Their common vehicle was a popular narrative about the proud virgin who spurned her village suitors and chose a stranger who ruined her life. Of her play *Anowa* (1970), set in the nineteenth century, Aidoo says, 'It's more or less my own rendering of a kind of . . . legend, because, according to my mother who told me the story, it is supposed to have happened. The ending is my own and the interpretations I give to the events that happen are mine' (Duerden and Pieterse, 1974: 23).

Anowa is marked from girlhood by an uncommon destiny. Six years after puberty, she at last chooses a feckless husband against her parents' advice. Her years of toil and self-sacrifice make her husband a rich trader, but she is conscience-stricken when he turns to slaves as his chief commodity. Anowa is unable to dissuade him and assumes the guilt for their ill-gotten wealth. The psychological burden merely aggravates an already-troubled spirit. Her 'restless soul' (p. 28) keeps her from bearing children, yet her devoted husband refuses to heed her entreaties that he take a second wife. Furthermore, because her personhood is wholly bound up with her work, she is torn between prolonging an evil occupation and giving up her sense of self. Her competence poses a challenge to her husband's self-respect, and she laments: 'Someone should have taught me how to grow up like a woman . . . here, they let a girl grow up as she pleases until she is married. And then she is like any woman anywhere: in order for her man to be a man, she must not think, she must not talk . . .' (p. 52). In what Aidoo calls a 'Freudian ending', Anowa's husband sends her away and in so doing knocks out the only prop that supports him. He shoots himself and Anowa, alone and without choices, commits suicide by drowning.

In Sutherland's play *Foriwa* (1964) the same heroine returns, but in a happier mode. The drama of Foriwa, maid of Kyerefaso, unfolds in a small, backward village caught in a destructive cycle of unreflective habit. The Queen Mother of the settlement favors progress, but every new proposal is spurned by reactionary elders. 'When you restricted women with taboos', says one to the ancestors, 'you damned well knew what you were doing' (1967 ed., p. 38). Against this background the refusal of Foriwa, the Queen's daughter, to marry her suitors is a symbolic rejection of the selfish interests that flourish in the old structure. The enlightened girl joins the cause of Labaran, a stranger and university graduate, who sets up a bookshop in town. When the elders refuse his proposed school, the emboldened Queen achieves a turning point. At the yearly first fruits ceremony she openly confronts the elders: 'Is this the way to praise [the ancestors]? Watching the walls crumbling around us? . . . Letting weeds choke the paths they made? Unwilling to open new paths ourselves because it demands of us thought, and good-will, and action?' (p. 50). In the year that follows, Foriwa accepts Labaran as her partner and thereby inaugurates a new era. She achieves what Anowa could not. A harmonious conjunction of old and new restores sweetness to a tired, embattled society.

Transitional literature was also marked by Okot p'Bitek's *Songs*. Adapted from Acholi (Ugandan) women's laments and mocking verses, they comprise a series of poetic works that turn on the theme of domestic change. 'I found the [traditional] poetry was rich, the oral literature was full-bloodied', the writer said (Duerden and Pieterse, 1974: 150). *Song of Lawino*, first in his series, records the voice of a traditional woman fighting for her husband's affection against the corroding influences of his Western education and modern junior wife. The robust dignity of the traditional form is perfectly suited to the ardent message that bursts out from her wounded heart. Lawino is ashamed of her husband's strange behavior, not for herself, but for him: 'All I ask/Is that you give me one chance/Let me praise you/Son of a chief!' (p. 215). Lawino is a woman; she is also the personification of traditional Africa. Indignant, she mocks her rival Clementine, the embodiment of foreign sophistica-tion. Powdered, lipsticked, and bewigged, she 'looks like a guinea fowl' (p. 22), 'head huge like that of the owl' (p. 24), so slim 'You can hear the bones rattling' (p. 26). Against Tina's grotesque sterility, Lawino sings the virtues of Acholi womanhood: erect breasts, a bright mind, shining skin, body tattoos gleaming 'like stars on a black night' (p. 34).

But change, whatever its ills, must come for women and for society's view of them. If Tina is artificial, Lawino—unable to imagine herself in any role other than in the service of her 'master and husband' (p. 205)—is enslaved by the tradition she extols. And so the husband lifts his voice, and his song (*Song of Ocol*, 1970) calls for her self-liberation: 'Sister/Woman of Acoliland/Throw down that pot/With its water . . .' (p. 38). Ocol longs for a wife who is free and at ease with her person-hood: 'Woman of Africa/Whatever you call yourself/Whatever the bush poets/Call you/You are not/A wife!' (p. 43).

Modern expressions: women seek a new place

With the advent of literature wholly conceived and composed for the press, the African heroine underwent further re-examination. Traditional images of sweetness survived in echoes of old songs and tales. They filled many early novels and poems as complements to nostalgic tales about the pre-colonial way of life. Yet close upon the heels of this golden age, literature followed a wave of feminist rebellion. Its credo was the 'anti-sweet'. As women began to enter the ranks of published authors, they took the old images, prised them apart, examined them critically, and frequently denied them outright. In their work wives, mothers, and courtesans moved through a world charged with fresh possibilities and there awakened to inner talents that would forever alter their sense of self. A new 'sweetness' was coming into being, one that would readjust the inequalities perceived in the old. In Hegelian fashion the old synthesis would give way to antithesis before finally engendering a revolutionary vision of the woman's new place.

Men in the early years were the first educated and hence the first authors. They populated their literature with women, but most were idealized portrayals of traditional feminine personalities. In a recurrent image, woman was mother-nurturer and, by extension, symbol of a sweeter, more secure Africa which the educated man left behind. Camara Laye of Guinea, for example, opens his lyric, autobiographical novel *The African Child* (1953) with a praise poem to his mother:

> Black woman, woman of Africa, O my mother, I am thinking of you . . .
>
> O Daman. O my mother, you who bore me upon your back, you who gave me suck, you who watched over my first faltering steps . . . how I should love to be beside you once again, to be a little child beside you!
>
> Black woman, woman of Africa, O my mother, let me thank you; thank you for all that you have done for me, your son, who, though so far away, is still so close to you!
>
> (1959 ed., p. 1)

The Malinke woman, says Laye, was never despised, but enjoyed 'fundamental independence' and 'personal pride' (p. 58). Daman's presence anchored each passage in his life. Of childhood mealtimes, he says, 'my mother, by the mere fact of her presence . . . saw to it that everything was done according to her own set of rules' (p. 56); of initiation, 'she was waiting secretly to proclaim that I was still her son, that my second birth had done nothing to alter the fact . . .' (p. 112); of courtship, 'those girl-friends she did not like were shown the door' (p. 143). She protested about his departure for France: 'Any excuse is good enough for you to run away from your mother!' (p. 155).

Meanwhile, the few women writers of the early period fit their art to the same apologistic trend. Too pragmatic to idealize their sex (and perhaps already aware of the limits tradition had placed on their liberty), they offered a more generally idealized view of Africa in its physical, cultural, and philosophical dimensions. Pioneer poet Gladys Casely-Hayford Africanized her turgid Victorian style by turning to Krio language and themes; even her English language verse was inspired by a patriotic zeal. Her poem 'Freetown' (*c.* 1935) argued for an anti-colonial vision of the African continent by depicting a shoreline sanctioned by Almighty God and built to meet divine requirements:

> Freetown, when God made thee, He made thy soil alone
> Then threw the rich remainder in the sea. . . .
>
> (Casely-Hayford, 1937: 6)

Soon the political realities of the independence struggle and its aftermath worked upon the sweet vision until it soured. Insiders as much as outsiders became perpetrators of oppression. If woman equalled Africa in her literary persona, she was recast as the symbol of a continent grown ailing and corrupt. Mozambique's Noémia de Sousa created a tortured characterization of woman to portray her country's protracted struggle for independence. Her poem 'If You Want to Know Me' (1972) echoes a recurrent theme of *négritude* poets who read the marks of an anguished, paralyzed continent in the iconography of an African mask:

This is what I am
empty sockets despairing of possessing life
a mouth torn open in an anguished wound
huge hands outspread and raised in imprecation and in threat
a body tattooed with wounds seen and unseen
from the harsh whipstrokes of slavery . . .

(de Sousa, 1975: 85-6)

In a similar way, Mother undergoes distortion and reappears as traitor in the dislocated world of Congolese poet Tchicaya U'Tamsi. In his verse woman is a surrealist symbol that attracts a constantly shifting set of values. She is Africa, the fertilizing waters, the moon. Yet running like a cross-current through these idealizations is the image of a treacherous and diminished being. Dehumanized by colonial disruption, woman becomes the sterile temptress, the agonized mother, the abandoned wife. She lives in a tortured landscape peopled with aimless wanderers. Unanchored and confused, she develops a dual personality: 'I can console', she says, 'I can betray' (U'Tamsi, 1970: 82). In 'Cradle-song' (1962) she is seen lulling her child into a soothing, but sinister sleep. Her 'love' lures her child into a dreamworld that lays him vulnerable to unhealthy influences borne by 'moths' who dance in witchlike patterns round his head (p. 83).

As the 1970s approached, post-colonial protest literature abandoned symbolism for the directness of social realism. The anti-sweet became a favorite theme. Political institutions underwent hard scrutiny, and such writers as Senegal's Ousmane Sembène, Kenya's Ngugi wa Thiong'o, Ghana's Ayi Kwei Armah and South Africa's Bessie Head studied their impact on the lives of ordinary men and women. Playwright Athol Fugard, always searing in his criticism of South African apartheid, added a woman to his list of political victims in his grimly humorous play *Boesman and Lena* (1969). Lena, an 'angular, gaunt cipher of poverty' (p. 1), is locked into a marriage that mirrors the fruitless contest between oppressor and victim characteristic of the apartheid system. Boesman tortures Lena. He beats her, claiming that she has broken a few returnable bottles on which their income depends. He is bitterly contemptuous of her appearance and speech. He wilfully deprives her of sympathy and compassion. Lena's counterweapon in the battle is her stubborn refusal to give in. She bombards Boesman with hard questions: 'Why must you hurt me so much? What have I really done? Why didn't you hit yourself this morning? You broke the bottles' (p. 44). Desperate for human warmth, she seizes on an old Xhosa man and gives up her food, wine, and place in their temporary shelter in exchange for permission to house him overnight. The man reciprocates by managing, despite barriers of language and culture, to recognize and repeat her name. This opened channel of human exchange is a challenge to Boesman's private claim to Lena; it undermines his whole reality. For Lena the victim is the 'only real thing in his life' (p. 44), and that is why he hits her.

The erosion of feminine well-being was a popular subject for women writers, but they most often saw it from the vantage point of their domain, the home. If the world was changing, so too was marriage, the family, and notions of women's work. Curiously, romantic love became a focal point in the budding feminist debate; it challenged family authority in marriage and extolled the virtues of individual freedom. The idea was new to African literature. Traditional folktales argued that private desire, fulfilled without public sanction, isolated young people, made them vulnerable, and thereby posed a threat to social cohesion. In an early short story, 'The Rain Came' (1964), Grace Ogot of Kenya reversed this view by adapting the style of the traditional storyteller to a narrative in which love is equated with courage and free will. Her story builds suspense in two interlocking dilemmas. Oganda dreams of marriage to Osinda, her favorite among three suitors; meanwhile, Labong'o, her father and a Luo chief, has learned that he must sacrifice his only daughter to a lake monster who threatens the community. Despite compelling alternatives, both father and daughter choose to fulfill their society duty: 'It was an honor for a woman's daughter to be chosen to die for the country' (p. 184). Oganda is sent to the lake, and at the eleventh hour she—and by implication Africa—is rescued from slavish submission to religious dogma by her courageous and free-thinking intended, Osinda. Here folktale is transmuted into the counter-face of itself by preserving traditional motifs and yet breaking with ancient themes. The young couple is condemned to permanent exile from home, but Ogot's story makes plain that personal happiness is adequate compensation.

The wrenching battle between free choice in marriage and social prescription receives a sophisticated treatment in Buchi Emecheta's modern psychological novel *The Bride Price* (1976). For Aku-nna the conflict escalates into a struggle between reason and a conditioned unconscious. A sickly *ogbanje* since childhood, Aku-nna ('Father's Wealth') resolves to make up for her inadequacy by fulfilling the prophecy couched in her name. She will marry a rich man able to endow her parents with a large bride price. Her father dies prematurely, and the beneficiary becomes an uncaring and mercenary uncle who takes Aku-nna's mother Ma Blackie as his wife. Emecheta builds a pathetic figure of the girl who uncritically accepts the notion that the bride price is the sole measure of her worth. Only Chike, her schoolmaster and eventually her lover, attempts to cure Aku-nna's psychological submission to a cruel destiny. He, member of an outcast class forbidden to Aku-nna, sadly compounds her guilt when he rescues the girl from a rival's kidnapping attempt. Their elopement deepens her crippled sense of duty; for Chike has not paid the bride price, and Aku-nna's life ebbs away, sucked, she believes, by her uncle's vengeful spirit.

Structure is the key to the message of this story. Emecheta has conceived the novel around a classic pattern in which the negative, anti-social personality must be removed from the society he disrupts. Here, the author switches the narrative positions of good and bad characters, and thereby moves the plot in two opposing directions. If Aku-nna is somewhat unrealistically driven to death, it is not because of her own wrong behavior but because society is wrong in granting her uncle the right to sacrifice a woman's happiness in the name of custom.

For most African women writers, it is on this psychological battle-ground that freedom from external limits must finally be won. When society does not grant women the power to make choices, women must summon the courage to claim that right for themselves. Bessie Head, one of Africa's most gifted authors, traces one such struggle in her finely wrought study, *A Question of Power* (1973). Elizabeth, a South African Coloured woman, loses hold of her personality because it is over-whelmed by the destructive male egotism of her husband, Dan. A nervous breakdown follows, and she retreats into a private world. There her psyche pits Dan against his male opposite Sello, the incarnation of compassion and love. The battle, of course, is a mental invention, and her cure from madness rests on the choice she makes between these two kinds of power. Either she will submit to the old cycle of oppressor-victim, or she will find happiness in Sello's scheme of universal harmony. She chooses Sello, and thus restores herself to the sweetness of non-aggressive human bonds.

Wives and mothers in literature were not the first women to realize the feminine potential unlocked by social change. For this part, male authors seized upon 'free' women who were seasoned participants in a man's world. Prostitutes and courtesans openly challenged the estab-lished norms of sexual politics and roles. A degree of personal independ-ence offset their marginal social position and often propelled them into the service of the larger society through politically significant acts. Early examples of these self-willed heroines filled the pages of popular chap-books sold in Nigeria's Onitsha Market. Their exploits often provoked disapproving clucks from their narrators, but old-fashioned moralizing could not dull their vibrant charm.

With Cyprian Ekwensi's novel *Jagua Nana* (1961) the Onitsha heroine was transformed into a brassy, good-hearted, but heart-breaking prostitute who hurtles through dangerous encounters with picaresque abandon. At forty-five, Jagua was still sure that 'she could outclass any girl who did not know what to do with her God-given female talent' (1975 ed., p. 6). A hard-loving woman, Jagua foresakes romantic security for the freedom of the street, feeding her sense of sexual power as much as sucking her clients of their wealth. In her trade, she finds an equality with men unthinkable in any sanctioned feminine role (p. 101).

Jagua is a complex character. Her dizzying array of traits ranges from amorality to political activism to altruism. Yet tragedies mark her life. She grieves for the children she cannot bear, for the murder of her young lover Freddie by her older lover Uncle Taiwo, for the disappoint-ment she brings to her churchman father. And when she returns home to her village Ogabu, she grieves for her newborn who stays a mere two days before he dies. Transformed by this sweet moment of motherhood, Jagua resolves to stay at home and become a trader. 'I don' wan' to be me ol' self who suffer too much', she says (p. 192) and awakens to the knowledge that the 'equality' she sought was the wrong kind.

In a more serious context the prostitute may also feature as a symbol of the human community degraded by a loss of moral conscience. Wanja in Ngugi wa Thiong'o's *Petals of Blood* (1977) and Penda in Ousmane Sembène's *God's Bits of Wood* (1960) are examples of 'free' women who redirect their rebellion against sexual inequality to the higher emancipation of an errant society. 'We are all prostitutes', admits Wanja's lover Karega, 'in a world of grab and take, in a world built on a structure of inequality' (p. 240). The women are admirable, indeed heroic, characters. Others benefit from the sweetness borne of their new-found altruism, yet neither manages to resolve her own unhappiness. From start to finish they remain angry, dissatisfied, and unfulfilled.

Of the two Wanja is the more complex. As a schoolgirl she is betrayed by the businessman Kimera, who makes her pregnant and then scoffs at his promise to marry her. From then on her life is a constant cycle of new beginnings. Three times this 'virgin-prostitute' (p. 76) puts aside the seductive power of her body in feverish dedication to improving her grandmother's village Ilmorog. She welds the drought-stricken villagers together in a spirit of common destiny and leads them on an epic march to the capital to demand relief. She joins the Ilmorog women in creating a self-help collective labor scheme. During these chastened moments Wanga attempts to unlock her woman-ness. She passes from the schoolteacher Munira to a gratifying affair with the leftist Karega. Later, she and Abdulla crown their love by building a distillery for the local Theng'eta gin. The intoxicating spirit seems to fuel the on-rush of developers who transform Ilmorog from a village into a bustling town. At the height of this flowering, Wanja loses the distillery in a fraudulent foreclosure. Succumbing to a bitter philosophy, she opens a brothel for the exploiters: 'Eat or you are eaten . . . [If you are a woman], you are doomed to either marrying someone or being a whore . . . what's the difference whether you are sweating it out on a plantation, in a factory, or lying on your back, anyway?' (p. 293). The new development is cut short by a fire in the brothel, started by the puritanical Munira. Inside, Ilmorog's exploiters are consumed in the fire, caught pants down in the act of consuming.

Penda's appearance in *God's Bits of Wood* expresses the growing political consciousness of women in French West Africa during the 1947-1948 railroad strike. Faced with shortages of money, food, and water, the women are spurred on to a series of revolutionary acts. Fifty-year-old Ramatoulaye, for example, finds new strength 'born beside a cold fireplace in an empty kitchen' (1970 ed., p. 74), and openly defies her collaborator brother by murdering his fat and spoiled ram when he dares attack her store of rice and groundnut cakes. Street battles break out between the women and the colonial police. In Thiès the feminine revolt is organized into a mass march that gives dramatic shape to the 'different countenance' women have assumed (p. 33).

It is Penda who leads the women on the march, passes out their rations, settles their quarrels, and urges them on. In her new role the prostitute forces even the men to respect her. She and her women have done more than their men could do. Penda is killed by the police as the women enter Dakar, and she dies a hero of the revolution. Strike leader Bakayoko tells a dreamy schoolgirl admirer: 'You will probably never be worth as much as Penda, and I know what she was worth . . . There are many ways of prostituting yourself, you know . . . what about you?' (p. 221).

Prostitutes make appealing revolutionary figures because their lives bring them in touch with big issues without challenging the structure of family and home. Women writers, however, argue that change is illusory unless it also touches the domestic world. Committed writers Buchi Emecheta of Nigeria and Mariama Bâ of Senegal—Francophone Africa's first major woman author—squarely address the issue of feminine equality in voices edged with protest.

In her semi-autobiographical novel *Second-Class Citizen* (1974), Emecheta sets Adah, a resolutely independent girl, into an Igbo family structure that vests all decision-making power in senior males. They grant her few choices, but the young woman acts with awesome determination when blocked from an important goal. She meets the world with such resilience that the reader feels no pity for her situation; still, we are angered that she must continually leap the hurdles of absurd social rules.

A young man of limited intelligence, her husband Francis applies the prerogatives of his sex like a mindless automaton. Stereotypically Francis wants—and receives—sex on demand, his wife's paycheck, minimal responsibility for his children, sexual freedom for himself, absolute fidelity from his wife, no feminine competition, and uncompromised obedience. Adah, who resolved at a tender age 'never in her life . . . to serve [her husband's] food on bended knee' (1977 ed., p. 20), finds that she must serve him in ways that humiliate her far more.

When Adah joins Francis in London, the inequality of her marriage is compounded by the inequality of color prejudice. Her life becomes an endless list of battles against incompetent baby nurses, hostile landlords, unwanted pregnancies, and her husband's increasing physical abuse. Adah meets each confrontation head on and often wins. When Francis destroys the manuscript of her first book, she abandons hope for the marriage: she rents a separate apartment and sets about the task of building an individual identity.

The matter-of-fact reportage of Adah's story contrasts with the lyrical reminiscences of Ramatoulaye in Mariama Bâ's novel *So Long a Letter* (1980). The lengthy epistle explores the full range of Ramatoulaye's marital experience, recently ended by her husband's death. To her lifelong friend and correspondent Assiatou she reveals her own despair at her husband's decision to take a young friend of her daughter as his second wife. Ramatoulaye translates her emotional distress following the second marriage into a personal yet philosophical commentary on the plight of women in a polygamous society. Even her wedding, says the letter-writer, was a moment 'dreaded by every Senegalese woman, the moment when she sacrifices her possessions as gifts to the family-in-law, and worse still, . . . she gives up her personality, her dignity, becoming a thing in the service of the man who has married her . . .' (1981 ed., p. 4).

The usual course for a widow such as Ramatoulaye would be remarriage to one of the several suitors who wish to add her to their own households. 'I cannot lightly bring myself between you and your family', she tells an admirer: 'You think the problem of polygamy is a simple one' (p. 68). Ramatoulaye's loneliness is eased by the generosity of her friend Assiatou, who alone achieves a solution to the injustice of polygamy: she divorces her husband rather than share him, and becomes a successful career woman.

In these times, when traditional images of women do battle with modern women's reason, a new generation of women authors urge their women characters to be the pilots of their own lives. The successes of Adah and Assiatou are literary creations made by women who demand the fulfillment of feminine potential; their work anticipates the sweetness that will come with equality between men and women. Until that new golden age, it should be expected that the sweeter voice will for some time to come take on a sharper edge with repeated honing against the grindstone of modern life.

8 Women in the arts

Lisa Aronson

African women play a major role in art production. In nearly every ethnic group south of the Sahara, some women work as artists, in addition to carrying out their other activities. The arts women produce demonstrate an extremely broad range of media, including pottery, weaving, embroidery, cloth dyeing, basketry, calabash carving, wall painting, beadwork, leather work, and body decoration.

Women's and men's arts often constitute very separate spheres of activity, however. Two art forms generally not practiced by women are wood-carving and metal-smithing, the exclusive domain of men. Through boundaries that female (and male) artists impose, these spheres are kept divided. Nevertheless, it is equally true that women's arts can complement those of men; women can affect the arts that men do and, occasionally, they can enter art professions traditionally dominated by men.

The domestic orientation characteristic of women's arts must also be emphasized. Unlike men, women most often produce their arts within a domestic context, around other domestic activities and, at times, as part of their interaction with other women. This would explain why certain arts such as the painting of compound walls tend to be exclusively female. However, while produced in the context of their domestic work, many women's arts can have considerable economic value and serve important functions in social, religious, and political segments of society, therefore assuming a major role in the public domain.

Changes in these various spheres of society are among the many factors which account for innovations and change in women's arts. When these changes occur, women find the need to establish new boundaries, enabling them to protect their own social and economic interests.

It is on these main issues concerning women's arts that this chapter is focused. Beginning with a discussion of the boundaries dividing women's from men's arts, it examines factors explaining their existence and focuses on where they become blurred or re-defined. The arts that women perform in terms of their domestic orientation will then be discussed, using weaving and wall-painting to illustrate the dynamics of such compound-centered media. Since pottery is a highly professional activity of considerable economic worth, being an important medium for the making of household, religious and political artifacts, it serves as the main focus for a discussion of the socio-economic function of women's art. To conclude, and to demonstrate how change in society affects change in women's arts, the chapter again looks at weaving, dealing with the Igbo weavers of Akwete, Nigeria, and how they adapted to shifts in their economy brought about by new trading patterns.

Boundaries separating women's and men's arts

The introductory paragraphs have already implied that women's arts differ very much in type from the arts that men perform. Women dominate
pottery production[1] and do wall painting while men do wood-carving
and metal-smithing. Although both men and women weave, do cloth
dyeing, embroidery, beadwork, and basketry, it is rarely the case that
both sexes produce them in the same geographical area. If they do, the
types of objects each makes and the tools and techniques of production
differ, suggesting that the same art is either rooted in separate traditions
or is for exclusive use by one or the other sex. For example, in West
Africa (mainly Nigeria) women usually weave on an upright frame loom,
a type presumably of indigenous origin (see this type illustrated in

*Fig. 1 Anoke Lawal, a Yoruba weaver from Ijebu-Ode. She is weaving an
'Itagbe' cloth worn over the shoulder as insignia by members of the Ogboni
Society and traditional Yoruba chiefs.*

Fig. 1). It is more common for men to use a horizontal, foot-operated loom producing narrow strips, a portable variety possibly introduced via nomadic groups from the north. North Africa may also be the source of one indigo dyeing technique in which men utilize pots sunk into the ground, in contrast to the placement of dye pots above the ground that characterizes women's methods. Among the Gurensi, of north Ghana, both men and women weave baskets. However, men exclusively make bags and hats while women weave the flat-bottomed cane basket (*piou*). Men claim they never make the flat-bottomed variety because it is only women who use it to carry goods to market; thus from their perspective it is 'part of the woman's world' (Smith, 1978a: 78).

Women and men often desire to keep their artistic domains separate and it is through taboos and other means of social avoidances that the lines of division are kept intact. One frequently hears of taboos which prevent women from doing men's wood-carving and iron-work, but it is also true that taboos prevent men from entering arts dominated by women. Weaving in the Yoroba town of Oyo and the Igbo village of Akwete is strictly a woman's domain, and it is believed that men who attempt weaving will become impotent (Poyner, 1980: 49; Aronson, field-notes). Taboos such as these also prevail amongst women dyers of Liberia who believe that the dye vats are sacred to them and therefore are off-limits to men. Such attitudes, also prevalent amongst women potters throughout Africa, are a conscious effort on the part of women to keep the lines of division intact and thus protect their own profession.

The exclusion of men from women's arts and vice versa can also be a function of the rules that artists must follow to ensure skill and precision in art production. Zulu blacksmiths, like blacksmiths in other parts of Africa, adhere to certain dress codes, food and speech restrictions as well as sexual and social taboos, the latter involving the exclusion of women from the area where men are doing their work. If a Zulu blacksmith does not abide by the prescribed codes of behavior, 'his work would come to naught,' he would become mad, he would be wounded "by iron" or killed for disregarding the taboos of iron work' (Raum, 1973: 216).

Women artists and their arts can also be subject to these kinds of controls aimed at guaranteeing mastery over their art. Women potters will often prohibit menstruating, pregnant or uninitiated women (who are perceived as potentially dangerous) from entering the area where the more crucial stages of pottery production, such as firing, are in progress.

While boundaries exist, men and women can cooperate in the production and use of certain types of art. Among the Baule, women spin and dye the cotton which men use to weave cloth strips on horizontal foot-treadle looms (Etienne, 1980). Similarly, among the Kuba, men weave the plain woven raphia cloth to which women then apply elaborate brush-pile embroidered designs (Adams, 1978). The social context in which men's and women's arts are used can also coincide; an example is the paraphernalia used by members of the Yoruba Ogboni society, a secret judicial body whose power is derived from its link with spirits of the earth. As their insignia, Ogboni members use brass cast figurative staffs (*edam ogboni*) and intricately patterned shoulder cloths (*itagbe*), the former produced by men, and the latter by women.

Women can also influence and affect the arts traditionally done by men. Recent research is revealing interesting information about the vital role that women, as diviners, can have in the utilization of shrine sculpture, which men carve. Because of their close ties with spirits, gods and ancestors, women are thought to have easy access to their requirements for shrines erected in their name. They can thus play a crucial role in commissioning shrine sculpture and in determining the configuration of artifacts placed in the shrines. Among the Ijo of Nigeria, Anderson has noted that women diviners (*buroyara*) are told by the spirits which items (such as sculpture or cloth) must be placed in a shrine. Men are commissioned to carve only if sculpture is requested by the spirits. The Buroyara are also instrumental in the arrangement of the shrine objects (a key factor in the efficacy of each object) because only they receive that type of knowledge from the spirits (Personal communication, 1980).[2] Similarly, among the Senufo of the Ivory Coast, the aesthetic of placing the figures on the shrine enhances the prestige of the owner. And there too, it is only the Sando diviners (mainly women) who learn from the spirits what the appropriate configuration should be (Glaze, 1975: 65). Women also have considerable decision-making power in the Poro society, ostensibly male dominated, and the arts associated with it, because of their close link with the spirit world (Glaze, 1975).

There are also instances where women enter into arts traditionally dominated by men. For example, when the horizontal foot-treadle loom was introduced into the Yoruba town of Ijebu-Ode, women took over the once male-dominated task of weaving cloth for the Ogboni society on the vertical frame loom. With the introduction of foreign jewelry into Yoruba society, the number of men involved in jewelry production has decreased. Women, who traditionally were excluded from the profession, are now becoming bronze and gold metal-smiths (Awe, 1975: 66). Even in the case of blacksmithing in iron, a profession traditionally restricted to men, it has been possible for women (especially family members) to assist in the process and even smelt the iron itself. Among the Oyo Yoruba, for example, the blacksmith's wives and daughters will pound the ore, wash it in the river and burn it in the furnace (Williams, 1973: 146). They can even describe the design of the furnace and the process of smelting. Among the Bambara, blacksmiths (*namu*) are both men and women of a particular lineage. All *namu* have access to the supernatural powers associated with blacksmithing, including knowledge of the smelting process itself. As a rule, a division of labor exists among *namu* such that men work with metal and wood while women are confined to clay, as potters. While women rarely smelt the iron, McNaughton notes that they occasionally do so (Personal communication, 1982).

Women's arts and domestic work

For the most part, women's arts remain distinct from those of men, a tradition consistent with the separation of other areas of labor common to men and women in Africa. One principal role for African women is the domestic one, that is, raising children, preparing meals, and supervising activity within the compound. Peculiar to women, this role can explain certain differences their arts can exhibit, both in type and in organization, from the arts of men. Women's domestic responsibilities often govern where their artistic production is to be confined within the village, how the arts are organized economically and socially, and how younger women are taught the traditions. It also determines what types of arts women perform.

Weaving

A comparison of women's and men's weaving in the Yoruba town of Ilorin illustrates differences, explained in part by women's domestic roles. Weaving for men is generally a full-time activity which takes place in centralized areas of the village. Drawn from disparate regions of the town, the men work under the organization of a guild headed by one person who receives the commissions and pays the younger weavers to make the cloth. He also apprentices the young boys wishing to learn the craft. By way of contrast, young girls learn by observing their mothers from early childhood. Ilorin women weavers, unlike men, most often confine their work to their living quarters where weaving can be done as a part-time activity along with domestic responsibilities. Consistent with this, they avoid working in public arenas of the village, within centralized guild structures that require them to work away from their domestic domain. Regardless of how many women weave within a compound, each tends to work independently, earning her own wages. Much of their weaving is for domestic use. Other cloths are done on commissions which the women receive directly from the patron. Surplus cloths are arranged to be sold in the market through intermediary traders.

Like Ilorin weavers, those of the Igbo village of Akwete, Nigeria, also work in their compound and it is this factor which seemed to hinder the success of a weaver's cooperative begun in their village in 1950. At that time, male chiefs wishing to centralize weaving production organized a cooperative and built a center, illustrated in Fig. 2, where women wove one month out of the year. Forced to close during the Biafran War, it was officially re-opened in 1977. At that time, I noted that the project was only marginally successful because the women, preferring to weave in their compounds, rarely used the center. Excuses for avoiding responsibilities as coop members often hinged on their need to be near the family. When approached to pay fines for not appearing at the weaving center, they explained: 'My daughter is about to give birth and I need to be close to her' or 'An ailing family member requires my close attention'. Clearly the immediacy of domestic work governed where they wished to weave. Similar motivation underlies the fact that pottery production, basketry, embroidery, and calabash carving are done near women's living quarters where they can be easily integrated with their domestic activities. The domestic orientation of Shai potters in Ghana is discussed below.

Fig. 2 Akwete Cooperative Weaving Society Center, Nigeria. The cooperative center was built in 1958-1959. It was shut down in the late 1960s during the Biafran War. This photograph was taken in July 1977 on the day it was officially re-opened.

Certain arts are also an outgrowth of social relations with other women. For example, women among the Tera and neighboring groups along the Benue Valley region of Nigeria decorate calabashes which they circulate amongst themselves as part of their dowry and for use as domestic ware (Rubin, 1970). Ndebele women make and wear beaded garments bearing designs which communicate their own social status (Priebatsch and Knight, 1978). Hair plaiting and body decoration are also done within the women's social spheres, at a time when they are free from other work.

Wall painting

The art of wall painting, like those arts mentioned above, is an activity which a woman integrates with her other areas of productive labor and her social interactions with other women. In addition it is confined to her own compound. The motifs themselves often refer to objects and events familiar to her daily experience or to information about her social identity. By virtue of public visibility, the images applied to the walls communicate information to others in the village. Thus, while done within a domestic area, wall painting can be an important public concern.

Most domestic architecture in sub-Saharan Africa is made up of mud wall construction. While men are mainly responsible for laying the foundation and building up of mud walls, it is the woman's task to finish the wall surface, an extension of which can be the application of decorative painted motifs.

Two regions of Africa are known for wall painting. It occurs frequently among a number of Voltaic-speaking groups along the Sudanic stretch of West Africa and among the Zulu, Sotho, Ndebele and related groups of Southern Africa. In both regions, wall painting is something women do when they have leisure time from agricultural work. Among the Gurensi of northern Ghana, women paint the compound wall during the dry season, when the weather is suitable for such work and when work in the fields is at a minimum. It is also only done when the walls are in need of refurbishing, every four or five years (Smith, 1978b)

Among the Gurensi, when wall painting is needed, the senior wife of the compound organizes her co-wives and the wives of her husband's brothers to work collectively at resurfacing and painting the walls (as seen in Fig. 3). Young girls participate and, by so doing, learn the patterns and how they are to be applied. No formal training is required. While the senior wife usually decides on the pattern and the compositional layout, the final decisions are made through collaboration and cooperation with the other women. Thus, wall painting, for the Gurensi, constitutes a collective effort recognized by the women as a vehicle for their group identity. An exception occurs when the senior wife does her own room. Here, the choice of designs and execution on the walls is her work alone, as a statement about herself (Smith, 1978b:80).

Fig. 3 Wall painting being done by Gurensi co-wives of the Atia Compound in the town of Zuarungu in the Fra Fra region of northern Ghana (Photograph courtesy of Fred Smith).

While women's wall embellishments are contained within the compound, the designs have considerable public impact by virtue of their visibility to individuals beyond the compound walls. Recognizing this potential, women use the medium to communicate information about their social status and the status of the owner of the compound. Gurensi wall painting, when done well, can reflect positively on the male owner of the compound (Smith, 1978b: 40), a fact which may explain the incorporation of male-prestige objects as decorative motifs, such as cloth strips (*tana*) which men wear. But more often the patterns which women paint are oriented towards their own social sphere. Coupled with the cloth strip motif, Gurensi designs refer to items such as the 'broken cala-bash piece' (*wanyagese*) or 'fiber nets' used to hold calabashes in their living quarters (*zanlengu*). In other regions of Africa, wall designs can derive from various forms of female body decorations which enhance the beauty and communication information about the social status of women. Among the Sotho women of South Africa, wall designs relate to patterns on their beaded garments; the colors used to paint them correspond to those painted on women's bodies during initiation (Matthews, 1977: 31; Rohrmann, 1974: 18). For unmarried women of the Transvaal area of South Africa, the aim is to attract male suitors. The same may be true for Igbo women whose wall designs often relate to body designs which communicate their social status as uninitiated women (Aniakor, 1979).

Gurensi women regard any negative criticism of other women's work as 'anti-social and disruptive behavior' (Smith, 1978b). While no explanation was given for this attitude, it could be viewed as a function of the very personal kind of referencing that wall painting can have for the women. Because Gurensi women regard the medium as a statement about other women, they feel inhibited from passing judgement on the designs, tantamount to making a value judgement of the individual who painted it.[3]

The socioeconomic importance of women's arts

Women's wall painting, while confined to the compound, can function as a network through which social status is communicated. In this manner and through other media as well, women's art performed in a context with domestic work serves significantly in the society's principal non-domestic realms, the economic, political and religious spheres.

Most arts which women perform are economically valuable as a means through which they earn an independent income. At times that income can be quite substantial. Akwete weavers, for example, earn a subsistence wage which they use to support themselves and their children. They only give a portion of their earnings to their husbands if they so choose. The economic value can influence how the arts are performed. Sometimes it motivates artists to achieve a high level of skill at their craft as noted among calabash carvers of numerous groups along the Benue

Valley area of Nigeria (Rubin, 1970). The economic value can also explain the boundaries that women establish to maintain domination and control of their art. Such boundaries often involve the exclusion of other women, thus permitting artists to keep the profession within their economic domain. These protective strategies are similar to those followed in the more specialized occupational associations described in Chapter 5.

In addition to their economic value, women's arts can be of political and religious importance. Many serve as emblems to validate the power of individuals of rank. An example is the cloth woven by the Ijebu Yoruba women for use by traditional chiefs and members of the Ogboni cult. Figure 1 illustrates such a cloth being woven. In Zaire, Kuba women embroider raphia cloths which serve as important emblems of traditional wealth and status in Kuba society in their use in bridewealth payments, divorce settlements, and ceremonies legitimizing the power of the king (Adams, 1978). Other important leadership arts are the terracotta portrait heads which Akan-speaking women make for deceased chiefs and elders. The terracotta heads also serve important religious functions, because these leaders are often divine in nature.

Pottery

Ceramic pottery, the technique used for making such heads, is the most pervasive and perhaps the most important of art forms which African women perform. In addition to serving important religious and political purposes, it is economically vital as is indicated by the degree to which women impose rigid boundaries and controls to protect their profession and the processes with which it is associated. And yet, most stages of pottery production are confined to the women's domestic areas of the compound.

Pottery production involves five important stages of activity: the gathering of clay from clay reserves; the building of the pots; the predrying of them in the sun; firing; and marketing. While some women trade pots from a home base, most must travel to distant markets to sell their wares. Clay reserves are also frequently situated beyond the village boundaries, and in order for women to gather the clay, they must often go some distance from their compound. All other phases of pottery production, building of the pots and firing, are activities which the women do at home, within the domestic realm.

It is here, for example, that learning takes place, starting in early childhood, through observation and imitation. Girls begin before the age of five beating lumps of clay, a first step in acquiring the necessary familiarity with the medium. Pots are hand built; the wheel is not used in Africa. Learning to build pots, done either by the coiled or pulled method (the latter illustrated in Fig. 4), takes considerable skill acquired gradually through persistent trial and error and positive instruction. Young Marghi girls of northeastern Nigeria are neither ridiculed nor admonished by the older women when their newly formed vessels crack while drying in the sun. Instead they are encouraged positively to try again (Vaughn, 1973: 184).

Most potters in Africa do not master the art of building clay and

Fig. 4 Mo potter of west-central Ghana making a large water pot by the 'pulled method' of working the clay—pulling the clay up to form the walls of the pot (Photograph courtesy of Roy Sieber).

decorating the pots until they have reached adulthood. Among the Ikombe Kisi of Tanzania, women potters claim to continue learning into motherhood and middle age even though they began before the age of ten (Waane, 1977: 265). Skill in production of sophisticated, sculptured wares created among the Akan-speaking groups of Ghana or the Yoruba of Nigeria may not be acquired until very late in a woman's life. Abatan, a woman potter from the Egbado region of Yorubaland, admits that it was not until she had reached middle age (30 to 40) that she became skilled at creating sculptured pots for the Erinyle deity, the most sophisticated and religiously complex of the many types with which she is familiar (Thompson, 1969).

The majority of pots Abatan and other women potters make are for domestic use, a fact which may explain why the craft is predominantly women's work. Pots made by the Yoruba of Moro serve the following functions: cooking, dyeing cloth, smoking meats, frying foods and storing ashes, charcoal, firewood, water, food or clothing. Another type is used as a brazier to hold other pots for cooking (Wahlmann, 1972: 325).

For whatever use, their methods of production can be complex. The most difficult stage is firing, always done in the open air, without a kiln. It is often done collectively with other women, since the larger the quantities of unfired pots placed in the fire arena, the more effective the firing will be. When a sufficient quantity of pots have been pre-dried in the sun, they are carefully stacked one on top of another and then covered with broken pot sherds, palm fronds and leafy twigs to help retain the heat while being fired.

Careful preparation is necessary to ensure that the temperature is kept under control, thus preventing pots from cracking or exploding, disasters which could cause the loss of many hours of productive work and thus considerable revenue. It is therefore at this crucial stage of production that taboos and rituals are observed and strictly enforced. It is taboo for menstruating, pregnant or uninitiated women to approach the area where Shai women are firing pottery (Quarcoo and Johnson, 1968: 68). Among the Mossi of Upper Volta, sacrifices are made before firing to ensure that the ancestors will not interfere in a harmful way (Roy, 1975).

The clay reserves, the source for their materials, are also an important focus for women potters. Often the reserves are located near riverbeds, beyond the village boundaries. Thus, the women must travel a considerable distance from home to gather quantities of clay, which they keep stored in their huts. Shai potters of Ghana trek an arduous trail up and down a steep hill to acquire their clay. When queried as to why they prefer carrying the clay over such a distance to building pots close to the clay source, they responded that they would prefer working close to their families. Such a response reinforces the notion that women's domestic responsibilities determine where their artistic activity occurs.

The clay reserve is also an area where women come in close contact with the spirits and ancestors residing in the earth. Thus it, like firing, is an important focus for ritual activity. Among the Shai potters of Ghana, a priestess is placed in charge of each clay pit to ensure that the pit is kept 'healthy' and free from danger. The Barikiwa of East Africa have a similar practice (Cross-Upcott, 1955: 25).

Even though women produce pots within the compound, such activity can be highly professional, lucrative, and prestigious. Like most potters in Africa, Gwari women of Ushafa market their own pots traveling as far as 25 miles from the home to do so (Bandler, 1977: 31). Men may assist women potters in the transport. Among the Ikombe Kisi of Tanzania, pots made in the village must be carried to a market some distance away. While pots will be carried overland by women, they can also be transported by canoe, which only men navigate (Waane, 1977).

Ikombe potters, being the only potters in the region, exchange their wares for foods or implements produced in other villages. Women carry on this exchange among themselves, traditionally not using cash in these transactions. When cash is received for the sale of a pot, the money often becomes the property of the men. In most cases, women potters benefit from the sale of their pots, often substantially.

A song that Shai potters sing indicates their own awareness of the economic necessity of their profession:

Hear oh, hear, we continue in the work so we shall lack nothing. The work of the great grand-ones, that is our heritage. Good omens we ask. Come ye mothers and drink. Come and eat. Drive bad luck from us. Teach us pottery. Flourish the work of our hands.

(Quarcoo and Johnson, 1968: 68)

Because of the lucrativeness of the pottery market, it is not uncommon for women to establish boundaries which prevent outsiders from learning the profession. Non-Shai women are not permitted to learn the potter's craft, and men, in general, will not participate in it for fear of impotency. Ikombe Kisi potters of Tanzania also claim complete ownership of their art and thus exclude others from capitalizing on it. In such instances, exclusivity is aimed at protecting economic interests and a sense of identity in relation to their art.

In addition to its economic value, women's pottery can also have religious significance in the society, and because of such importance, its production is given special attention. Ritual pots made by the Yoruba of Moro must be treated carefully because of their close association with the gods. Clay used to make Shango pots is pounded separately from that

Fig. 5 Krinjabo woman, Krinjabo, Ghana, hand-building a terracotta funerary portrait head used to commemorate a deceased elder in the village (Photograph courtesy of Roy Sieber).

Fig. 6 Terracotta funerary portrait head, before firing, made in Krinjabo, Ghana (Photograph courtesy of Roy Sieber).

used for domestic ware and the pots are never left in the sun to dry (Wahlmann, 1972: 329). Because sacrifices must be made during the production of ritual pots, they are generally more expensive. As a rule, they are also made on commission and thus are not produced in large quantities.

A highly sophisticated sculptural form of pottery used in funerary rites is produced among Akan-speaking groups of West Africa (such as the Krinjabo, Attie, Anyi and Baule). While men are known to make such figurative pots, it is also an important artistic tradition for women. Figures 5 and 6 show such heads being made by a Krinjabo woman potter in 1964 (Sieber, 1972). Such clay modelled figures represent idealized portraits of deceased chiefs or important elders in their society. When an important individual dies, these ceramic portrait heads are commissioned and then carried in procession and used in ceremonies in their honor (d'Aby, 1960). Similar ceremonial uses of these heads for royalty were noted by European merchants in the 17th century, thus dating this tradition at least 300 years. Given the continued importance of Ashanti royalty, there is every reason to suspect that this centuries-old tradition continues to be as vital today as it was when documented in the seventeenth century and more recently in the early 1960s when it was researched.

Women's arts and change

While women's art traditions may persist over centuries, their artistic styles and roles can undergo change. Often changes can be linked to the preferences of patrons. In response to the newer demands of urbanized upper classes for European pots, several pottery centers are now adapting traditional hand-built pottery methods to European pot designs and finishes. One noted Gwari potter, Ladi Kwali, now makes hand-built pots bearing traditional shapes and designs but stoneware clay and transparent glazes (Wahlmann, 1974).

Change need not be the result of external influence. The Yoruba potter Abatan introduced numerous innovations in design to her pots, stemming in part from inspiration she received from the god, Erinyle, for whom the pot is made (Thompson, 1969). Among the Kuba, women embroider patterns on raphia cloths which, while relating structurally to the traditional royal designs on men's wood-carved objects, also show a propensity for innovation. Kuba legends telling of Kashasi, the legendary inventor of the embroidery technique, suggest that it was her desire to please the king that prompted her to devise new ways for executing royal designs (Adams, 1978).[4]

Economic changes through trade or a fluctuating market can precipitate changes in the artist's role. Among the Mo of Ghana and the Gwari of Nigeria, pottery production had once been widespread, but over time it became localized in one group who took control of the craft and began practicing it on a full-time basis (Bandler, 1977; Sieber, personal communications, 1981).

Akwete weaving

It was an economic shift due to the increase in trade that caused a change in the weaving of the Igbo village of Akwete in southeastern Nigeria. In the process, Akwete weavers set up boundaries enabling them to claim ownership of a craft once the prerogative of women throughout their clan. Amidst heavy trading with the coastal Ijo in the nineteenth century, innovations and changes were introduced into the weaving. Weaving evolved into an elaborately decorated type, mainly woven by Akwete women within the clan. In spite of a history of weaving throughout the clan, Akwete women now believe that they invented weaving and are sole owners of their craft. This belief is reinforced by a legend telling of an Akwete-born woman who invented weaving in her dreams. Boundaries are also kept intact by the rigid rules Akwete women follow regarding who is permitted to learn the craft. The need to establish such boundaries

stems from Akwete women's desire to take control of
lowing major changes in the craft. The remainder of th
devoted to discussion of the changes in Akwete weavin
red and how the women adjusted to them.[5]

Akwete is one of twenty-five villages withir
Ndoki clan. It is situated on the bend of the Imo
Nigeria, approximately 50 miles from the coast. Whi
exists in other Ndoki villages, it is in the village of Akwete wher
is most dominant. There Akwete women are expected to weave cloth
full-time basis. Before the age of five, Akwete girls begin imitating their
mothers by playing at weaving on upturned stools (see Fig. 7). At that
time they are already demonstrating some knowledge of the craft in the
way they mock their mothers' gestures and movements. Girls, such as the
one noted in Fig. 8, begin weaving on an upright loom as soon as they
are physically able and will continue to do so as long as they remain in
Akwete.

*Fig. 7 Child playing at weaving on an upturned stool in the Igbo village of
Akwete, Ndoki clan, southeastern Nigeria.*

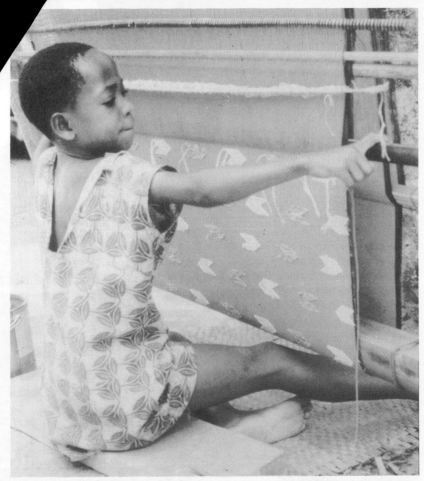

Fig. 8 Young girl weaving her first cloth on an adult loom in the Igbo village of Akwete, Ndoki clan, southeastern Nigeria.

At this early stage, girls are also told of a legendary figure, Dada Nwakwata, who invented weaving in her dreams. It is through Dada Nwakwata that weaving purportedly began in Akwete; no women before her had woven cloth. The following is a shortened version of the legend told to me on August 11, 1977:

Dada Nwakwata was from the Uhuobu compound in Akwete . . . of the Egbe family. Nobody taught Dada Nwakwata how to weave. She learned the designs in her dreams; she said the ancestors taught her. She did not allow anyone into her backyard where she was weaving her cloth except one deafmute slave who therefore could not teach the weaving art to other women. But by carefully studying Dada Nwakwata's art, she learned the craft and started to teach other women secretly after Dada Nwakwata's death. Dada was not aware that she could teach Ngbokwo to weave.

Other versions of the legend state that Ijo traders so preferred Dada

Nwakwata's cloths that they would pay twice as much to buy them. (With such profits, Dada Nwakwata could purchase two slaves instead of one, a monetary incentive which prompted other women to learn her weaving secrets.) Such legends, told time and time again in Akwete, serve as an historical document about change in weaving in the mid-nineteenth century when Akwete and other Ndoki villages were involved in active palm-oil trading with the coastal Ijo.

The palm-oil trade, which gradually replaced that of slaves after 1807, required both the use of intermediary markets situated near channels of water and greater numbers of individuals, including women, for the manufacture and distribution of the oil. Women from Ndoki and particularly Akwete, situated close to the Imo River, assumed an important intermediary function in the trade. They sold palm-oil products, brought down from northern Igbo areas where they were made, directly to Ijo traders who sold them to European merchants on the coast. Coastal Ijo traders, wishing to maintain control of the channels between Ndoki and the coast, frequently travelled up river to purhase the goods from Ndoki women. At that time, they also began buying the women's cloths and influencing how they should be woven. While weaving throughout Ndoki changed in the process, the Dada Nwakwata legend informs us that it was cloths from Akwete which underwent the most significant changes.

Prior to this time, cloths throughout Ndoki were said to have been plain woven or of simple stripes, woven with handspun cotton. They were also narrow in width, approximately 8 inches (20 cms), occasionally

Fig. 9 Akwete woman weaving a pattern inspired by imported Indian Madras traded to the coast of West Africa by the British as early as the eighteenth century and introduced to the Akwete women through trade with the Ijo.

sewn together in twos or in threes. In response to Ijo demands, Akwete cloths were widened, making them the widest variety of women's weave produced in West Africa (see example of such cloth in Fig. 9). Imported cotton threads were also introduced to Akwete women, presumably through the Ijo, who were in direct contact with the Europeans through trade. The greatest impact was on the patterns themselves. One pattern in particular, IKAKI, an Ijo word for tortoise, is the most important design the Ijo introduced to Akwete's repetoire. IKAKI, illustrated on the cloth in Fig. 10, constitutes one of a hundred or more patterns familiar to Akwete women. Many of these are copied from cloths owned by the Ijo. Scores of others are derived from such designs. Still others stem from the weaver's own imagination, for Akwete women place a strong emphasis on innovation and change, an artistic accomplishment of which they are exceptionally proud (Aronson, 1982).

Akwete weavers were able to dominate this newer form of weaving when palm-oil trading declined, after 1900. Because of the decrease in trade, the Ijo visited Ndoki less frequently for the purchase of palm-oil and cloths. And yet, Ijo demands for Akwete cloths persisted. To meet these demands, Akwete women began traveling south directly to the Ijo patrons to sell their cloth and cloths from other Ndoki villages. As marketeers, they were able to take economic control of weaving in their clan, selling all cloths with the name *akwa akwete* (Akwete cloth). This pattern continues today. Cloths woven in neighboring Ndoki towns, such as the one illustrated in Fig. 10, are invariably sold to Ijo patrons by

Fig. 10 Akwete cloth with IKAKI (tortoise) design, woven by women in the neighboring Ndoki village of Ohanso. However it carries the Akwete label because women from Akwete will very often purchase it from these weavers and trade it themselves to the Ijo.

Akwete traders, bearing the Akwete village name.

Weaving is now also a full-time activity for Akwete women, who are less involved in farming than women elsewhere in Ndoki. As a full-time activity, weaving has become an important aspect of their identity both as women and as members of their own village. Rules to which Akwete women adhere insure that this identity is reinforced. Young Akwete boys may play at weaving and occasionally assist the mother in winding the threads, but they will never be permitted to weave on an adult loom for fear of impotency (*isu otiti*). More importantly, other Ndoki women are denied the right to learn weaving in its newer form. Akwete women will never reveal their secrets. If ever suspected of doing so, they are severely reprimanded by other Akwete women. For it is their belief that all weaving must be rooted in their own village. Whatever weaving does exist elsewhere in Ndoki, Akwete women claim had to have been introduced through an Akwete-born woman who married elsewhere.

Such claims were frequently denied by weavers of these other Ndoki villages who often asserted that weaving had once been the prerogative of women throughout Ndoki, taught from generation to generation within their own villages. Such assertions are confirmed by oral histories and ceremonies recorded from these villages. During burial services honoring a senior woman from the Ndoki villages of Ohambele and Obunko, her eldest daughter danced with the deceased woman's beater stick (*otiti*) in praise of her weaving profession as a source of her sustenance in life.[6] While weaving is now only a minor occupation in those towns, the persistence of such ceremonies suggests that it was once economically significant to the women. Oral histories also cite the types of cloths these villagers were once weaving, narrow, handspun cloths of plain or striped designs.

Evidence that weaving had once existed elsewhere in the clan would then explain the very possessive behavior now characteristic of Akwete women. In essence women from Akwete have taken economic control of a new and improved craft, which caused the extinction of a simpler and once more prevalent form of weaving. In order to maintain ownership of the craft, Akwete women deny women outside the village the right to learn weaving. They justify this exclusive behavior by claiming that weaving was invented by their own village. This belief is legitimized by the legend of Dada Nwakwata continually told by the women, which states that no other women ever taught her to weave. Born in Akwete, Dada Nwakwata learned the art of weaving in her dreams.

Notes

1 There are exceptions, such as among the Hausa of northern Nigeria and the Baganda in East Africa, where both men and women are potters.
2 Martha Anderson is currently writing a Ph.D. thesis at Indiana University, Department of Fine Arts, on Ijo shrine sculpture.
3 Fred Smith notes that Gurensi women are inclined to make aesthetic criticism

about other women's pot designs, because of the economic value that they have to the women (Smith, 1981).

4 Patricia Darrish, a Ph.D. student in African art at Indiana University, has recently completed her field work on women's embroidery designs among Kuba-related groups in Zaire.

5 This section is based on the author's own research in Nigeria; similar occupational associations are discussed in Chapter 5 above.

6 Akwete women informed me that this ceremony was once also practiced in Akwete. However, the impact of Christianity in Akwete has brought about the end of such ceremonies that focused on communication with the ancestors.

PART THREE

Women in politics and policy

9 African women in politics

Jean O'Barr

The political roles African women play must be described by two seemingly contradictory statements. On the one hand, women's political roles in pre-colonial Africa provide stimulating examples of how social systems have been organized to include positions of power for women. On the other, a survey of contemporary Africa reveals few women in decision-making roles and an underlying tension in gender relationships which impedes the exercise of political power. Then, as now, the relationship of women to politics has been based in the nature of African societies themselves and the changes those societies have undergone.

The purpose of this chapter is three-fold. First, we will discuss the avenues of political participation open to African women, stressing the importance of going far beyond Western notions of electoral activity and recognizing the fusion between politics and other aspects of social life. Second, we will review women's political activity in pre-colonial times, the reversals imposed during colonial times, women's involvement in the nationalist period, and women's contemporary political power. Third, we want to suggest a way of thinking about political participation and its attendant power, whether on an individual or group basis, which will help us chart likely future events.

The exercise of political power

African societies have been characterized by a fusion between the social, economic, and political spheres of activity. As earlier chapters have suggested, it is not only difficult but often misleading to try to differentiate economic power from political influence, or religious authority from political clout. Thus in looking at the exercise of political power by African women, we will constantly refer to the economic and social realms.

Three ideas underlie our discussion here:

1. Political power refers to the ability of A to get B to do something that B would not otherwise have done. Power is derived from the resources (influence, material goods, or contact with the sacred, for example) which A possesses. A gets B to do the desired thing by suggesting it be done, by threatening what will happen if it is not done, or by coercing B to do it through emotional or physical force. Politics then is the process

by which resources are allocated in a society.

2. The distinction between power and authority is crucial to understanding African women. African women often have power (they are As who can get Bs to do something) but they often lack authority, the culturally accepted beliefs that they have a legitimate right to power. Universally, women have more political power than they have authority.

3. Most accounts of political systems assume that the action is with males and that women are peripheral to the events of politics. While this is less true in Africa than elsewhere, the bias of Western observers comes through in their interpretation of the data. The first and most important step in political analysis is to accept the fact that women are social actors with agendas and strategies of their own. We must look at women not exclusively as appendages of men but as social actors in their own right.

What then is the range of political activities open to African women? The modes of political power utilized by African women, individually or in groups, include indirect ones, such as withdrawal, evocation of the supernatural, or manipulation through males, as well as direct ones, such as selecting leaders, holding elected or appointed office, and wielding resources for desired ends.

Withdrawal is often the simplest mode African women have used to exercise their power. In the ethnographic film 'N!ai, The Story of a !Kung Woman' (Public Broadcasting System, 1980), the narrator depicts a series of scenes in which N!ai refuses to abide by her family's decision to marry. For her, the exercise of autonomy is brief but effective; by withdrawing from social interaction she manages—albeit temporarily—to assert her own will. Faced with the impossibility of permanent withdrawal because she has no other options (no other place to live, no other source of support or status in her community), N!ai eventually agrees. Clearly, withdrawal is not an effective strategy for the long-term exercise of control. Yet it allows a woman to take a position, it forces others to deal with that position, and it produces control for a brief period of time.

Resort to the supernatural is a more frequent and often a more effective method of exercising political power. Chapter 6 in this volume suggests several ways in which women utilize the supernatural (see also Berger, 1976; Strobel, 1982). Commonly cited examples center around women employing ritual to bring desired ends—fertility for themselves, punishment for those crossing them, benefit for their agricultural labors or the community's well-being, or protection and favor from the ancestors. Whether the ritual involves a chant said while preparing a dish, a cleansing ceremony performed prior to visiting sacred places, or specified behaviors undertaken to insure agricultural productivity, Africans have long believed that women's activities controlled some aspects of the supernatural and that this control was a political resource women could employ to bring about desired ends.

By far the most frequent means used by African women to control their destiny is working through men. By this we mean that where women do not occupy officially recognized positions in the society, they must influence the men they are personally connected to in order to influence policy. Women use their fathers, their brothers and cousins, their husbands, or their sons to influence outcomes in the desired direction (Rosaldo and Lamphere, 1974). Lacking a place on the chief's council, women will convince some men over whom they can exercise authority to make their point. Even more subtly, women will get men to put items on the political agenda by convincing them of the salience of an issue. Such manipulation need not be conscious for it to be either effective or observable.

One of the most interesting facets of the exercise of indirect political power is the fact that both parties often deny its existence. Yet the observer sees the dynamics at play. Men in a given community may never have considered the question of moving a farm plot, building a communal area, or promoting a particular person for office. Women's gossip, indirect suggestion, and the set-up of situations may cause men to accomplish the women's objective without even knowing they did. Using the first example, I could write a script based on my field work among the Pare of Tanzania in which the women complain about the condition of the present plot, fantasize about the attributes of another, and predict the low productivity from the present plot. The men, whose job it is in this society to clear land, would undertake to clear a new plot, overtly at their own discretion, in fact as a result of having the decision-making climate created for them by female political actors. The female actors had the power, but not the authority to achieve this desired end.

Direct modes of exercising political power seem more familiar. The first example is selecting leaders through voting, through decision-making in groups, through covert support when a would-be leader assumes power. The second example is the exercise of power by an elected, appointive or inherited office-holder. Women who have official positions—and the African material tells us that there were many official positions for women in pre-colonial times—can exercise political power directly (Paulme, 1971). As described below, several state systems in pre-colonial Africa had women's positions as part of the normal fare of politics. In some cases, the king's wife or sister ruled over women's affairs and was responsible for the performance of those under her authority.

The exercise of power as a result of group membership is a third example of a direct mode. As Chapter 5 shows, women belong to many groups, based on kin, ethnic, age, and occupational relations. Those groups are often politicized and thereby empower the women who are members. There were many examples of this kind of mobilization during the colonial period, and some will be described below. Here perhaps it is sufficient to reiterate that African women operated groups for collective ends long before European-style organizations were introduced. In addition, many African societies were divided into complementary spheres where women conducted women's affairs and men tended to their own, with neither controlling the other. African women have long been in charge of affairs in their realm; their realm was important to the society as a whole and was not subject to male control.

Finally, women wield direct political power where they use resources in their possession to support a person or policy. As one person has put it, it is indeed more blessed to give than to receive, for the giver controls the situation. African women may possess knowledge of the supernatural which endows them with the ability to handle nature. Some African women possess the means of production and its yield; through this control of production they can and do allocate food and shelter. Other African women possess group solidarity which can be placed at the disposal of a person or a project.

Women in pre-colonial politics

Recent work on women in African societies has shown that we cannot make a simple statement that easily summarizes how women fare politically. In some systems women have economic status, but lack religious control. In others, women seem dominant in ideology but lack day-to-day political power. It is almost as if each system had worked out a way to balance power between the sexes, to give a slight edge to the men in that system, but to vary the areas of women's control across systems so that no universal pattern of asymmetry emerges (Whyte, 1978; Quinn, 1977).

Prior to the systematic penetration of the European colonial systems, African women had a much broader role in decision-making than they did under colonialism or than they have had since independence. As described in Chapter 1, the hunting and gathering societies of Central and southern Africa were characterized by relative political equity between women and men. There was no continuous formal political leadership, and each sex had its own sphere of activity, over which its leaders exercised control. Women organized the hunting of small animals, the gathering of roots and berries, the provision of water, and the care of small children; men were involved in the hunting of larger animals, the division and storage of the kill. Both participated in the ritual and communal activities of their societies (Collier and Rosaldo, 1981).

In the agricultural societies of most of black Africa, where the majority of African women lived, women derived their political status from the key role they played in production. Whether the society was matrilineal or patrilineal, women usually (1) had political control over some area of activity, be it farming, marketing, trading, or household and family affairs; (2) had political institutions (usually councils) to decide how to rule their own affairs or to influence the affairs of men; and (3) were not subject to general control by men as much as they were autonomous in their own areas of responsibility (Hafkin and Bay, 1976; Rosaldo and Lamphere, 1974). Women's solidarity groups, based on kinship, age, culture, or economic production tasks, played a critical role in providing formal relationships for women in the community as well as in endowing women with a psychological sense of self-esteem. African women were bound to other women through a complex set of associations; that sense of belonging provided the base from which they carried on their day-to-day affairs.

Several African polities had a 'dual-sex' system in which a woman was responsible for women's affairs and a man for men's affairs and the general community. For example, an official called the Omu among the Igbo of eastern Nigeria was in charge of women's affairs, including the regulations of market trade, as described in Chapter 5 (Okonjo, 1976). Similarly, the Iyalode among the Yoruba in western Nigeria had jurisdiction over all women and represented women on the king's council, which was otherwise dominated by men (Awe, 1977).

Some women in high political office were not restricted solely to women's affairs, however. Thus the Queen Mother among the Asante of Ghana represented the matrilineage, not women's interests, and was generally responsible for the fertility and good fortune of the kin group as a whole (Lebeuf, 1971). And among the Mende and Sherbro of Sierra Leone, women held chiefships on the same basis as did men, their gender being seen as irrelevant to their political role (Hoffer, 1972; 1974).

One author has recently described the differences between the roles of sister and wife, showing it would have been better to be a woman in some systems than in others, if by better we mean that women as individuals and as a group had more control over their lives. A *sister* in this sense is one who has economic control and is in a social system which is neither patriarchal nor excessively hierarchical, while a *wife* is one whose position derives from her husband and whose cultural system is patriarchal. *Sisters* fare better than *wives* politically; the cultural situations in which sisters flourish tend to be those without patriarchy and without a capitalist base. This argument, while clearly subject to debate, provides a clear distinction between conditions favoring political power and those which do not (Sacks, 1979).

The key idea to grasp from a discussion of women's political positions in pre-colonial Africa is that there were well defined and respected political roles for women. Women's prerogatives were never equal to those of men across all types of systems, nor were there ever as many women in leadership positions as there were men. However, African women did have considerable power—more than they have had in subsequent periods.

Politics in the colonial period

The advent of the colonial period in the nineteenth century and its intensification in the first half of the twentieth century had a profound impact on African women's position in politics. In general, women were ignored and deprived of their power. All colonial officials shared a basic belief that the role of women was that of household helpmate to men, and that women were outside the proper realm of politics. The colonial powers did not try to manipulate female leaders; they often did not even know that female leaders existed. Among the Igbo, for example, the British made the male Obi into a salaried official, but by-passed his female counterpart, the Omu, thus destroying the 'dual-sex' political system

(Okonjo, 1976). One hundred years of neglect, coupled with the relatively rigorous implementation of new political forms in the male sphere resulted in the eclipse of African women in politics.

Occasionally, African women struck back. We have at least three well documented cases of women's resistance to colonial imposition. In these situations, involving taxes and the control over land and farming practices, women took affairs into their own hands. In the Pare highlands of Tanzania, among the Kom of Bamenda Province in the former British Cameroons, and most spectacularly among the Igbo of eastern Nigeria, women were mobilized into active political participation.

The tax riots in Pare District, Tanzania, in the 1940s precipitated the first active roles for many Pare women in modern politics. The riots grew out of a Pare District Council decision to levy a graduated income tax, on the advice of the British district officer. In 1942-1943, the colonially instituted council, composed of the nine male chiefs or native authorities, decided to institute the tax, in addition to the poll tax already in force. The new revenue was to be used solely for development projects in the district.

The direct cause of the riots was confusion arising out of the imprecise and unclear procedures for tax assessment and collection. People demanded more information about the basis of assessment and objected to the use of the traditional name and form for the tax. Pare men became indignant, taking the position that people had a legitimate right to question the governing authorities. The chiefs, for their part, sensed that people were attacking their position, and not simply their stand on the tax. They became determined to impose the tax without any modifications, as evidence of their authority. Stymied in their discussions with the chiefs, people chose a more direct course of action. Early in 1945 thousands of men representing the various parts of Pare District marched on the district headquarters at Same, announcing their intention to remain there until the tax was abolished.

After the demonstrators set up camp, the chiefs and their assistants moved to the district headquarters as well. Several meetings were held among the people's representatives, the native authorities, and the officers of the colonial government, but little progress was made. After several months, the mobilization of women began in one subdivision. The wives, mothers, sisters, and daughters of the demonstrators marched twenty-five miles to the district headquarters, to show their support for the stand the men had taken. The women presented themselves as a delegation to the district officer and demanded that he either effect a settlement and allow the men to return to their homes, farms, and jobs, or that he himself should impregnate all of them. The women claimed that the controversy had so disrupted the normal life cycle that, if Pare society were to continue, they would be forced to follow their husbands to Same. Since the British officer had forced the men to abandon their wives and their work, he should assume their roles as husbands. For them, the officer symbolized the deadlock between their husbands and the native authority structure.

The local officer, who foresaw no easy resolution to the tax controversy, requested assistance from both the provincial and territorial governments. When the national officials arrived in Pare in 1946, they were stoned by crowds of angry women. Sensing that the situation had taken on new and uncontrollable dimensions, the chiefs relented. They remained firm that a tax should be levied, but consented to a new form of assessment. Still dissatisfied, more than 2 000 Pare taxpayers (about one-fourth of the total) paid their 1946 tax in the neighboring district of Kilimanjaro, even though the rate there was slightly higher than in Pare District. Informants, remembering this event, claim that the taxpayers believed their action demonstrated to the colonial government that they were indeed willing to pay taxes, but were protesting its form and the manner in which it had been levied. The idea of graduated tax was dropped the following year, and the existing poll-tax rate was raised. Other reforms in local government increased popular representation in district decision-making, although none guaranteed direct involvement for women.

The involvement of Pare women was essentially a conservative reaction. During the tax riots, women asked that the order in their lives be restored. They wanted their men home, and the dispute settled. By asking to be impregnated, they vocalized their demand for a continuation of life was it was. Pare women were mobilized into this new form of political activity by the new circumstances in which they found themselves (O'Barr, 1976).

Among the Kom of the former British Cameroons, the involvement of women in politics during the first part of the nationalist period stemmed from the utilization of a traditional practice which was transformed into a tool of contemporary power (Kaberry, 1952). The custom of *anlu*, in which women used to bring community shame on offending individuals by dressing in vines and singing derisory songs, has been described in Chapter 5. In 1957 the *anlu* tradition was transformed into a modern political organization. Grievances against the colonial government—such as the rumor that land was to be sold, the failure to restrain the invading cattle of neighboring groups, and the inadequate enforcement of a contour farming program—were all felt acutely by the Kom women. Urged on by some enterprising men, the women formed an organization using the traditional mechanism. Within a year, the organization grew to include virtually all Kom women. They proceeded to seize authority from the representative councils and exercised it in mass public meetings. By mid-1958, the premier visited the area and was faced with an *anlu* reception. Working with the district officer, he convinced six thousand women mobilized for the occasion that there was no substance to the rumor that their land would be sold and that the contour farming scheme would be postponed. Subsequently, *anlu* activity continued in reduced proportions until it faded from public importance.

While this episode has cultural dimensions, its primary dimension seems to have been political. The Kom women reacted to the lack of control over their farming activities. After they had gained some concessions and realized they had been used as a vehicle of protest for the entire community, they began dropping out of the *anlu* organization. The political situation turned on other issues, not exclusively women's protest. But women's initial involvement was pivotal in mobilizing wider community opposition.

The most amply documented case of a women's uprising occurred among the Igbo of northeastern Nigeria in 1929-1930 (Van Allen, 1974, 1976). As in the Kom case, Igbo women had a mechanism for exercising their influence in pre-colonial times; their institution of 'sitting on a man' was described in Chapter 5 above. When Igbo women utilized that mechanism during the colonial period, their activities were misinterpreted, in fact punished, and they found themselves on the eve of the nationalist period with even further diminished influence. There is one final irony in the Igbo situation: unlike the Pare and Kom cases, several official and scholarly inquiries into the events were conducted; not until Van Allen analyzed the Igbo women's revolt within a feminist framework, however, did observers understand what they were seeing.

In 1929 in one province of Igboland, a zealous district officer decided to recount the households to verify them for the tax records. This recount came at a time when rumors were out that the government was going to increase taxation and might even tax women's property. Entering one homestead, the officer got into a scuffle. Word spread of the encounter and the 'Igbo Riots' were launched. 'Riots' is the term the British chose to apply, because they did not understand either their origin or structure.

When the tax collector and the women in this province tangled, the local women punished him according to custom. They sounded the traditional alarm, assembled, and marched on government headquarters. They brought into action their strongest sanctioning mechanism, 'sitting on a man' or 'making war'. While traditionally force had been legitimate in getting compliance with their rules, they extended and elaborated upon its use—buildings were burned down, jails broken into and prisoners released, native courts attacked and sometimes destroyed, and European stores and trading centers attacked and looted. At the height of the uprising, thousands of women in many provinces were said to be involved. At one point, the military was called out and eventually fifty women were killed, with another fifty injured. No colonial officer or assistant, however, was injured in the 'riots'. The situation abated as men came to speak with the colonial powers on behalf of the women.

These three cases suggest that African women resisted colonial encroachment on their prerogatives. We do not know how frequent women's protest was, because observers at the time left only a biased and inadequate record of women's roles. The cases do demonstrate that African women had indigenous political institutions which were powerful, and that when they utilized them they were able to challenge the new institutions being imposed upon them.

The nationalist movements

As the colonial period came to a close in the 1950s and 1960s, we have additional evidence of the political roles played by African women.

Unable to maintain their earlier range of options, women participated in the nationalist revolutions in diverse ways. The various kinds of nationalist movements, as well as the period in which they occurred, provide the context within which women acted. The earliest, relatively non-violent and non-Marxist revolutions of West Africa were followed by similar movements in East and Central Africa. A second set of nationalist movements occurred in the entrenched 'settler' economies of Kenya, Algeria, and Zimbabwe, where violent struggle was necessary. A later wave of more self-consciously socialist and Marxist-Leninist movements led to intense fighting in Guinea-Bissau, Angola, and Mozambique. Finally, there is South Africa, where nationalist activity continues, in the face of strong repression.

In this chapter we will discuss examples from Nigeria, Sierra Leone, Guinea, and Algeria, all of which attest to the fact that women helped bring about the expulsion of colonial authorities, though the forms of participation differed in each case. We will also consider the ways in which women did or did not build on this power in the years after independence. Women's roles in the armed national liberation movements in Guinea-Bissau, Angola, Mozambique, Zimbabwe, and Namibia will be discussed in the next chapter. South Africa will be treated in both chapters.

In Nigeria, where the nationalist movement was less violent and centered on electoral struggles, organizations of market women were key supporters of the political parties during the elections. Market women's support became the leading factor in a party's control of an area. The women themselves were active in endorsing and financing candidates, extracting promises, and generally participating in the political process (Johnson, 1981; Mba, 1982). However, they limited their politicking to demands related to market activites and continually underestimated their own more general political strength. Thus, as time went on, the political clout which they had once exercised tended to decline.

In other West African cases, such as Sierra Leone, women did institutionalize their participation both during and after the nationalist period (Steady, 1975). The career of Constance Cummings-John is an excellent example of how some women became effective political leaders.

Mrs Cummings-John's early career demonstrates how an elite woman became politically aware through family participation in local politics, reinforced by radical contacts she made while studying in Britain. The experience of racial discrimination at home and in Britain was a motivating influence, but not the only one. Her ideas developed partly as the result of discussions with West Africans and other black colonials about the colonial situation, and partly because of her own upbringing in a home in which politics was an important concern. Cummings-John's early success was due to her connection with Wallace-Johnson, one of the most astute politicians of the inter-war period. From him she learned the techniques of mass organization, protest demonstrations, and the necessity of keeping in touch with the people. The people in her constituency noticed that she listened to their complaints, took note of their needs, and helped them obtain what redress was possible. In the process, she became conscious of the power residing in the market women, although she did not seek to harness that power for political purposes until much later. For her the lesson of the inter-war years was that the parochial concerns of the established elite inhibited self-determination and limited development for the masses. In the 1950s she utilized her insights about the colonial situation to create a dynamic new movement, the Sierra Leone Women's Movement. That association united Creole and Protectorate women in a fight against colonial policies inimical to their economic and political interest. She aligned the women's movement with the Sierra Leone People's Party, the Protectorate-based party which was much more in tune with the interests of the masses than the other, elitist colony-based parties. Thus Cummings-John became one of the most important women politicians in West Africa in the fight for independence (Denzer, 1981: 31-2).

In Guinea, in former French West Africa, the nationalist movement assumed a more socialist ideology and had a greater commitment to political roles for women. Here women played a direct role in the rise to power of Sekou Touré, the principal nationalist leader, and they maintained that power thereafter. Touré appealed early to women as active participants. They responded with active involvement—they gave money, they provided communication links among the revolutionaries, and their leadership participated in policy formation. After independence, women stayed in the party and in power (Dobert, 1970). In comparison to other regimes of that period, Guinean women exercised political power extensively as a result of recognizing and building on the support they had given the winner, and as a result of his eagerness to use them. Like the leaders of nationalist movements in Angola and Mozambique discussed in Chapter 10, Touré worked from a dual base vis-à-vis women. On the one hand, he had an ideological basis for his socialism which demanded the equal participation of women. His view of the body politic required equal involvement of all citizens, male and female. On the other hand, he was an astute judge of his limited resources and well aware of his need to mobilize all of them. Guinean women, by tradition and through modern market involvement, were key resources, and he reached out to them.

In Algeria, a former French settler colony in North Africa, the nationalist movement became an armed struggle against the colonizers. Women's activities were extensive and varied, but eventually self-defeating. As in the other armed struggles discussed in Chapter 10, women played important roles. Garbed in traditional clothing, Algerian women became the primary means of transmitting food, weapons, and information. They were able to traverse the cities unknown to the French authorities, providing the communications link necessary to the rebels' success. Some became involved in policy-making. Accounts of the period describe how difficult Algerian men found it to listen to the advice of women but how the demands of the revolution forced them to lay aside gender stereotypes and incorporate women as fellow comrades.

The French too saw a political role for Algerian women; for them, the political role was a modern one. In their propaganda, they appealed to Algerian women to stick with France as the primary means to reduce their oppression and to take advantage of a new life style. Some Algerian women supported the French, seeing alliance as the means to a new equality. With the achievement of independence, Algerian nationalists rejected that which had been French, including the proposed political roles for women, and stressed the return to an indigenous state. The fact that women had taken enormous individual political risks to bring about the revolution was pushed aside in the fervor to restore legitimacy. Male leaders, both Algerian and French, had perceived that as a practical matter they needed female support and participation in order to win. In the intensity of the revolution, the constraints for an appropriate gender role behavior in both cultural traditions went by the board, creating new opportunities for women. But once independence was achieved, the crisis past, women were edged out, and were not rewarded with the power they had earned. Algerian women, active in the revolution, did not have an organizational base to utilize in order to capitalize on their work afterwards, when the political agenda shifted (Gordon, 1972).

A survey of the highlights of women's participation in the African nationalist movements would be incomplete without mention of the experience of South African women, black and white, in the protracted struggle of that country. The nature of South African politics makes it difficult to compile a full picture of how women have aided the yet unfinished anti-colonial struggle. Accounts of earlier history demonstrate how white women's roles were interrelated with national politics during the Anglo-Boer War (Spies, 1980). The Black Sash, since 1963 a multiracial, liberal organization of women opposed to apartheid laws, stands as an important example of how South African women have found ways to resist the dominant political culture (Michelmann, 1975). The link between apartheid policies and the intersection of gender, race, and class in the South African cultural system is described in *For Their Triumphs and for Their Tears* (Bernstein, 1975). Bernstein demonstrates how the sex-gender system of white South Africa is fundamental to the policies of apartheid, policies which systematically manipulate black family life and the place of women in society. In South Africa, as elsewhere, women were active in the political movements, in this case the African National Congress in the post-Second World War period. Our knowledge of women's participation in resistance is limited. Nonetheless, it appears that women, black and white, individually and collectively, have demonstrated the same resistance to intolerable situations, usually by finding ways around the constraints, sometimes by initiating protest, often by joining with men in opposing repressive conditions. One area in which black women continue to be active is in labor organization (see Berger, 1982).

These mini-cases of African women's involvement in politics during the colonial period and in the nationalist struggles suggest that women, using ideas and tactics derived from traditional experience in politics, were able to exercise some clout, in spite of the anti-feminist impact of Western colonialism. In the years since independence, however, the situation has been less conducive to women's power.

The contemporary scene

The perspective on African women in politics we have outlined points out their progressive disenfranchisement, though there have been occasional outbreaks of protest and a few exceptions to the rule. In this section on the contemporary scene, we want to sketch the situation as it appears now. Table 4 lists a number of African women prominent in the political affairs of the continent. While the list is neither exhaustive nor representative of the total of politically active African women, it illustrates the fact that there are some women in leadership positions, and it underscores the fact that they are found in many countries and come from diverse areas of professional expertise. Actual statistics on women at the national, regional and local levels of representative assemblies, of the bureaucracy, of the judiciary, and of political party

TABLE 4 African women in national leadership positions: an illustrative sample

Jeanne-Martin Cisse: Guinea's permanent representative to the UN, and one-time president of the UN's Security Council

Judith Irma: Ethiopia's former deputy foreign minister and leader of the Ethiopian delegation to the non-aligned nations' conference in Guyana, 1971

Geosihwe Chiepe: Botswana's minister for commerce and industry, and former ambassador to several European countries

Angie Elizabeth Brooks: Liberia's permanent UN representative and former president of the UN General Assembly

Julie Manning: Tanzania's minister of justice, who was the country's first woman law student in 1963

Dorothy Njeuma: Cameroon's vice-minister of national education and former professor of zoology at the University of Yaoundé

Annie Ruth Baeta Jiagge: Ghana's first woman lawyer, judge, and Supreme Court justice who is internationally active in church and legal circles

Julia Ojiambo: Kenya's assistant minister of housing and social welfare, an international expert on rural development and housing

Eugenia Stephenson: Liberia's first woman ambassador and a lawyer long active on women's issues

Ms. Tambo: a founder-member of the All African Women's Conference now known as the Pan African Woman's Congress and an activist in the liberation struggle

Petronella Kawandeai: member of Zambia's Central Committee

Honoraria Bailor Caulker: Sierra Leone member of Parliament and a paramount chief

Aduke Alakija: Nigerian director of Mobil Oil, and president of International Federation of Women Lawyers

Louise N'Jie: Top-ranking Gambian education officer and women's advocate

Source: A list of the women selected for interviews in one year, 1976, by the magazine *African Woman*.

posts are simply not available. A global survey of women in politics found that everywhere the pattern was pyramidal, with many women at the bottom, and few at the top (Newland, 1975). In a few of the socialist countries, the percentage of women in the national legislature, or in the top party hierarchy, may reach twenty. Most countries register 5 percent or less of women at every level, in every sphere of government. Africa appears to be no exception to the global rule.

The participation of a few outstanding women in politics, however, must be contrasted with the lack of participation of the many. One important reason for this gap is suggested by the data presented in Table 8 in the Appendix. These show that about 80 percent of African women were illiterate in 1970, and that only about 30 percent of them went to school at any level. Of those in school in 1970, women compose only about 40 percent of primary enrollment, 32 percent of secondary enrollment, and 26 percent of university enrollment (McGrath, 1976: 29). Some of the differences between African countries in relation to female literacy and school enrollment are discussed in the Appendix. The high female drop-out rates in secondary school are mentioned as well. In addition, using data from one country, Tanzania, we see that even those women who do reach university level concentrate in the more 'feminine' subjects, such as liberal arts and education, rather than in areas such as medicine, engineering, or agriculture which would be more likely to give them access to money and prestige. These data on education illustrate the conflict for contemporary African women: while their heritage of political power is impressive, it is receding with time, and their preparation for attaining the contemporary tools of political power is quite limited. The contradiction in the present position of African women can be further illustrated by considering the following social trends, all of which reinforce one another to restrict women as political actors.

The first factor is the transformation of African political systems themselves. With the imposition of the nation-state form and the increasing bureaucratization of society that accompanies modernization, politics is separated from other realms of social activity and local initiative gives way to national control. African women have been most politically active when political institutions have been fused with social and economic ones, and where the political arena was communal rather than distant. Thus the process of change itself conflicts with the areas of political expertise African women have possessed. Universally, there are many more women politically active at the local base and very few at the top of the pyramid. While we have no hard data on numbers of women active by level and by country, it would be safe to assume that fewer than 20 percent of local activists are female and no more than 2 or 3 percent of any country's top leadership is female. The socialist countries may be an exception to this, as the next chapter suggests.

The second factor, however, is that women have benefited in many ways from the process of social change engendered by colonialism and carried on by African governments. They have better health care, more links to the outer world, a higher material standard of living, and greater access to education and employment. While statistical indicators of any measure will show women's share of the resources increasing absolutely over their previous share, they also show that women gain proportionately less than men over time. In a word, while both men and women have more of whatever is being discussed, the gap between men and women grows and women are relatively less well off vis-à-vis men than they were in the past.

Access to education and to employment are the key ingredients for individuals in a modern society to obtain if they want to exercise political power. The relations between the individual attribute of education and the acquisition of public political power are complex, but some links are apparent. The education of an individual, both formal and non-formal, enables her or him to have access to a job or profession which guarantees economic control of some resources. (Some people, of course, may begin with economic resources and acquire education as the situation demands.) These resources, coupled with an organizational base which teaches leadership skills, give a person self-esteem. From a psychological point of view, it is this self-esteem which then enables a person to gain political power and to exercise it effectively when the occasion arises. Thus, without education and without the kind of employment that prepares them for public life, African women will not be competitive in the contemporary political world. While they derive strength from their legacy of political expertise in traditional society, it is not sufficient in a world where men have a greater share of new resources.

A third factor is the role of African women's organizations. They have been a powerful force in helping bridge the gap between past and present as well as the gap between men and women in terms of political power. The great variety of African women's organizations has been described in Chapter 5. African women value participation in these groups because it offers them resources not available to them as individuals—the exchange of money and ideas, a larger scale of operation, a communications link to other groups, a source of leadership training. Like their colonial predecessors, however, contemporary governments often disregard the contributions of women's organizations. Given the separate spheres of gender-based activities in Africa, women's organizations want to retain their autonomy and often refuse to be considered political, thereby reinforcing their ineffectiveness. The older women's organizations concentrate on improving the home-making skills of individual women; some of the newer ones emphasize the creation of economic opportunities for women. In either case, every African woman's organization must debate the question of whether to go it alone, remaining autonomous and gaining the advantages of skill-building for members, goal-setting for themselves, and the effectiveness which comes from control, or to become part of a larger mixed group with men, thus trading off political subordination for more general access to influence. The struggle over which organizational form best suits women's needs varies by country and by circumstance. The tendency at this point, however, is to remain a separate women's organization.

However, the organizational form of the movement—whether formal association with the ruling political party, or nominal independence—may not be so important as its strength and ideology. One case in which a strong women's organization, with formal ties to the party, was able to gain significant reforms was that of Guinea in the 1950s and 1960s, described above. Here women gained reform of the marriage laws, access to education, and representation within the party and the government. In addition to the commitment of the women themselves, an important factor was certainly the responsive ideology of the ruling party.

A different case may be found in Kenya, where the absence of an ideology addressing women's situation among either party leaders or women's leaders has meant that the national women's movement has remained largely ineffective. Though nominally independent from the party, the Maendeleo ya Wanawake, described above in Chapter 5, has suffered from its national leadership being coopted and a drying up of grass-roots support (Wipper, 1975).

Finally, the Tanzanian national women's organization illustrates a case in which although the rhetoric of women's important place in development appears widespread, the practice falls short because there is no challenge to the pattern of unequal gender relations. (Rogers, n.d.) The women's branch of the ruling party, the Umoja wa Wanawake wa Tanzania (UWT) is relatively large (one quarter of a million members) and extensive (some 3 000 branches), built around a series of committees from the village to the national level. Program and projects are coordinated with overall development projects. Concern with maternal health and child care issues are the mainstay of UWT projects, although home-industry efforts and some marketing and retailing projects are also undertaken. These programs and projects enjoy moderate success, given the lack of leadership and material resources endemic in a poor country. Their lack of greater success may rest not on a lack of resources, however, but on the fact that most of the monetary benefits derived from women's efforts are controlled by men. It was assumed that women's income-producing projects would automatically enable women to better meet the health, clothing, and food needs of themselves and their children without in any way challenging the 'gender system in which men *control* the lives of wives and children but are not economically *responsible* for them' (Rogers, n.d; see also Caplan, 1981).

Conclusions

The imposition of Western-based gender-role attitudes and behaviors continues to have a detrimental effect on African women's political potential. In the urban areas, for example, women are deprived of the kin and community supports, both materially and psychologically, which allowed them in the past to direct events in their lives. Without these supports and without access to the educational and employment opportunities of the modern sector, African women are increasingly without a base of operation. Many become dependent on men—men who expect women to continue to provide the traditional services of educating and feeding children and who themselves subscribe to Western stereotypes that view the male as an independent actor with little concern for women's situations.

A realistic projection for the resolution of the gender role debate must be somber and long-term. Such changes come slowly and painfully for both individuals and societies. We might expect Africa's struggle with these changes to be a bit briefer than that in the West, given the heritage of African women, but certainly not much easier.

Beginning in the mid-1960s and increasingly in the late 1970s, African women have participated in a series of regional, continental, and international forums which address women's issues. Participation in these tribunes provides knowledge on topics of importance—how child care centers can be most effectively run, what makes for successful craft cooperatives, and how to reduce female attrition in secondary schools, for example. It gives African women a comparative perspective, emphasizing, for example, that they are less restricted by hierarchical patterns of authority than their Latin and Asian sisters. Above all, participation in international forums gives African women the ability to analyze their situation on a global basis, reinforcing the idea that women world-wide have problems that cut across the usual political dimensions of haves and have-nots. The public recognition given to such problems on an international level reinforces the efforts of African women to seek solutions on a country-by-country basis. The premise from which such solutions proceed is that women must be incorporated into the decision-making process in order to improve their situations. Having generally lost that participation under colonialism and now seeking to participate in a vastly more complex system, African women are dealing with both continuities and conflicts as they seek to regain political power.

10 Women in national liberation movements

Stephanie Urdang

By the late 1950s and early 1960s, the map of Africa had changed radically. One after another, the many colonies of Britain and France, which for decades had been exploited and oppressed by colonial rule, achieved their independence. For the most part, victory was procured at negotiating tables, though for some independence was possible only after nationalist movements had organized intensive protest. Certain countries, however, were conspicuously absent from the independence celebrations. Portugal refused steadfastly to relinquish its rule over Angola, Guinea-Bissau and Mozambique. The white settlers in Rhodesia, fearful of Britain's threat to grant independence to the African majority, declared their own unilateral independence, with little response from London. South Africa continued to strengthen its hold on Namibia (then known as South West Africa) in defiance of United Nations condemnation and the World Court's ruling that their occupation was illegal. And in South Africa itself, the white government, technically independent since 1910, continued to impose brutal minority rule on the blacks.

In these territories, revolutionary wars of liberation were launched, which achieved notable successes. As a direct result of the wars in Portugal's African colonies, the fascist Caetano regime in Portugal was overthrown in 1974 and Angola, Mozambique, and Guinea-Bissau won their independence, led respectively by the Popular Movement for the Liberation of Angola (MPLA), the Front for the Liberation of Mozambique (FRELIMO), and the African Party for the Independence of Guinea and Cape Verde (PAIGC). A five-year armed struggle in Zimbabwe, led by the Zimbabwe African National Union (ZANU) and the Zimbabwe African People's Union (ZAPU), eventually forced the settler regime to the negotiating table and majority rule became a reality in that country in 1980. In Namibia the guerrilla struggle led by the South West African People's Organization (SWAPO) continues to intensify against the considerable military force employed by South Africa. And in South Africa itself the last few years have seen an upsurge of militancy, towards the inevitable path of armed struggle. The Organization of African Unity recognizes two liberation movements in South Africa, the African National Congress (ANC) and the Pan Africanist Congress of Azania (PAC).

Ideology is perhaps the most striking difference between these liberation movements and the earlier independence movements which achieved generally peaceful transfers of power. For many of the latter, the main goal was to take power. In many cases, black faces supplanted white faces, while independence made little impact on the material conditions of life for the majority of people in the country. In contrast, each liberation movement was both founded upon and further developed ideologies that have many facets in common. Particularly important is the insistence that their fight stretches beyond victory on the battlefield to the more fundamental question of establishing a new and just society in each of their countries, one that brings an end to all forms of exploitation. Within this context, the liberation movements have all—in varying degrees—emphasized the liberation of women.

The movements' commitment to women

The words of Mozambique's President Samora Machel at the founding conference of the Organization of Mozambican Women (OMM) are a clear statement of this view: 'The liberation of women is a fundamental necessity for the revolution, a guarantee for its continuity and a precondition for its victory' (Machel, 1973). Machel's statement is a compelling one. But what does the 'liberation of women' mean to FRELIMO and the other movements? Why do they view it as so important? How successful are their efforts?

One reason for a guerrilla movement's efforts to involve women is sheer need; every man, woman and child has to be called upon to participate in some way to overthrow repressive regimes. The ideology of these movements, however, has provided a basis for women's involvement to flower into something far more profound and to become a 'precondition for victory'.

While all movements acknowledge the need for the liberation of women, those who fought longer and were able to set up the elements of new societies in the areas they liberated—such as FRELIMO in Mozambique, MPLA in Angola and PAIGC in Guinea-Bissau—were the most effective in establishing programs and mechanisms to put theory into practice. Nevertheless, the belief of all the movements that women need to liberate themselves is an acknowledgement that women are considered oppressed. The extent of this view differs from one movement to another—again, to some extent dependent on the length of struggle.

This oppression has been acknowledged in different ways by the movements' leaders. Samora Machel asserted that 'generally speaking women are the most oppressed, humiliated and exploited beings in society' (Machel, 1973). Similarly, Robert Mugabe, President of ZANU and head of state of Zimbabwe explained:

Custom and tradition have tended more to favor men than women, to promote men and their status and demote women in status, to erect men as masters of the home, village, clan and nation. Admittedly, women have . . . been allowed sometimes a significant, but at other times a deplorably insignificant role to play. The general principle governing relationships between men and women has, in our traditional society, always been that of superiors and inferiors. Our society has consistently stood on the principle of masculine dominance—the principle that the man is the ruler and the woman his dependant and subject (Mugabe, 1979).

How African women view their own situation was, for example, described by Maria Sá, an elderly peasant woman in Guinea-Bissau:

We women really suffer. First it is the women who pound, it is the women who cook for the men. And then sometimes he says, 'Ah, your food is not well prepared'. With all the work we have to do, and he protests! It is these kinds of things, this discrimination that we have suffered and continue to suffer from. When there is a lot of work to do, we women go and help the men. When the men are tilling the land, we have to cook fast and take it to them. And we must be sure that we are not late with the food! It is our responsibility also to find rice supplements such as fish.

It is very hard, our life. In addition to all of this, if his clothes are dirty, it is we women who must wash them. Very nice and clean. Because if a man walks outside wearing dirty clothes and people see him like this, who gets the blame? Why the women! Not the men. We do not like this or want this. All these things are ways in which women suffer. As for men, the only thing they do is till the land. We are responsible for everything after that. The women alone harvest the rice and we have to transport it without their help, to the village.

This I tell you, is how all women are suffering (Urdang, 1979).

Travelling through the liberated zones of Guinea-Bissau at the beginning of 1974 and later through independent Guinea-Bissau and Mozambique, I could appreciate Maria Sá's words, which were born out of the heavy load of work performed throughout the day. Before the sun had risen, and while the men were still asleep, the women were already preparing the food, sweeping the ground, getting the children up, cleaning. For hours they would pound, the back-breaking work that processed grains for the daily needs of the family. There were infants and children to care for, water to get from the wells, often a number of miles away, and firewood to gather. This was in addition to the agricultural work in the fields and the frequent childbearing.

The African peasant woman's role in domestic labor includes the provision, not just the preparation, of food. Her work includes helping to clear the land and sowing the seeds, as well as harvesting and the pounding or grinding necessary to process the staple food for cooking. Guinea-Bissau and Mozambique are no different from the rest of sub-Saharan Africa where women are generally responsible for well over half the work in production, and are often estimated to be responsible for as much as 80 percent (Boserup, 1970; United Nations, 1978). This sexual division of labor, which delegates to women the sole responsibility for household tasks, is a critical factor in the continuing subordination of women.

Despite the fundamental importance of the provision of food, women did not have equal decision-making power in village life, except in women's affairs. The PAIGC recognized the situation: 'In spite of the importance of women in the life of African peoples, it is only rarely that they take an active part in political affairs. In our country, women have almost always been kept out of political affairs, of decisions concerning the life which they nonetheless support, thanks to their anonymous daily work' (Urdang, 1979).

Women's predominant role within the household and their absence from wider political affairs go hand in hand with attitudes that perceive women as inferior and assume their subservience. While these attitudes are perpetrated by males, they are also internalized by women who acquiesce in their own subordination. Samora Machel acknowledged that 'the centuries-old subjugation of women has to a great extent reduced them to a passive state, which prevents them from even understanding their condition' (Machel, 1973).

Certain customs entrench these traditional attitudes and those singled out as the most detrimental to the society as a whole and women in particular include polygyny, bride-price, forced marriage and lack of divorce for women. Machel recognized the link between these customs and the village economy:

Polygamy [played an important role] in primitive agrarian economy. Society, realizing that women are a source of wealth, demands that a price be paid for them. The girl's parents demand from their future son-in-law the payment of bride-price before giving up their daughter. The woman is bought and inherited like material goods, or any source of wealth (Machel, 1973).

Antagonism against such customs is felt by many women. 'It's just as if a woman is being sold to a man,' said a PAIGC militant of bride-price. 'Its like selling babies or young children. A woman is sold for a pig or a cow,' said another (Urdang, 1979). These customs were discussed at the 1979 ZANU women's seminar. A woman militant who attended reports that:

We spoke of how women always looked to men for guidance and the right answers, and this must stop. We analyzed *lobolo*, the bride-price paid by a man for his wife, so we could understand better how this made us into commodities who were not respected by others and did not respect ourselves. We discussed how women are at a disadvantage under polygamy so we can better oppose that as well (Barnes, 1979).

Once these areas of women's oppression were identified through the movements' analysis of their own societies, measures were taken to try to correct the inequality. Let us look at how, in the context of armed struggle in Guinea-Bissau, Mozambique, and elsewhere, these problems—the lack of political rights, traditional attitudes, detrimental customs, and the sexual division of labor—have been tackled.

Political mobilization of women

To encourage women to participate in the political affairs of their society is far from simple. It is not only that the men resist this incursion into their domain. Life-long experience of subordination, and lack of confidence in their own capacities, leave most women reluctant to take such a step. The development of political consciousness through political education plays a vital role in such changes. But also playing their part are the oppressive practices of the regimes in question which have pushed women into making the first move. Once women are part of the movement, the encouragement they receive to play a political role has developed their commitment further.

Netumbo Nandi, a SWAPO militant, recalled her feelings when she first decided to join SWAPO:

SWAPO came into existence in Namibia in 1960. Even though I was young then, I could still not fail to be impressed by SWAPO's militant activities . . . Seeing what SWAPO was doing and realizing what SWAPO said about the exploitative conditions existing in Namibia, I felt the urge to join. I found out that it's only through SWAPO that all the Namibian people could be united to face the colonizers. So that's why, in 1966, I joined SWAPO. I was just 15 years old at the time (Collins, 1977).

Other women militants speak of their consciousness of the subordinate position of the female sex and the added level of political consciousness that they derive from being able to join the movement as equals. Teodora Gomes, a political worker in the liberated zones of Guinea-Bissau, and a ranking member of PAIGC, is one:

I saw how women lived in misery, struggling to survive. They had to contend with a lot of problems from their husbands. But what could we do at the time? What the men wanted was for the women to stay home. They had control over all the money. If they chose to give some to their wives they gave it. If not, they didn't. We could do nothing because we were oppressed. To me [the thought of marriage] meant that I would enter a life of hardship, but one that could be avoided.

Her father joined PAIGC and although he did not tell his family, she suspected that something was afoot:

Knowing that my father would refuse to answer my questions, I began to plague one of his workers. Eventually he agreed to talk about PAIGC and took me to visit a camp (one night when my father was asleep). I was welcomed as a friend and for two hours they talked about the struggle and the mobilization. It changed my life.

A while later Portuguese soldiers rounded up ten well-known people in her town, all supporters of PAIGC, and shot them to death in full view of the townspeople. That day her whole family decided to join the guerrillas, and since then she has become an active and responsible militant in the movement. She added: 'We [women] did not know how to fight together to change our lives as women. This we have now learned through PAIGC' (Urdang, 1979).

At the other end of the continent, Sarudzia Churucheminzwa spoke of her experience in growing up in Zimbabwe and joining ZANU: 'As I grew up I strongly resented the attitude of my society which deliberately underrated and underestimated women's capabilities to mold society. Such an attitude deprived many women of giving assistance where they could and all incentives to cultivate their talents as human beings.' After she finished school she could not find a job. Her family was destitute so she and her mother went to work on the land of a settler farmer. They were paid a meager wage and had to work long and difficult hours on land so vast that much of it was left idle: 'From this inhumane treatment we were getting, it was easy for me to see how it was possible for the boer to own a big luxurious house, several cars and a huge store. My experiences at this farm increased my hatred against these rapacious boers.' When Churucheminzwa heard of ZANLA, the armed wing of ZANU, she decided to find them. She and a friend eventually did, and were admitted to a base where they joined ZANU. They were the only two women in the military base: 'After political education, the comrades introduced us to the rigors of the strategy and tactics of guerilla warfare . . . As women we felt pride in being able to tackle tasks which at home [were] regarded as men's tasks.' But their pride grew to exaggerated self-importance, until one of the commissars rebuked them: 'A gun is not an object for you to use as an instrument of showing off; neither is it a certificate that you are equal to men comrades. A gun is only for killing the fascist soldiers of Ian Smith and the eradication of . . . exploitation in Zimbabwe.' The two young women grasped this point more fully when they were sent with others to set an ambush; they exchanged fire with the enemy and bullets whizzed past their ears: 'Then I learned more of the use of my sub-machine gun. It's either you kill the boer or the boer kills you. With more of such experiences in ZANLA we became more enlightened about our convictions and our freedom-bound duty' (Churucheminzwa, 1974).

But what about those women—the considerable majority—who did not seek to join the movements from their own initiative? It was here that political education played a critical role in mobilizing women. It was often found that women were particularly adept in undertaking such mobilization. Josina Machel, one of FRELIMO's top women cadres until her untimely death from illness at the age of 25, explained: 'Firstly, it is easier for us to approach other women, and secondly, the men are more easily convinced of the important role of women when confronted with the unusual sight of confident and capable women militants who are themselves the best examples of what they are propounding' (Machel, Josina, n.d.).

It was sometimes found that women responded more readily to political mobilization than the men, because of their understanding of their double oppression. They had more to fight for and more to gain, and once in motion they often surpassed the political commitment of their male comrades. Francisca Pereira, one of the top women in PAIGC and, since independence, president of one of Guinea-Bissau's eight regions, made this point:

[Women] realized that this was a great opportunity for their liberation. They knew the attitude of the party, and understook that, for the first time in the history of the country, they would be able to count on political institutions to safeguard their interests. This was important because they also knew that the burden of colonization had rested more heavily on their shoulders. In this respect, we can talk about various forms of colonization — by the colonizers themselves, by the men and by the tribes (Urdang, 1979).

But generally, women were hesitant to come forward, and special measures have often been taken to ensure that women participate. Once the process has begun, there is potential for it gaining momentum. For instance in Guinea-Bissau, few women attended when the early mobilizers began calling village meetings. So they would insist that at least a few women be chosen by the other women to attend. They could then return home after the meeting and discuss what had been said. The next time, a few more women would attend, and slowly the numbers grew until the majority of the village population would set off for the secret gathering place.

In order to translate theory into practice more concretely, PAIGC stipulated that at least two women be elected to the five-member village councils that were established once a zone was liberated. In order to break resistance to women candidates, the task initially assigned women members related to the work they traditionally performed, namely the provision of rice for the guerrilla camps. It was an extension of the work they did daily and, as such, was acceptable to both men and women. Nevertheless, a qualitative change had taken place. Women were integrated into a decision-making body which brought with it recognition and increased status for women's work. For the first time the 'anonymous daily work of women' was being given status more in keeping with its real value in the society. Once on the councils, the women could take part in all discussions and decision-making, giving them an opportunity to develop self-confidence and leadership abilities. As time passed, women began to take on tasks other than the provision of rice. There were councils that had three or four women members, as well as a few with women vice-presidents or even president. This 'two-out-of-five' stipulation was repeated for councils at district and regional levels.

A woman member of the first council elected in the south of the country Bwetna N'dubi, stressed how much these changes had meant to women. She became very active, a member of a regional council which entailed regular travel back and forth from her village, leaving her husband at home:

Today I work together with men, having more responsibility than many men. This is not only true for me. I understand that I have to fight together with other women against the domination of women by men. But we have to fight *twice*—once to convince women, and the second time to convince men that women have to have the same rights as men . . . The party has brought new ways and a new life for women. But we must continue to defend our rights ourselves (Urdang, 1979).

The wars of liberation in Mozambique and Guinea-Bissau lasted over a decade, and during that time extensive areas of the countries were liberated. It was possible in those liberated zones for FRELIMO and PAIGC to demonstrate in practice their stated commitment to the liberation of women. A similar process was underway in Angola, led by MPLA. Thus there were women political workers, health workers, and teachers; women were elected to political councils and justice tribunals, and they generally played an increasingly active role in the support network for the revolution.

Women's roles in armed struggle

Teurai Ropa is an example of the new Zimbabwean leaders. By nineteen she had completed her military training and was appointed to the General Staff of ZANLA, the liberation army. In 1977, at age 22, she was the youngest member of ZANU's Central Committee and National Executive, and was appointed secretary for women's affairs. She is now minister of community development and women's affairs, the only woman to hold a ministerial post in Zimbabwe. She described the way in which Zimbabwean women (like those in Mozambique and Guinea-Bissau) were beginning to enter many areas of work:

> Our women's brigade is involved in every sphere of the armed revolutionary struggle. Their involvement is total. In the frontline they transport war materials to the battlefield and . . . fight their way through enemy territory . . . . They teach the masses how to hide wounded comrades, hide war materials and carry intelligence reports behind enemy lines . . . .
>
> At the rear our women comrades' tasks are even more extensive. They are involved in every department of ZANU. They work as commanders, military instructors, political commissars, medical corps, teachers, drivers, mechanics, cooks, in logistics and supplies, information and publicity, as administrative cadres. There is no department where their beneficial presence is not felt (Ropa, 1978b).

Perhaps the most visibly dramatic evidence of a change in women's roles was the sight of women carrying guns. Women's participation in the military has varied to some extent among the movements. Recently SWAPO has been training women in Namibia for combat, and women are among those sent to the training camps of the African National Congress of South Africa. Both FRELIMO in Mozambique and ZANU in Zimbabwe had women's detachments, while women fought in combat with MPLA in Angola and PAIGC in Guinea-Bissau. A closer look at this aspect of women's roles in the context of Mozambique and Guinea-Bissau gives us insights into this dimension to the revolution.

An important step in the hastening of the involvement of Mozambican women came with a 1966 decision of the FRELIMO Central Committee to encourage women to participate more actively in the struggle for national liberation at all levels. Women should receive political and military training in order to carry out all tasks that the revolution demanded. A few months later the first group of young women from Cabo Delgado and Niassa provinces began their training. This first experiment was highly successful, and the young women of this new group became the founding members of the Women's Detachment. Josina Machel pointed out that they played a very important role in the revolution, 'both in the military field and in the political field, but principally the latter' (Machel, Josina, n.d.)

The involvement of women brought with it considerable resistance by the population in general and the men in particular. A militant in the Women's Detachment recalled that:

> When we started to work there was strong opposition to our

participation. Because that was against our tradition. We then started a big campaign explaining why we also had to fight, that the FRELIMO war was a people's war in which the whole population must participate, that we women were even more oppressed than men and that we therefore had the right as well as the will and the strength to fight. We insisted on our having military training and being given weapons (Liberation Support Movement, n.d.).

A seventeen-year-old commander of the Women's Detachment, Pauline Mateos, spoke about her experience during the war. She was in charge of 200 women guerrillas from the age of fifteen in liberated areas of Cabo Delgado province. One of the early tactics used was to mobilize the wife, who in turn, pressured the husband to join. 'Some men have no heart for fighting. They are afraid or they don't want to leave their families and fields. But once a woman tells her man to go and fight he feels more inclined' (Cornwall, 1972).

PAIGC had similar experiences of women coercing their husbands into joining PAIGC. A woman militant commented that they would chastize their husbands saying 'Go and join the fight. If you don't, I'll wear the pants and I'll go.' Or, 'If you don't join the fight, you can stay in the kitchen and do all the cooking and I'll go and join the guerrillas' (Urdang, 1979). A form of pressure found particularly effective by the movements was simply to confront men with women guerrillas. As Josina Machel of FRELIMO said, ' . . . the presence of emancipated women bearing arms often shames them into taking more positive actions' (Machel, Josina, n.d.). A regional commander for the PAIGC local army reminisced about how, at the beginning of the war, recruiters would often go to a village with a group of armed women. 'Then *all* the men would join up so as not to be shown up by the women!' This was found effective in Zimbabwe as well (Ropa, 1978a).

When training for the FRELIMO Women's Detchment, women were not spared. The course was strenuous. Pauline Mateos described her experiences:

We undergo the same program as the men because we will be doing men's work. We stay in the same camps often and we regard them as our brothers. We suffer hunger and thirst and heat as they do, and we learn to handle all kinds of arms. When we first begin our training we think that we will die of hunger and fatigue. With the men we are marched past water holes and rivers and not permitted by our trainer to drink although we might be near collapse with thirst. This is done to toughen us for the time when we might want to drink water from sources suspected of being poisoned by the enemy. Finally, when we are strong enough to have overcome all of these trials, we find that we can suffer as much and march as long as any of the men, even with our packs and rifles. Sometimes we overpass men who have collapsed (Cornwall, 1972).

The Women's Detachment to the FRELIMO army was formed three years after the beginning of the armed struggle in 1967. At about the same time, the role of women in combat in Guinea-Bissau was, if anything, being phased out. Unlike Mozambique, women had been trained as guerrillas in Guinea-Bissau from the beginning of the war. Many women underwent guerilla training, and fought alongside men in combat. But when the guerrilla militia was reorganized into the national army, women were no longer encouraged to go into combat. They remained members of the village militias and to a lesser extent the local armed forces. By the beginning of 1974, the difference between the two countries in this respect was marked. Whereas I seldom saw women armed in Guinea-Bissau, other than cadres who were armed for self-defense, visitors to liberated Mozambique during the last years of the war were impressed by the large number of women carrying rifles.

PAIGC reasoned that since there were more than enough men available for the army, the situation in their country was very different from that in Mozenbique, whose population and territory were ten or more times the size of Guinea-Bissau. In addition, PAIGC felt that overcoming traditional opposition would slow down the war. The leaders carried out their recruitment of women in the liberated zones instead, where time was on their side and where improved conditions, directly attributable to PAIGC, created a more favorable atmosphere for change. Towards the end of the war, women were again being trained along with men in military camps in the south of the country, but independence came before they could see action. After independence, Guinea-Bissau had no military threats from across its borders, and it could minimize the role of the army. This was certainly not the case for Mozambique, and women soldiers continued to fight in the attacks against Rhodesia's invading forces.

Guinean women were always emphatic that PAIGC policy was correct for their situation, because of the very different conditions obtaining in the two countries. Certainly, it seemed, no special heroism was attached to being an armed soldier, and any tendency in this direction was consciously discouraged. At the same time, all work for the revolution was heavily emphasized. As Amilcar Cabral, PAIGC founder and leader until his assassination in 1973 was to say, 'Between one man carrying a gun and another carrying a tool, the more important of the two is the man with the tool. We've taken up arms to defeat the Portuguese, but the whole point of driving out the Portuguese is to defend the man with the tool.' (Chaliand 1971). This concept was conveyed by a twenty-one-year-old woman cadre when she said, 'but we do not see some work as being more important than other work. The important thing is to work for the revolution. And there are many different and equally essential ways of doing that' (Urdang, 1979).

FRELIMO's experience seems to show that the Women's Detachment was able to provide impetus for the mobilization of women, although women's military actions tended more often to take the form of defense of the liberated zones rather than combat on the front. As Josina Machel reported:

> As in the case of military units composed of men, one of the principal functions of the Women's Detachment is naturally, participation in combat. In Mozambique, the military activities of the women are *generally concentrated, together with the militia, in defense of the liberated zones*. In this way, the men are partly freed from the task of defense and can concentrate on the offensive in the advance zones.

Nevertheless there are women who prefer to participate in more active combat and fight side by side with men in ambushes, mining operations, etc. They have proved to be as capable and courageous as their male comrades (Machel, n.d.; my emphasis).

It appears that in Mozambique, women fighting in direct combat tended to be the exception rather than the rule. President Machel himself paid tribute to the effectiveness of the Women's Detachment in changing attitudes in the liberated zones and in raising the consciousness of men as well as women, as well as to their heroism displayed on the battlefield (Machel, 1976).

Women's roles in production

As we have seen, the sexual division of labor in social and political activities outside the home has been positively influenced by women's involvement in the military as well as in other work within the revolutionary process. The integration of women in areas of responsibility, authority, and status has afforded them the opportunity to become active outside the home and begin to step out of their traditional roles. Although equality is certainly not yet a fact and men continue to dominate this world, women have begun to make noticeable inroads. However, the tasks that are relegated to women within the household have not been similarly challenged.

Although political education has been effectively directed towards breaking down the barriers to women's political participation and to their involvement in economic and social affairs beyond the family, the reverse has not been true. Men have not, in general, been called upon to share women's work, and thus the burden of the double work load for women looms large. Given the circumstances of war and the non-negotiable precedence that ousting the colonial and oppressive powers takes, it is understandable that this would be fairly low on the list of priorities. But in fact, not only is it, for the most part, absent from any such list, it has been seldom acknowledged as a problem. For African women a particularly pressing need is the reorganization of the economy in order to release them from such heavy responsibility for subsistence agriculture. This would have far-reaching effects on women's subordinate role in society. It would make it possible for a family to produce its needs without extra workers in the form of wives and children, and thus customs that ensure this could be uprooted. Similarly, reduction in women's work in the fields would leave them more time for political and/or paid wage labor which would give them more status and strengthen their development as more independent and militant members of society. Once this is on the agenda for a new society, there would be more room for confronting the sexual division of labor in household tasks, particularly for a woman who is becoming active herself. Without this measure, it is quite possible that the ultimate and full liberation of women will be undermined.

What is possible for the future can be seen in Mozambique, one of the African countries that has seriously attempted the process of transforming rural agricultural production. With 90 percent of its population living in the rural areas, the problem is urgent. The eventual goal is collectivization of both cash crops and family agriculture. A key to this process is the establishment of communal villages throughout the country. But a closer look at these efforts provides a sober lesson in just how difficult the process of reaching such goals remains in poor, underdeveloped countries, devastated by years of colonialism and war and plagued by ecological problems such as floods in one region, drought in the next.

Communal villages are envisioned as the basis for building a new social order that will embody the government's socialist principles—stressing equality between people, curtailing oppressive practices and providing a basis for collective production. A look at one such village, Três de Fevereiro in Gaza province, vividly demonstrates that one of the most challenging problems being confronted is the realization of equality between the sexes.

What has changed thus far for the women of Três de Fevereiro? Perhaps the most striking turnabout—which also acts as a barometer for other changes—is the very visible role that women play in political affairs. Of the thirty-three members of the elected People's Assembly of the village, for instance, twenty-three are women. Of the five members of the executive council of the Assembly, two are women. A woman sits on the Justice Tribunal of the village. The secretary of the women's organization is a strong leader in the village more active than other leaders such as the secretary for the party cell or the president of the Assembly, in confronting problems, making daily decisions needed to resolve conflict, and mobilizing villagers for collective work.

There are other changes. The schools and health care services that were denied the vast majority of Africans under the Portuguese are now found in the village, along with literacy and adult education classes, a consumer cooperative (store), and an agricultural cooperative for cash crops.

What about the changes in women's roles within the household? Here far less has changed. While stated goals for the new Mozambique include the collectivization of all agricultural production—family as well as cash-crop production—the former remains a tantalizing objective for the future; as yet it has no footing in concrete plans. Thus the day of an active woman militant in Três de Fevereiro is very full. In addition to the hours spent in domestic labor and child care, there continue to be the long, hot hours in the fields from just after sunrise to midday. Then there might be literacy classes to attend for two hours, meetings to go to, problems to help solve and a finger to be kept continually on the pulse of village life. These women work hard. They are effective. But their burden has *tripled*: work in production, work in the home, and political work.

Some inroads have been made into alleviating this work. Some villages do have day care centers. The fact that the older children are in school much of the day means they are cared for elsewhere (although this does deprive mothers of their labor, often a real difficulty). Then there are technological improvements. These include four new, mechanical water pumps, which give families constant and easy access to clean water. This is no small achievement in rural Africa, since it frees women from the drudgery of trekking to the nearest water source and walking home with a container of water so heavy that it often requires the help of two others to lift it onto the carrier's head. But this new technology speaks to the broader problems confronting development in Mozambique. On my first visit to the village, three of the four pumps were out of order, and has been for a few months. By my second visit they had been fixed, but one subsequently broke again. The critical lack of mechanics, spare parts, and the foreign exchange to purchase the latter frustrates attempts to mechanize.

Yet other changes affect the customary practices that are viewed as detrimental to women and abhorrent to the new Mozambique. Through political education, backed up by decisions of the justice tribunal, practices such as the payment of bride-price, arranged marriages, polygyny (and in the north of the country, initiation rites), have noticeably declined in Três de Fevereiro. This has a significant impact in freeing women, particularly younger women, for making their own decisions and controlling their own lives.

These are some of the changes that are beginning to transform women's lives in Três de Fevereiro and the many other communal villages in the country. The key to further changes lies, in the end, with women themselves and their willingness to make demands for the restructuring of the household so that men accept equal responsibility and equal work within it. The women's perceptions of their own situations are an important part of the process of transformation. For the many women who have benefited from FRELIMO, the transformation already achieved is so remarkable they will speak of being 'liberated.' They themselves seldom mention their role within the family as a problem. While objectively some contradictions are apparent, it is for the women themselves to begin to make other demands that will change their lives even more.

Conclusions

The manner in which the revolution has often accelerated the involvement of women in both the armed struggle and the fight for their emancipation has been expressed by women from the different movements. Teurai Ropa described this impact on Zimbabwean women:

The revolutionary armed struggle has been the biggest blessing for the Zimbabwe women. Within a few years it opened the doors which would probably have taken decades to loosen. The struggle for national independence has opened our womenfolk to a world even they would not have dreamed of (Ropa, 1978b).

The struggle made possible the politicization of women, without which the social gains could not have been made. As SWAPO militant

Nethumbo Nandi put it, 'It is only when the women themselves are armed with a high level of political consciousness that our movement can guarantee that reactionary ideas such as male chauvinism and female docility will have no place in liberated Namibia' (Collins, 1978).

As we have seen, the armed struggle accelerates fairly dramatically the process of transformation. The social, political, and economic upheavals that it imposes on people provide conditions for the establishment of a totally new life. If this process is guided by an ideology that arises out of the genuine concern of the leaders for the welfare of the people, then a very different society is possible once independence has been won. The foundation can be laid for a future that breaks from the exploitation of the past and provides the possibilities of the emergence of the 'new man' and the 'new woman,' as FRELIMO states it.

The visible enemy and the tensions of life in a war zone helped to break down barriers—ethnic, class, religious, and sex—in order to build unity. The strength and all-pervasiveness of the oppressive powers demand that the people launch a strenuous counter-attack. Unity is the key. But the exploitative barriers that exist between people extend into peace time, when the visible enemy has fled. This means that the struggle for unity and to bring a final end to all forms of exploitation—the subjugation of women included—is in many ways harder after independence. What countries like Mozambique demonstrate is that the socialist principles upon which their revolution was based, can nonetheless be extended beyond wars of liberation and can affect the changing roles of African women.

11 The impact of development policies on women

Barbara Lewis

Getting African women farmers on the development agenda

African women have been called the invisible farmers of African agriculture because their extraordinary labor contributions to farming—the livelihood of most Africans—is regularly overlooked in national statistics and development plans. Planners too often see African peasant women as farmers' wives, as houseworkers rather than farmers. But, as the foregoing chapters have shown, African women are usually the primary food-producers in the countryside. Rural women typically work two to six hours per day longer than rural men. On the average in African societies, women put in 70 percent of all the time expended on food production, 100 percent of the time spent on food processing, 50 percent of that spent on food storage and animal husbandry, 60 percent of all the marketing, 90 percent of all beer brewing, 90 percent of time spent obtaining water supply and 80 percent of time spent to obtain the fuel supply (Blumberg, 1982:10; see also McSweeney, 1979, 1980; Goody and Buckley, 1973). Failure of development planners to recognize this important role of women has both undermined the status and well-being of African women and limited the effectiveness of governmental efforts to increase agricultural productivity.

Recently, however, African peasant women have gained some visibility within the international development community, and processes of education and legitimation have been triggered which may alter the syndrome of unconcern and neglect of the past (see Nelson, 1981). The two major causes of this shift are the international women's movement and the appreciation of the food crisis in Africa.

Advocacy of women's interests

The resurgence of feminism in the last decade has led to explicit and direct attention of the UN community to the needs of women in the development process. Third World women, including rural women, have been the subject of discussion and of conference resolutions of UN meetings such as the International Women's Year and Mexico City Conference of 1975, the World Food Conference of 1975, the World Conference on Agrarian Reform and Rural Development of 1979, the Technology and Development Conference of 1980 and the Copenhagen International Women's Conference of 1980. These have called for national and international action to promote equal access of men and women to land ownership, to vocational training in agriculture, to cooperative membership, and to agricultural extension sources. Attention has also focused on women's particular tasks which limit the productivity of their labor and thus their opportunity to earn cash: water porterage, food processing and firewood collection. Proposed solutions involve technology to alleviate burdens and improved political representation to ensure access to productive resources.

These formal declarations responded, in part, to the growing documentation of women's unequal access to the benefits of development. The paucity of past efforts to assist rural women has been criticized, but perhaps more significant is the recent emphasis on women as agents of production as well as of reproduction. Much past development assistance for women was geared to improving their nutritional awareness, health practices, childrearing techniques and cooking skills; this approach has been judged too narrow, as women's continued poverty and enormous labor burdens left them unable to benefit from such programs. Despite the evident involvement of African women in agriculture, the women's programs of some African national governments still focus on home economics, including baking, sewing, embroidery and handicrafts intended to enhance the home.

African food crisis

The growing awareness of rural women's productive roles converged in the late 1970s with a sharp realization of the world-wide food crisis, which is particularly pressing in Africa. Development strategies in which industrialization is to be financed by highly taxed agricultural surpluses have clearly foundered. Efforts to promote agricultural production have been inadequate, and funding has been concentrated in cash crops, and particularly in export crop production. Spiraling import costs are not covered by meager returns on agricultural exports, and rising urban populations necessitate importation of food staples—a cost which primarily agricultural societies cannot meet. In addition to pressing shortages in subsistence production in rural areas, entire national economies are staggering under food import costs, for which foreign exchange is wholly inadequate. Thus national planners are under great pressure to reevaluate their agricultural strategies, both to increase exports and to pursue agricultural self sufficiency, so that economies can fill their own food needs.

Data on the food crisis is ominous. The following figures are based on actual consumption, and thus do not reflect the widespread mal- and under- nourishment of Africans. The most pressing cases are Nigeria, where a 2 percent defict in 1975 is projected to be 35-39 percent by 1990; the Sahelian countries, with a 9 percent deficit in 1975 rising to 44-46 percent in 1990; and Ethiopia, with 2 percent and 26-28 percent respectively. The projections for other African countries are less devastating, but rising prices of food imports have made agriculture the central issue on development planners' current agenda.

Development theorists, planners and government leaders differ in their emphasis on which to promote in response to the food crisis—export crops, food crops for consumption within nations' cities, or food for rural inhabitants. In addition, conditions vary greatly from country to country. But in most African nations small-holder agriculture has undeniably come to have a greater priority; concomitantly planners' focus is closer to the actual work of rural women than it has been in the past (see for example, Bryson, 1981). But whether this new focus will really serve to benefit women farmers depends on how policies affect the actual division of labor between men and women and the control of goods produced.

The sex division of labor

At first glance, the division of labor by sex in African agriculture often seems to correspond to the division between cash crops and subsistence crops. As described, for example, in Chapter 2 for the cocoa-producing Ewe of southern Ghana, women are typically assigned separate plots on which they produce for home consumption while men manage production of crops grown solely or primarily for cash sale. Similar systems are found among those who produce peanuts and coffee for export.

But the 'men's' cash crops/'women's' subsistence crop dichotomy over-simplifies the sex division of labor in misleading ways. The choice is not typically whether to increase production of one or the other by aiding one sex or the other. The family economy in much of rural Africa depends upon the exchange of labor between men and women. Men may clear the land for women's food crops, while women are charged with certain tasks, such as weeding and transplanting men's crops. Some of these tasks are sex-typed in a relatively inflexible manner (men rarely join in women's farming tasks, but women may be called upon to assist men with their crops).

Although women may work widely in cash and export crops, they rarely control the profits derived from them. Thus the exchange between men and women tends to be unfavourable to women; a man may give gifts to his wife to compensate her for work done on his crops, while she feeds him and his children with food grown on land he has set aside for her use and has possibly cleared for her.

Thus the sex division of *control of production* corresponds more closely to the cash/subsistence distinction than does the sex division of labor. Improving women's status probably requires increasing women's leverage over, or control of production, while increasing production requires increasing the incentives and efficiency of both men and women.

In those areas of Africa where the division of labor and control is different, where women process and market men's production, women seem to fare much better. For example, in the southwestern Ivory Coast, women purchase fish from the fishermen, and smoke or dry the fish before marketing them. In this case, and analogous ones in southern Nigeria, women's strategic role in commercialization offers them far greater social leverage and access to income. On a smaller scale, women who are able to market the surplus of their subsistence food crops are also better off, and they may be little motivated to assume production tasks in men's crops for which their compensation may be variable, uncertain, or nil. But their preference for autonomy may change if they understand that they will be rewarded for their work on the men's crops.

In general, plans to increase production in any aspect of agriculture must rest upon an awareness of how projected changes will alter the work loads and rewards of each sex. For planning to be effective, the household must not be seen as a collective of undifferentiated workers whose time can be reallocated according to a plan which is rational at the community level. Rather the community labor force is composed of people occupying distinct social roles who are responsive to relative and absolute gains and need to be motivated accordingly.

A note should be added on households headed by women alone. They are an especially numerous category in those parts of Africa where male out-migration in search of employment is the entrenched pattern. One estimate for the continent as a whole places the percentage of rural households headed by women at 33; another finds a range of 10 to 40 percent (Blumberg, 1982; Newland, 1980). More reliable are the data from particular countries, which suggest the range of variation. In Cameroon 17 percent of coastal area farm managers are women, while the northwest has only 7 per cent (Bazin-Tardieu, n.d.) In western Kenya, women manage 40 percent of the farms (Staudt, 1975-76; Moock, 1976). In Lesotho, a pure case of a labor exporting economy, women head 80 percent of the farms. Despite their numbers, these women have been markedly bypassed in development efforts. Often they have less land, poorer quality land, and lower yields of cash crops. They face legal and political barriers to land ownership, credit and cooperative membership, and informal but equally effective obstacles to agricultural extension services. Their plight is particularly serious.

The impact of policy on the division of labor

It is quite possible that a policy of increasing food production might affect the division of labor and control of produce in ways which would not be to the benefit of women. For example, in the savannah areas of Mali and Upper Volta, men generally control the production of grains consumed nationally (millet, sorghum) as well as peanuts (grown for export as well as for domestic consumption), while women control truck gardening. Women market their own surplus production, but also work on men's crops, of which they receive a small share for household consumption. A policy of national food self-sufficiency would indicate increasing production of both millet and garden crops. But garden crops are often more difficult to market due to storage problems and their unsuitability for long or rough transport. Further, substituting millet for imported rice most directly meets the goals of self-sufficiency. Thus planners are likely to give millet priority over garden crops. Women's labor in millet production will subsequently increase, to the detriment of their own garden crops. In this case, promoting food self-sufficiency through millet production benefits women far less than through increasing garden crops: the prime beneficiary is the one who markets a crop.

In other regions, women have established control over both the production and the marketing of food crops. In southern Ivory Coast, men control highly profitable export crops such as coffee and cocoa, while women have established control over their own food crops (such as yams, manioc (cassava), tomatoes, eggplant, and pepper) which they grow for household consumption and for sale in urban markets. Agricultural extension and the commercialization of the (men's) export crops is institutionalized and effective, while little government attention has ever been paid to women's crops, so that this sector produces far below its potential. Thus, should the Ivoirian government be committed to increasing food production, furnishing agricultural extension benefits to women farmers seems an obvious and feasible solution. Men are not entirely dependent on wives' labor; wives join the numerous migrant laborers in work on husband's coffee and cocoa cultivation, usually receiving a gift or some cash when the crops are marketed. Is this then a case in which policy could promote the cultivation of women's crops to the benefit of women without undermining men's crops?

It is unlikely that increasing production of women's crops would have no effect on the production of men's crops. The conflict may be less rather than more severe, however. For example, the growing cycles of the crops in question may permit women to increase cultivation of their crops and yet continue to contribute labor to men's. However, this situation is rare in Africa, where labor shortages are typical and severe for short periods of the year. Increased migrant labor or labor saving technology (applicable to men's or women's crops or both) may offer solutions. Land shortage is often another constraint to the expansion of women's crops; this may be softened by innovations permitting more intensive land use. While such feasible solutions are unlikely to be wholly without social costs, they must be put on the planners' agenda.

If raised to a national priority, commitment to domestic food crops is unlikely to ensure both increased productivity *and* women's control over production without a *specific commitment* to women's interests. These two distinct goals are, we believe, reconcilable, but they are not automatically identical. A national commitment to improving domestic food production does favor peasant women in as much as it favors new understanding of peasant women's economic roles. But whether resulting projects actually benefit women depends on the design of the project in relation to the existing division of labor and control. In addition, it depends critically on the manner in which the project is implemented.

Implementation strategies

Protecting women's interests throughout the dual processes of project design and implementation has proved extremely difficult, perhaps more difficult than gaining official recognition of women's legitimate interests in development. Advocates of women's interests have debated how best to ensure the delivery of needed resources to women. One strategy is to seek out rural development projects which promote women's interests in project design and implementation. The tendency of many planners to make a symbolic bow toward women's interests, or for women's components of larger projects to be side-tracked during implementation, has led some proponents of peasant women's interests to prefer 'women's only' projects (WID, 1980; Dixon, 1980). In this view women's interests will be fully defended in the complex process of project design and implementation only when women are the sole beneficiaries and, in addition, when women's agencies fill all or most of the managerial and delivery functions. Attitudes, bureaucratic inertia, and the permeability of bureaucracies to other competing interests are all barriers to the realization of the women's components of 'integrated development projects' (that is, projects whose designated beneficiaries are both men and women).

However, the 'women only' project strategy has drawbacks as well. Because rural women ae rarely the constituency of greatest importance in the eyes of national decision makers, 'women only' projects are unlikely to gain more than a small, perhaps only symbolic, share of development resources. Second, while a women's organization may indeed be more sympathetic to women's interests than a ministry of agriculture or of commerce, it is unlikely to have sufficient technical expertise to execute many desirable projects on its own. Thus, the 'women only' strategy may not avoid dependence upon less sympathetic ministries. A third problem lies in the local population's response to development projects. Should men perceive that women are getting development assistance while they themselves are not, they are more likely to block the project than if the men see both themselves and women as beneficiaries. A fourth problem lies in the interconnectedness of male and female activities in a community. As noted above, women supply not only food and children for men, but also commonly work in conjunction with or for men. Altering women's time-use patterns, land requirements, or capital needs is likely to affect men's vital concerns. Thus striving for integrated development projects which explicitly include benefits for women has substantive merit in all but very simple projects (establishing a childcare center, or introducing technology to reduce women's household, rather than farm, labor). But typically, community development is a complex process which affects all community members (see Grindle 1980). Integrated development planning holds the promise of coordinating the changing needs and capabilities of all community members, while recognizing the political weakness of women as a pressure group.

Because planning for women as producers is so recent and so partial, neither strategy can be declared more effective at this time. The debate is perhaps best understood as symptomatic of the difficulty which proponents of women in development have had in getting projects funded and implemented which respond to their critiques of past development efforts. For example, the record of agricultural extension workers' low responsiveness to women has led to efforts to train women extension agents. Should these new agents be integrated into the national extension service, where they will surely be a minority voice? Or should they be employed in a separate women's branch, where they may be by-passed and underfunded? A women's bureau may be best suited to manage the search for labor-saving technology in exclusively women's domains, such as cooking and food preparation. But should the national bureaucracies responsible for energy or agriculture be permitted to sideline women's concerns, with the excuse that women's interests are taken care of elsewhere? The debate does not so much pose a soluble problem as it underlines the partial nature of women's victory to date. Peasant women have been recognized rhetorically and officially as producers and rightful beneficiaries of development efforts. Now women's advocates must gather the technical administrative support and political resources to ensure the implementation of rhetorical claims. No strategy is suited to all contexts and no strategy is without pitfalls and limitations.

The effects of colonial development policy on women

Current patterns of African agriculture and current agriculture policy are rooted in colonial practice and institutions. The syndrome of high labor inputs and low productivity in women's agriculture, discussed in earlier chapters, was reinforced by colonial and contemporary officials' tendency to overlook both subsistence crop production and women's role as agriculturists. This neglect has contributed to women's loss of access to productive resources and to their increased labor burden. While African women have continued to provide much of their family food needs, they have become increasingly marginalized relative to the modern sector of the economy.

Access to land

In the pre-colonial economy, land was acquired by men and women for use rather than for sale. Custom varied: women were granted access to land by village authorities, by their own kin group, or by their husbands. While women were granted use rights by men (kinsmen or spouses), the lower population densities and lesser demand for export crops ensured the relative importance of their subsistence farming, and their relatively easy access to land.

The dual forces of the increased private ownership of land by men and the declining value assigned to subsistence crops in the colonial and post-colonial economies have undermined women's access to land. The spread of export and cash crops and growing populations have both increased demand for land, and women have disproportionately borne the brunt of land pressure. Women's plots now tend to be smaller, located on the less desirable land in the village, overtilled and left fallow for shorter periods, and furthest from home. At best this increases the labor women must expend to maintain constant production levels.

Not only do women receive land of declining size and quality, their use-rights are becoming increasingly insecure (Jones, 1982). This is particularly true for divorcees and widows. While societies vary in custom and adherence to custom, individualism has nearly everywhere made inroads into the obligations and interdependence among members of the extended family. Use-rights become increasingly tenuous as traditional prescriptions become less respected. In some countries, post-colonial legal reforms have addressed these problems; whether they have actually benefitted rural women is unclear. The new civil codes of African states vary in the extent to which they have altered and codified customary law. Furthermore, many governments have not attempted to apply these codes nationally; rather they have selectively applied the codes in urban areas, projecting their future penetration into outlying areas. Thus the actual situation in a rural area must be documented by case law and histories of land ownership. (See Jones, 1982 for an excellent discussion and rare case law documentation; also Pala Okeyo, 1980).

Village settlement schemes offer an example of how state authorities have allocated land to inhabitants on a 'clean slate,' uncluttered by accumulated and conflicting claims of use and ownership rights. Governments' response to this opportunity reflects the presumption that women cannot or should not be farmers independent of a husband. While joint ownership may exist in theory, here too it is a legal fiction in which husbands have the sole voice, and indeed, women cannot acquire or even inherit land from their spouses. Thus, in Tanzania, where women have been formally given full citizenship rights and registered as farmers in 'Arusha villages', women cannot inherit land from a spouse or join co-operatives (see also the discussion of women's status on the Mwea scheme in Kenya, below). After divorce, a Tanzanian woman living on a settlement scheme may find herself without either settlement village land *or* land from her kinsmen, for she has effectively forfeited her use-rights by moving out of her own home area (Brain, 1976; see also Fortmann, 1978; 1979).

The settlement schemes appear to formalize the more slowly emerging legal practice in villages. A woman's legal identity is subsumed under that of her spouse, reflecting the emphasis on the nuclear family as the unit of production. Thus women become solely dependent upon their spouses for land.

Agricultural extension and women farmers

Agricultural extension in independent African states, greatly expanded to reach African farmers, continues to bypass women farmers. The reasons for this vary according to the marital status and crop specialization of women, but the pattern is consistent. Typically agricultural extension is still oriented solely to exported crops or relatively large-scale production of cash crops, which are in turn the domain of men. Thus in coffee or cocoa growing areas of Ivory Coast, the potential to increase garden crops or local staples produced by women has been largely ignored (my observation, 1976). But even where the women farm cash crops, agricultural extension workers generally fail to include them among their constituents. A detailed study of agricultural extension in Kakamega District, western Kenya, shows that the gap between services provided to male- and female- headed households increased as the value of the service increased. In this area women head about 40 percent of the rural households, because of the extensive male out-migration. These Luyia women grow maize and beans for sale and also for consumption;

some of them grow coffee and tea as well. In the Kakamega area studied, women heads of household were much less likely to have been visited by an extension agent, to have received training at the Farmer Training Center, or to have received agricultural credit. These differences between the services received by men and by women heads of household were not explicable by differences in wealth or farm size, although lower-income women managers were the most disadvantaged category (Staudt, 1975-6; 1978).

Male extension workers generally avoid interacting with women farmers, whether the women are wives with husbands present or women heads of household (Staudt, 1978; also Newland, 1980; Bazin-Tardieu n.d.; Ashby, 1982). This may be because social customs proscribe contact between male outsiders and women. It may also be because the agents had been taught, implicitly or explicitly, that women are dependent laborers or home-makers, and thus need not be included in the worker's constituency. In any case, the result is that women are deprived of techniques which could increase their productivity; in addition, the extension workers receive a distorted picture of farm problems and practices. Researchers gathering information on food storage practices in Senegal discovered that their male informants were in fact guessing about the precise methods used in this, a women's task (Dulansey, 1976).

Female agricultural extension workers—the logical solution to the 'contact' problem—are unknown in some countries; and elsewhere, despite efforts to recruit them, women form only a tiny percentage of all agricultural extension staff (Ashby, 1982). (Women made up only 2 percent of the extension workers in the Kenya study just discussed). Despite efforts to train some female extension workers to be village para-professionals, most rural development services are directed to rural women at home: home economics, skills oriented to child care, family health and nutrition, crafts, and meal preparation. The reality of women farmers' dominant concerns and time-use patterns continues to be effectively denied by an image which presents them solely as home-makers and mothers.

Disaster relief and women

Disaster relief has also failed to address the economic concerns and responsibilities of women. Refugee schemes typically address women's maternal and housekeeping functions, at the expense of women's expected productive roles (Chaney, 1980). Relief to the drought stricken Fulani and Tuareg of the Sahel is illustrative. International efforts to reconstitute the herds of these pastoralists provided cattle only (cattle are the property of men). Small animals such as donkeys and goats, commonly owned by women, were not replaced. This not only undermined the status of women, but also crippled the social system in which women's livestock were used for bridewealth and dowry. Finally, it deprived the entire group of a major source of meat and milk able to feed on poorer forage and to reproduce more rapidly than cattle after droughts (Cloud, 1978: 72-4).

Innovative technology to increase productivity

The subject of technological innovation is vast, and the impact of technology upon rural women has been variable. Capital intensive commercial farming has perhaps been the change most undermining women farmers. When small-holder agriculture is displaced, only a portion of the male peasantry, and a few women, find salaried employment on the export-oriented plantations. The remaining population must resort to subsistence farming on greatly reduced acreage of poor land, or become landless migrants. In a few African cases, employment patterns are reversed: women have become salaried agricultural workers on sugar plantations in the northern Ivory Coast, and on plantations in western Cameroon.

Other innovations have also resulted in a loss of employment for women. Labor-saving technology reducing women's work often simultaneously deprives them of employment because men have owned and operated the new equipment. For example, Nigerian women boycotted petrol-run palm-oil presses when their introduction threatened to destroy women's vital cottage industry of hand pressing the palm kernels. Fuel powered grinding mills have had a similar impact where women have neither the capital to own them nor access to alternative employment.

Such productive technology has not always been a disadvantage for women. In western Cameroon, the corn milling cooperatives which were described in Chapter 5 were successfully launched in the mid-1950s, and persist today. The cooperative purchasing of equipment seems the ideal solution when costs are too high for the individual, or when use patterns prohibit amortization by an individual purchaser. But this requires start-up capital, organizational stability and sympathetic public officials; the scarcity of this combination makes such cooperative ventures the exception rather than the rule.

New technology has also had the reverse effect of increasing women's work load without concomitantly increasing benefits to women. Tractors introduced in Tanzanian settlement schemes permitted great expansion of the acreage under cultivation, so that women could not keep up with the weeding; the production achieved was well below planners' projections (Fortmann, 1979).

Such innovations which require greater female labor indicate faulty planning in a number of regards. Where cash cropping and subsistence crops both depend on women's labor, subsistence crop production must drop if women are to spend more time on cash crops without compensating labor-saving innovations. Where women sell some portion of their own 'subsistence' crops, they are not highly motivated workers on their spouse's cash or export crops. Planners must therefore consider women's work load, the impact of technology on the sex division of labor, and the differential rewards of innovations for men and women when they assess manpower availability in a given location. But planners often use the household or the community as the lowest level of analysis, and thus alter women's workload in ways which carry great disincentives for women.

National and international assistance organizations have supported projects that focus on labor-saving technology—wells nearer to residences, more efficient stoves and alternative fuel sources (badly needed in savannah areas), new food crops or new preparation techniques which require less preparation time—and all these directly diminish women's labor in non-cultivation tasks. They thus increase the potential labor women can allocate to other productive tasks. But such efforts often lack a clear grasp of the trade-offs and rewards of altered time-use patterns for women. Planners must ask who the direct beneficiaries are, whether the beneficiaries can pay for and maintain the technology, and whether others are in a position to undermine project success (Dulansey, 1976). Whether such projects will succeed at all, and whether benefits are distributed in the desired manner, are complex questions. The necessary first step, however, is to make women visible—to extend analysis to include women as a distinct group of laborers, whose assigned tasks, motivations, and benefits are usually separate from those of men.

Selected current projects aiding rural women

The range of rural development projects undertaken in Africa is enormous, as are the criteria by which we might evaluate them. Some projects include men and women, some women only. Some are implemented primarily by a women's agency; in others a women's agency is subordinate to another government agency. Some seek to train agents of change (such as planners, teachers, agricultural extension workers or even village paraprofessionals) while others seek directly to change the productive patterns of villagers themselves. Some seek to lay the groundwork for increased production by analyzing villagers' needs and by the design and trial of new technologies (seeds, farming tools, and methods of storage, food processing, and food preservation). Some seek to free women's time for production and processing through new technologies in cooking, water hauling, and storage; others seek only to improve current yields through the introduction of existing technology.

Every initiative generates its own problems. Some technology is costly or hard to maintain, while simpler technology, more accessible or more durable, may save much less labor. Another set of trade-offs concerns the scope of change or the number of goals. A single intervention such as well construction saves women a specified amount of time, but does not, in itself, achieve the use of that time in income-earning activities. A more ambitious project, with greater risk in implementation, aims at restructuring time-use patterns, perhaps by introducing new technology, by organizing a cooperative to pay for new inputs, by organizing collective labor or by improving access to markets. A project which entails implementation of existing techniques is simpler than one which will design and test a new technology before disseminating it. All these variations constitute elements of project feasibility, level of benefits, and definition of beneficiaries and implementors.

In this final section, we shall compare three different projects: (1) a single crop irrigation scheme (Mwea, in Kenya); (2) a project to restructure a regional economy away from cash monocropping and towards domestic food production (the Groundnut Basin Cereals project in Senegal); and (3) a multi-faceted rural development effort to increase the production and income of rural women in a region of heavy male out-migration (Swaziland Rural Development Project). The cases are suggestive of the range of organizational and substantive strategies by which development assistance can increase benefits to rural women.

The first, a rice irrigation scheme in Kenya, contrasts with subsequent cases in its clearly negative impact on women. But it is of interest not because of these shortcomings, but because of the critiques and solutions it inspires.

Mwea irrigation scheme in Kenya

The Mwea irrigation scheme in Kenya's Central Province has been called a success story by some development economists. Over 3,000 formerly landless settlers and their families are tenants of this, the largest and only consistently profitable of the National Irrigation Board's operations. Rice yields on the 1.6 hectare family plots are high, and tenants' incomes are generally higher than planned (Wisner, 1982).

Yet this 'success story' has negative aspects which exemplify the effects of planning which overlook women's socially-defined economic activities and responsibilities. Male heads of household are the sole legal tenants and contractors with the Board and they receive full cash payment for the rice marketed, although women contribute significantly to production. The planners set aside no land for growing food consumed by the household or for women's crops. They assumed that families would eat rice and other, purchased foods. Households have a ready supply of water, but it appears to be badly polluted. Household fuel, purchased at central marketing sites, is very costly. The scheme thus entails a single cash crop as the sole productive activity and its cash proceeds, controlled and allocated by males, must suffice for the purchase of all other household needs.

Two bold indices of social well-being suggest that the scheme is wanting, however well it serves its designated commercial function. According to one study, nutrition appears to have deteriorated from 1966 to 1976, while a more recent study reports that over a third of children aged 1-5 are less than 80 percent of the standard weight for their ages. Second, high rates of desertion by wives are reported. These women are articulate regarding their complaints: they have neither the cash nor the time to complete what they see as their tasks in the families. They cannot grow enough maize, beans and vegetables for their families on their plots outside the scheme, to which they must walk very long distances. They pay more and more for fuel. They have no legitimate access to rice or to the cash it brings. They are heavily dependent upon commodities which cost more (in part due to petrol, and thus transport, costs), and yet they have no cash with which to discharge their familial responsibilities. Women have not only found themselves reduced to unpaid household labor, but have lost the capacity to fulfil their prior role. They are cut off from the means of meeting their responsibilities and of having leverage and self respect. The scheme's basic design promotes the high cost of foods which women feel they must provide, while offering them no options for earning income. Although the men in fact give their wives rice to sell on the black market (thus circumventing the Board's legal monopoly), the money the women earn is inadequate in social and market terms. The nutritional data suggests that, beyond social and familial disintegration, basic needs are not being met, despite the scheme's extraordinary yields (Wisner, 1983; Rogers, 1980).

The Mwea puzzle illustrates the difficulties of isolating a feminist critique from a far-reaching critique regarding the nature of development itself. One approach would be to argue for economic and legal equality between the sexes: women might be made income-earning tenants, paid for rice directly by the Irrigation Board. If both women and men were rice farmers, however, the dietary complements to rice would be even more scarce than they are at present, and the constraints on women's time could be even greater, leaving no time for vegetable farming, visiting health centers, and other tasks of family maintenance. It would formally destroy the protective cushion from cash monocropping which these women currently strive to provide, as the women have for decades in Africa.

If women were given good and accessible land on which to farm crops for household consumption and for sale, they might come far closer to fulfilling their perceived household responsibilties and retain some leverage on their spouses. Critics might respond that this would be tantamount to 'tracking' women back into their established colonial role as subsistence farmers while their husbands raise cash crops.

The Mwea project is instructive because it is prototypical of an extractive mode of development. It appears to encapsulate the colonial economy both in the role assigned to women and in the manner male profits are dictated by official rather than by market forces. Its design precludes the diversification of productive activities among both men and women—a precondition for the development of a regional economy responsive to the communities' perceived wants.

Such schemes are predicated on a given level of profit in a given form, obtained through a hierarchy of state, scheme management, and male household heads: women's labor is assumed to be an asset of the male head of household. The cereals project in the Groundnut Basin of Senegal is appropriately seen as a response to the prototype illustrated by Mwea. The project marks a policy of withdrawal from the extractive monocrop production, and as such, it builds in a diversification which makes advances for women possible.

The Senegalese Groundnut Basin, Cereals II Project

The current development plan for the Groundnut Basin of Senegal (Thies and Diourbel regions) exemplifies a serious attempt to integrate the productive activities of women into a largely integrated development project. The Groundnut Basin is heavily populated, intensely farmed, and crucial to the Senegalese economy, producing a major national export (groundnuts/peanuts) and one-third of the millet consumed in Senegal. This region has witnessed declining productivity in recent years, due to low rainfall and deteriorating environment. Government policy until 1975 has sought principally to increase groundnut production. Following a major redefinition of national goals, national policy now seeks to diversify production, increasing cultivation for domestic consumption (millet and sorghum) as well as increasing productivity by improving inputs (fertilizer, new seed varieties). The main organizational vehicle of this policy will be SODEVA (the regional service) and its local counterpart, the village cooperatives.

The plan projects a battery of forms of assistance; agronomic research to improve inputs, application of this research through trials conducted within village cooperatives, additional training for current extension personnel, training for new village-level paraprofessionals, and audio-visual communications for villages. Projections include assistance in activities not previously touched by agricultural extension (feeding livestock the byproducts of peanuts and millet; financial and technical assistance to women's sheep raising cooperatives) and experimentation with labor-saving technology particularly for women. It also includes wider application of proven techniques; for example, in millet production, use of a drought tolerant variety, early thinning after germination and use of fertilizers (Cereals II, 1980).

This, then, is an ambitious project aimed at redirecting as well as increasing agricultural production in a region long a single export crop producer. There was no women's component in the first five year plan for this region reflecting this new orientation, but the second and current five year plan is marked by a major effort to integrate women economically, increasing both their productivity and their earned income.

In the Groundnut Basin, as among the Senufo discussed in Chapter 2 in this volume, both men and women work extensively in the principal cultivating activities of the region. Women traditionally cultivate up to 23 percent of the land in peanut production in addition to their activities in household food production, child care, food processing, and millet cultivation. But productivity on women's plots is as little as half as high as men's, due to labor constraints and lack of access to credit. Unable to get credit because they are excluded from extension services and cooperatives, women have not been able to get fertilizer and other agricultural inputs (Cereals II, 1980:13).

The project's design seeks to ensure that those women active in groundnut and millet cultivation receive full and regular access to SODEVA's services, permitting women to increase their productivity. In addition, extension services are to be broadened to include new activities which women have previously undertaken unassisted (cooperative vegetable gardens, and food preservation techniques). Labor-saving technologies are projected: these are to alleviate significant female labor constraints. More efficient wood burning stoves, hand operated millet threshers and mills, hand pumps for wells, and fish dryers are all elements of this effort — elements which village women themselves have chosen. Although extension workers and specially trained villagers will play a role in imparting new techniques and making technology accessible to women, groups of village women will be pivotal to implementing projects.

One can readily perceive possible problem areas in this ambitious project—problems which may affect men as well as women. Credit is a problem carrying over from the past: loans for inputs have been repaid at a rate of only 65 percent. It remains to be seen if the pattern of low repayment will be improved, and whether women will have a higher loan repayment rate, if credit is extended to them as planned. Such inter-organizational cooperation is always vulnerable and the problem is likely to be exacerbated by the fact that the extension of credit to women's cooperatives is a new responsibility for SODEVA.

The directive that SODEVA should be responsive to women's needs and extend credit to women's cooperatives will doubtless encounter at least some institutionalized resistance (few employees anywhere welcome increased tasks or bigger constituencies). Yet the effort to increase institutional extension capability to women may encourage inter-agency 'buck passing' by increasing the number of agencies undertaking this task (SODEVA plus a new agency). The Women's Extension Unit is supposed to program, coordinate and supervise all activities concerning women and to create a village trainee paraprofessional component. Thus not only is the women's cooperative component susceptible to all the difficulties inherent in collective action and collective liability; women's concerns may suffer from the ambiguity of organizational jurisdiction.

The interconnectedness of villagers' economic activities, the omnipresence of labor and capital constraints, and the impact of increased labor in one activity upon the viability of other productive activities provide the logic of integrated development efforts. Such projects attempt multiple innovations simultaneously and in a coordinated manner. The multiplicity of goals, and the number of implementing agents (both bureaucratic agents outside the village *and* village groups) are problematic aspects of many integrated rural development projects (Grindle, 1980). Thus the problems of bureaucratic cooperation and coordination in this project are not a function of the women's component. Nonetheless, the inclusion of women and their needs (a distinct constituency if only because of their long exclusion) in Phase II of the Groundnut Basin project necessarily makes implementation more complex and thus more problematic.

If women's components in this integrated development approach are in danger of 'getting lost', do projects of which women are the sole beneficiaries serve women better? The premise of basic interdependence of the village community's members suggests the need for a more holistic approach if the local economy is to be effectively restructured. Also local political forces may better tolerate innovations for women in integrated projects. In the Senegalese case, village men said that they would not do women's work, but favored increasing women's productivity because of the benefits to the family (Cereals II, Annex D, 1980). It is likely that these men would be less supportive if aid were channelled to women only.

The women's component of this project is fully compatible with the project's overarching goals. Certainly increasing women's productivity as planned will pronote economic diversification. And yet, the realities of development assistance in the face of inevitable competition for scarce resources means that the promotion of women's interests is far from guaranteed. The women's component would probably not have been included without pressures from women's advocates; its full implementation will similarly require the efforts of women's advocates within the several well established bureaucracies which carry Senegalese development plans to the villages.

Unlike Mwea and the Senegal cereals project, the Swaziland project is not an intensive, internally coordinated, and integrated effort to restructure a local economy. Rather it involves a series of distinct initiatives to increase productivity and earnings of rural women in a region exporting male labor to South Africa. Thus the project entails not the balancing of men's and women's share of development resources or of women's labor on their own crops and on men's crops. Rather it entails freeing women's time, providing women with productive resources, and ensuring markets for their produce.

The Swaziland Project of the UN Voluntary Fund

This project is an example of a low cost effort to increase women's income earning activities. Swaziland constitutes something of an island surrounded by white expatriates' large farms and highly industrialized South Africa. Swazi women make up the vast majority of the rural Swazi population; in 1976 over one third of the homesteads had no male present due to out-migration for cash employment. But because the Swazi economy is so fully commercialized, a central task is to increase these women's share of existing markets. To overcome the barriers of scarce time and capital, a combination of labor-saving innovations, training in new productive activities, revolving loan funds, and cooperatives are being introduced to raise incomes.

The Swazi project involves a number of local initiatives, each with three components: innovations which yield free time; start-up capital to obtain productive resources; and cooperatives to train members, repay the fund and sometimes to produce and market the products. Thus far improved stoves, wooden washers, and nursery schools have reduced the time demands of housekeeping. Pig and poultry raising, crafts (sisal and grass work, tie dying), dress-making, and knitting offer avenues for increased income. Markets have so far been able to absorb increases in production. The Swazi government has been willing to help Swazi women regain Swazi markets: school uniforms made by these women are being substituted for imported uniforms and the government has agreed to contract women's cooperatives to make policemen's jerseys and socks which the women can knit on simple knitting machines. Other efforts to introduce improved vegetable gardening and food preservation are also underway (UNVF).

The start-up capital for these various enterprises, supplied by the United Nations Voluntary Fund, becomes the basis of a revolving fund, from which the cooperatives can borrow with a low service charge. In some instances the capital serves as collateral for a bank loan, permitting a considerable multiplication of capital. In all cases, because the fund is replenished by repayment from borrowers, the initial capital permits women in a large number of communities to purchase equipment and stock. But even though the initial loans to these enterprises are small, repayment of the loans is difficult for the Swazi women, requiring a great motivation and commitment. For example, one knitting machine would cost a single woman six months' income; thus the cooperative structure is essential. The most striking aspect of these Swazi women's cooperative efforts has in fact been their ability to repay loans to the revolving fund through their cooperative.

Another potential problem is the maintenance of steady outlets for goods the women's cooperatives produce. While the high degree of commercialization of the Swazi economy makes production for sale feasible, the organizational task of capturing a share of that market is considerable. Marketing research continues but it is not yet clear that enterprises such as producers' retail shops will be fully viable, or that cooperatives' stocks and equipment will be maintained over time.

A number of international agencies are exploring the feasibility of additional income earning activities as well as accessible technologies to reduce time spent in household maintenance. The scope of these efforts to delineate cottage industries which can compete with imports from industrialized South Africa underlines a common dilemma of African development: locating low capital, labor intensive industry which is competitive with foreign imports. The consuming tasks of household and family maintenance are yet another constraint which faces planners seeking income earning opportunities for African women.

The Swazi project nonetheless has several mitigating characteristics. Despite the numerous areas of intervention — housework, loans, skills training, supply of stocks, marketing research and organization and co-operative — involving numerous international actors, tight coordination is not required due to the project's decentralized character. Also planners need not be preoccupied by trade-offs within communities between men's and women's crops and benefits. And perhaps because of the predominance of women in the rural labor force, government agencies have lent considerable support to this 'women's only' project. Finally women's support of the revolving loan fund has to date made possible continued multiplication of local enterprises.

Conclusions

The three development projects sketched above only suggest the kinds of efforts to assist women which have been initiated in the recent past. There are other, less ambitious village-level efforts to free women's time and energy by introducing a single change such as child care facilities, wheelbarrows, water pumps, cisterns to catch rainwater from roofs, or solar crop dryers (See for example, Carr, 1978; ILO, 1978; WID/AID, 1980). The range of agricultural inputs usually available to men is being distributed to women in some localities. Such projects are often pilot projects, funded at very modest levels and reaching only a small proportion of Africa's women farmers.

A different group of projects seeks to increase institutional capability and the predisposition to plan and implement projects which aid women farmers. Efforts to revise curricula, altering the assumptions about women's role in agriculture, have focused particularly on schools teaching agronomy and agricultural extension. Grants have been made to fund advance education in agronomy and other technical fields both within Africa and abroad. Past patterns of discrimination toward women in higher education mean that very basic changes are required: for example, the World Bank has funded the construction of a women's boarding facility so that women may attend technical school in Tanzania (World Bank, 1978).

In addition to efforts to train more enlightened cadres for the future, international donors have sought to strengthen women's advocates within existing institutions. Funds have been channelled to recently formed women's ministries and to women's voluntary associations, including national associations affiliated with political parties and to local and national nongovernmental associations. Research seminars and major research projects sponsored by national women's agencies have been initiated to supply badly needed empirical data on women in agriculture. Another particuarly promising effort is the establishment of a course on women and development planning for middle and upper level bureaucrats in African national development agencies. The first of these courses was given in 1981 at the Eastern and Southern African Management Institute in Arusha. Participants from five African countries spent two months studying empirical research on African women's economic roles and strategies for planning and implementing development projects benefiting women (See Bruce and Staudt, 1981).

While projects addressing women's economic interests are various and numerous, they represent a very small proportion of all development aid, and even these projects are not always fully supported by international and national government machineries. They seem, and doubtless are, wholly inadequate to reverse the process which has marginalized women in agriculture since colonization. Future initiatives, hopefully more extensive, will be built upon these current efforts to correct past trends.

But planning efforts to benefit women producers will address situations characterized by their historical legacies: planning never makes its mark on a clean slate. The three cases suggest how national context and policy shape the feasible, and how current local patterns of crops, labor allocation, and marketing constrain the research for alternatives. Success, even partial success, of women's advocates seeking to design projects to benefit women farmers will depend on their understanding of these constraints.

Appendix: Some selected statistics on African women

Sharon Stichter

The national-level statistics on women in Africa offer one important guide to what women do for a living and to the differences in women's economic and educational participation from country to country. Often they are the only means to approximate cross-national comparisons in these areas. The indices must be used carefully, however, for they have important limitations.

Tables 5 to 8 in this Appendix present available data on women's economic participation, status, and educational levels in a sample of African nations. The countries included represent those with the most available and reliable statistics for 1970 or near years. In some important cases, such as Nigeria, the censuses were not sufficiently reliable to warrant the inclusion of data based on them.

Table 5 shows the rates of economic activity for men and women. Here and in the following tables, the *economically active population*, or labor force, is defined as those (1) at work for pay or profit during a specified reference period (often the preceding week or month); (2) with a job but not at work; or (3) actively seeking employment. The *crude economic activity rate*, or crude labor force participation rate, is the proportion of the total population classified as being economically active. More refined measures of the labor force participation rate are age-specific; one measure, for example, includes only those above age 10 or 15. Although this standard concept of economically active population, or labor force, is widely used by economists and policy-makers, it has inherent limitations, especially when applied to women. There are at least four major problems:

1. *Subsistence and domestic production*   The concept excludes activities connected with subsistence and family production which do not result in marketed goods. Thus a 'housewife' is not considered to be economically active; nor is a subsistence farmer, which is the chief occupation of many African women. All in-kind exchanges and non-wage labor provided to meet social obligations are excluded, as are household food preparation, child care, and care of livestock for family consumption. Thus the major activities of the majority of rural African women are excluded, even though they may account for the bulk of the food production in that society.

2. *Unpaid family workers*   Most statistical departments do follow the International Labour Organization (ILO) specifications, according to which unpaid family workers are included in the category of economically active if they worked at a cash-producing activity at least one-third time during a short reference period. In practice, however, it is difficult

for census-takers to decide what constitutes one-third time, especially in the many situations where work is seasonal or intermittent. For this reason, many women workers are misclassified as economically inactive.

3. *Informal sector activities*   Large numbers of rural and urban women engage in trade and industry of various kinds—crafts, food products, beer-brewing, hawking, prostitution, and so forth. These activities are on the periphery of the formal wage-labor sector; they are free-lance or partly employed, for example on a commission basis. They are not adequately reflected in the census statistics, both because of the reference period problem—they are done irregularly or in conjunction with other economic roles—and because they are shifting in locale and perhaps quasi-legal. Also, no industry or detailed occupational breakdowns exist for these activities.

4. *Unemployment*   Those who have no job or economic activity, but are actively seeking work, are classified as in the labor force but 'unemployed'. In the case of women, however, there is a tendency for census-takers to automatically relegate a married woman who is not working to the status of 'economically inactive', or 'housewife', rather than 'unemployed', without probing whether or not she is looking for work or would accept a job if one were offered.

Clearly, the concept of 'economically active' needs to be expanded, and more categories added. In the actual census counts, more effort needs to be made by interviewers to report the work that women do. In addition to the other inaccuracies and inadequacies of coverage in census and employment data in most developing nations, present practices seriously undervalue and underenumerate the work of women (Youssef, 1981; Beneria, 1981).

Despite these rather severe limitations, however, Tables 5 to 8 do reveal some interesting information. The officially reported female participation rates are much higher in Africa than they are, for example, in the Middle East (25.16 for Africa as a whole, compared to 4.69 for North Africa), and are only slightly below the world average of 27.2, although much below it, of course, in the non-agricultural sectors (ILO, 1977). Africa is also unique among the world's major areas in that female activity rates increase steadily up to about age 50, with no drop during child-bearing years, and they remain high for the elderly population (ILO, 1975a: 6, 22).

Table 5 shows a good deal of variation among African nations, however. Those areas where women's activity rates are particularly high fall into two categories—first, West African nations, such as Ghana, Senegal, and the Ivory Coast, where there is a tradition of high female involvement in commerce; and second, Southern African areas such as Botswana and Lesotho, where many women are involved in wage labor, either in local towns or in neighboring South Africa. On the other hand, those nations with particularly low female activity rates are either quite underdeveloped areas, such as the former Portuguese territories of Mozambique, Angola, and Guinea-Bissau, or areas with strong Islamic

TABLE 5   Crude economic activity rates, male and female, 1970

	Female	Male	Total
Ghana	32.20	45.57	38.84
Kenya	27.37	53.83	40.63
Zambia	25.32	52.68	38.85
Botswana	46.76	49.84	48.17
Senegal	34.30	54.50	44.30
Mozambique	20.80	61.87	41.06
Lesotho	49.05	62.67	55.75
Angola	4.64	51.19	27.54
Sudan	6.64	56.94	32.05
Guinea-Bissau	2.36	62.75	32.37
Ivory Coast	47.26	59.38	53.38
South Africa	24.21	50.89	37.36
Total African	25.5*		
Total Non-African	22.6*		
African in 'White Areas'	33.4* +		
African in 'Black Areas'	18.2* +		

Source: ILO, *Labour Force Estimates and Projections, 19 50-2000* (1977), II, Table 2.

Notes: The ILO estimates are based on national population censuses and labor force surveys, adjusted to conform to a standard concept of labor force. They are thus more useful for inter-country comparisons than the national statistics would be.

* Source: Amelia Mariotti, 'The Incorporation of African Women into Wage Employment in South Africa, 1920-1970' (1979), Table 27, p. 205.

+ Includes women classified as 'foreign' by the Department of Statistics.

influence, such as the Sudan. The Eastern African nations of Kenya and Zambia fall somewhere in between these extremes. In South Africa, African women have a higher participation rate than do non-African women. Since African women who reside in the designated 'white' areas must be employed to remain there legally, it is not surprising that one out of three women is classified as active. Doubtless many more are in unreported or under-reported activities. The low activity rate for women in the reserves reflects the serious lack of economic opportunities there.

Table 5 also shows that in every case female rates of activity are lower than those for males. The difference between the two rates is very wide in the ex-Portuguese and Islamic nations mentioned above, but much less wide in areas with high female activity rates. In producing these figures, the ILO may well have underestimated female activity rates for certain countries such as Ghana, where national census data suggest that female rates increased between 1960 and 1970, and that the male/female gap was being narrowed. The ILO assumes on the basis of international experience that in the early stages of economic development, female participation rates always decline, and therefore has deflated the Ghanaian data accordingly (Akerele, 1979: 14-19).

Table 6 shows the percentage of women in formal-sector wage

TABLE 6   African women in wage employment: selected cases

	(a) As a percentage of economically active female population	(b) As a percentage of all wage employment
Ghana (1971)	2.7	9.9
Kenya (1970)	8.7	14.3
Zambia	5.7	6.7

Sources: Olubanke Akerele, *Women Workers in Ghana, Kenya, Zambia,* Addis Ababa, 1979, Table VI; Ghana, *Labour Statistics;* Economic Commission for Africa, *Summaries of Economic Data*, Addis Ababa, 1972; Kenya, *Employment and Earnings in the Modern Sector*, Nairobi, 1971; Kenya, *Economic Survey*, 1972 and 1971; Zambia, *Population Census*, 1969; Zambia, Cabinet Office, *Manpower Report*, 1969.

employment. Women who have these wage-paid jobs are generally a small minority of all economically active women (column a). In a West African country such as Ghana, the percentage of women in wage employment is particularly low; women are overwhelmingly self-employed, especially in trade. In Kenya and Zambia, on the other hand, the percentage in wage employ is much greater; the relatively larger figure for Kenya reflects the greater opportunities for women to earn wages in commercialized agriculture there. Of all wage employment, male and female, women do not form a great proportion in any African country (column b).

One might expect that as development proceeds in West Africa, women's traditional commercial skills would help them find jobs in modern commercial enterprises. Unfortunately, this does not appear to be happening. According to the 1970 Ghanaian census, there were 338 514 women self-employed in sales, but only 8 414 earning salaries or wages in sales, compared to 14 025 men formally employed in sales. Thus the business skills of the famous 'market women' of Ghana have not been translated into modern employment, perhaps because of low levels of literacy (Akerele, 1979: 39-40; Boserup, 1970: 99; ILO, 1975b: Table 2B).

Table 7 shows the concentration of women in certain occupations in three representative areas of Africa and the differences between the distribution of males and females in particular occupations. While the categories used here are standard, they do not reflect a true occupational breakdown based on skill levels. Only the first three categories are occupational ones, and correspond roughly to 'white-collar' jobs. The rest are industrial divisions of the 'blue-collar' work force, and include all skilled and unskilled workers below the clerical level.

Except for white women in South Africa, the percentage of women in professional, technical, and managerial occupations is very low in the countries shown, and in Ghana and Zambia is lower than the percentage of men. In South Africa, African women have actually had more access to the professions than have African men, through their entry into

TABLE 7 Occupational distribution of the economically active population: selected cases

	% of labor force women	men	Female/ male ratio	% of labor force women	men	Female/ male ratio
	GHANA (1970)			ZAMBIA (1969)		
Professional, technical	1.9	5.0	.38	2.8	4.5	.62
Administrative and managerial	.04	.6	.07	.3	.9	.33
Clerical workers	.9	4.0	.23	1.7	2.6	.65
Sales workers	24.8	2.8	8.86	1.4	3.6	.39
Service, sport, and recreation	1.4	3.8	.37	2.3	8.2	.28
Agricultural workers	52.5	56.5	.93	6.3	19.0	.33
Mine, transport and production workers	14.8	21.8	.68	2.3	23.0	.10
Other, unemployed, and unclassifiable	3.4	5.6	.61	83.0	38.1	2.18
	99.8*	100.0		100.1*	99.9*	
	SOUTH AFRICA (1970) African			SOUTH AFRICA (1970) White		
Professional, technical	2.7	1.0	2.7	17.9	14.2	1.3
Administrative, managerial	—	.1	—	1.1	7.1	.15
Clerical workers	.3	1.5	.20	51.7	12.8	4.04
Sales workers	.9	1.6	.56	12.6	9.4	1.34
Service	36.8	7.7	4.78	5.7	7.3	.78
Agricultural	43.9	38.5	1.14	.9	8.7	.10
Mine, transport and production workers	4.5	45.6	.10	6.1	38.0	.16
Other, unemployed and unclassifiable	11.0	4.1	2.68	3.9	2.5	1.56
	100.1*	100.1*		99.9*	100.0	

*effects of rounding

Sources: ILO, *Yearbook of Labour Statistics* (1975), Table 2B; Mariotti (1979), Appendix I, p. 286.

nursing and teaching. In all countries, the two occupations of nursing and primary school teaching account for a very large proportion of African professional women. The percentage of women in administrative and managerial occupations is even lower than in professional jobs, and the male/female gap here is particularly wide.

Women's participation in clerical work has been growing in Africa, in conformity with world-wide occupational trends, although clerical work has not become so completely feminized as it is in Western industrial societies. In the colonial period in Africa, clerks and white-collar workers were almost wholly men. Men still markedly predominate in clerical work in West Africa and among Africans in South Africa, but their predominance is much less in East Africa. In most countries, a closer look at the categories of typist and stenographer would probably reveal female predominance in these lower levels of clerical work. White South Africa shows the opposite pattern, with fully half of the female labor force in clerical occupations, compared to only 13 percent of the males. This contrasts starkly with African women's low degree of access to clerical jobs there.

The high concentration of women in the sales sector in Ghana, mentioned earlier, is quite evident from the table. This phenomenon is not found to a similar degree in East or Southern Africa, although the numbers in trade are doubtless underestimated there. Among service workers, men predominate in East and West Africa, but women predominate among Africans in South Africa, because of the heavy concentration of African women in domestic service jobs. Domestic work is one of the few urban occupations open to African women there. Of all domestic servants in South Africa in 1970, fully 78.7 percent were African women (Mariotti, 1979: Table 31, pp. 210-11).

In most African nations, the majority of economically active women work in agriculture. The low figure shown for Zambia under this head is suspect, given the high percentage of women who were not adequately classified in the 1969 census. In both Ghana and South Africa, there has been some decline in the percentage in agriculture in recent years. Among mine, transport and production workers, an interesting variation is evident; whereas in most African countries women are greatly underrepresented here relative to men, Ghana is something of an exception. In the garment and printing industries in Ghana, for example, perhaps 30 percent of the skilled and unskilled workers are women (Akerele, 1979: 41). In South Africa, the female labor force outside agriculture is still quite underrepresented in mine and production work, although during the 1960s, due to a shortage of white factory labor, the numbers of African women in the garment, textile and food processing factories increased greatly (Mariotti, 1979: 193-5).

A major reason for the difficulties African women face in the labor market is their relative lack of access to education. Of all world areas, Africa has one of the highest levels of illiteracy—in 1970 about 80 percent of the women were illiterate, and about 60 percent of the men (McGrath, 1976: 16). But there are wide variations among African nations in this respect, as Table 8 shows. Statistics on both literacy and school enrollments are shown here, since some people may be literate without having attended school, and conversely, attendance at school may not guarantee literacy. The West African countries of Ghana and Cameroon, and the Eastern African country of Zambia, have relatively high percentages of women who are literate or who are enrolled in school, and yet even in these cases, less than half of the female population is enrolled in school, whereas about half the male population is.

Botswana, a major exporter of both male and female labor to South Africa, has relatively fewer people literate or in school, but it is noteworthy that the percentages are about equal for women and men. At the other extreme is the Sudan, where the difference between male and female attainment is quite wide, although Ghana, Tanzania, and Mozambique also have rather wide sex differentials in literacy, as

TABLE 8 Percentage literate among African women and men, and percentage enrolled in school

A. Percentage literate (10 years old and over)

		Female	Male	Female/male ratio
Ghana[a]	1971	18.4	43.1	.43
Cameroon	1976	33.1	54.8	.60
Botswana[b]	1971	10.1	11.3	.89
Tanzania	1967	18.8	45.0	.42
Zambia	1969	40.2	63.1	.64
Ivory Coast	1975	14.6	29.9	.49
Sudan[c]	1973	17.9	44.7	.40
Mozambique[d]	1970	8.8	19.7	.45

B. Percentage of population enrolled in school (6-24 years)

Ghana	1970	38.0	52.3	.73
Cameroon	1976	40.2	52.5	.77
Botswana[e]	1971	28.4	27.7	1.03
Tanzania[f]	1967	14.5	24.8	.58
Zambia[f]	1969	31.4	44.0	.72
Sudan[g]	1973	22.0	39.9	.55

Source: Selected Statistical Data by Sex. Office of Development Information and Utilization, U.S. Agency for International Development, Washington, D.C., 1981

Notes:
[a] *15 years and over*
[b] *15 years and over; estimated*
[c] *all persons who ever attended school, including Islamic schools, considered literate*
[d] *literate defined as those who've completed primary school*
[e] *5-24 years; population bases and enrollments recognized to be understated*
[f] *5-24 years*
[g] *7-24 years*

measured by the ratio of female to male rates. As for absolute levels of female literacy, Botswana, Mozambique, and the Ivory Coast are on the low end of the scale, due primarily to the poor development of educational systems there during the colonial era.

The percentage of African women who have completed secondary school is much lower than the percentage enrolled in school, pointing to high drop-out rates among women. In Kenya, according to the 1969 census, only 1.2 percent of women had completed secondary school, compared to 3.8 percent of the men. In Tanzania in 1967, the percentages were 0.4 percent of the women, compared to 2.7 percent of the men. In general, the rates of secondary school attainment in Africa are still lower than those in other developing regions such as Asia and Latin America (US Dept. of Commerce, 1980: Table 10).

Bibliography

Note: items marked with an asterisk (*) are important books and articles which will be particularly useful for non-specialist readers.

Abbott, Susan (1976) 'Full-Time Farmers and Weekend Wives', *Journal of Marriage and the Family,* **38**, 165-74.

Abrahams, Peter (1970) *Mine Boy.* New York, first pub. 1946.

Abrahams, R. G. (1978) 'Aspects of the Distribution Between the Sexes in the Nyamwezi and Some Other African Systems of Kinship and Marriage', in J.S. LaFontaine (ed.), *Sex and Age as Principles of Social Differentiation,* London, pp.67-88.

Achebe, Chinua (1959) *Things Fall Apart,* New York.

Achebe, Chinua (1969) *Arrow of God,* Garden City, N.Y.

Adams, M. J. (1978) 'Kuba Embroidered Cloth', *African Arts,* **12**, 24-39.

Adams, M. J. (1980) 'Spheres of Men's and Women's Creativity', *Ethnologische Zeitschrift Zurich,* **1**, 163-7.

Aidoo, Ama Ata (1970) *Anowa,* London.

Akerele, Olubanke (1979) *Women Workers in Ghana, Kenya, Zambia,* Addis Ababa.

Al-Amin bin Aly Mazrui (1932) 'Wajibu Wetu kwa Wanawake' ('Our Duty Toward Women') and *Uwongozi* ('Guidance'), Mombasa reprint, 1955.

Albert, Ethel M. (1971) 'Women of Burundi: A Study of Social Values', in Denise Paulme (ed.), *Women of Tropical Africa,* Berkeley, Calif., pp. 179-216.

Alpers, Edward A. (forthcoming) 'The Story of Swema: A Note on Female Vulnerability in Nineteenth-Century East Africa', in Martin Klein and Claire C. Robertson (eds.), *Women and Slavery in Africa,* Madison, Wisc.

Alverson, Hoyt (1978) *Mind in the Heart of Darkness: Value and Self-Identity Among the Tswana of Southern Africa,* New Haven, Conn.

Amon d'Aby (1960) *Croyances Réligieuses et Coutumes Juridiques des Agni de la Côte d'Ivoire,* Paris.

Aniakor, Chike (1979) 'Igbo Architecture: A Study of Forms, Functions, and Typology', 2 vols, unpublished Ph. D. thesis, Indiana University.

Ardener, E. W. (1961) 'Social and Demographic Problems of the Southern Cameroons Plantation Area', in Aidan Southall (ed.), *Social Change in Modern Africa,* London, pp. 83-97.

Ardener, Shirley G. (1964) 'A Comparative Study of Rotating Credit Associations', *Journal of the Royal Anthropological Institute,* **94**(2), 201-29.

Ardener, Shirley G. (1973) 'Sexual Insult and Female Militancy', *Man,* **8**, 422-40.

*Aronson, Lisa (1980) 'Akwete Weaving and Patronage', *African Arts,* **13**, 62-6.

Aronson, Lisa (1982) 'Akwete Weaving: A Study of Change in Response to the Palm Oil Trade in the Nineteenth Century', unpublished Ph.D. thesis, Indiana University.

Arrighi, Giovanni (1970) 'Labour Supplies in Historical Perspective: A Study of the Proletarianization of the African Peasantry in Rhodesia', *Journal of Development Studies,* **6**, 2, 224-48.

Ashby, Jacqueline A. (1982) 'New Models for Agricultural Research and Extension: The Need to Integrate Women and the Crisis in Agriculture', in

Barbara Lewis (ed.), *Invisible Farmers: Women and the Crisis in Agriculture,* Washington, D.C., pp. 144-95.

Awe, Bolanle (1975) 'Asude: Yoruba Jewelsmiths', *African Arts,* **9**, 60-70.

*Awe, Bolanle (1977) 'The Iyalode in the Traditional Yoruba Political System', in Alice Schlegel (ed.), *Sexual Stratification: A Cross-Cultural View,* New York, pp. 144-95.

Bâ, Mariama (1981a) 'Interview' with Barbara Harrell-Bond, *The African Book Publishing Record,* **6** 3 and 4, 209-14.

Bâ, Mariama (1981b) *So Long A Letter,* Modupé Bodé-Thomas (trans.), Ibadan.

Balandier, Georges (1956) *Sociologie des Brazzavilles Noires,* Paris.

Bandler, Jane and Bandler, Donald (1977) 'The Pottery of Ushafa', *African Arts,* **9**, 26-31.

Barnes, Barbara (1979) 'ZANU Women Meet', *Southern African Magazine,* Jul./Aug., 8-9.

Bascom, W. and Herskovits, M. J. (eds.) (1959) *Continuity and Change in African Cultures,* Chicago.

Baumann, Hermann (1928) 'The Division of Work According to Sex in African Hoe Culture', *Africa,* **1** 3, 289-319.

*Bay, Edna (1982) (ed.) *Women and Work in Africa,* London.

Ben-Amos, Dan (1975) *Sweet Words: Storytelling Events in Benin,* Philadelphia.

Ben-Amos, Dan (1977) 'Introduction', in Bernth Lindfors (ed.), *Forms of Folklore in Africa,* Austin, Texas, pp. 1-34.

Beneria, Lourdes (1981) 'Conceptualizing The Labor Force: The Underestimation of Women's Economic Activities', in Nici Nelson (ed.), *African Women in the Development Process,* London, pp. 10-28.

Beneria, Lourdes, and Sen, Gita (1981) 'Accumulation, Reproduction, and Women's Role in Economic Development: Boserup Revisited', *Signs: Journal of Women in Culture and Society,* **7** 2, 279-98.

Berger, Iris (1976) 'Rebels or Status Seekers? Women as Spirit Mediums in East Africa', in Nancy Hafkin and Edna Bay (eds.), *Women in Africa: Studies in Social and Economic Change,* Stanford, Calif., pp. 157-82.

Berger, Iris (1982) 'Sources of Class Consciousness: The Experience of Women Workers in South Africa, 1973-1980', Boston University African Studies Center Working Paper No. 55, Boston, Mass.

*Bernstein, Hilda (1975) *For Their Triumphs and for Their Tears: Women in Apartheid South Africa,* Cambridge, Mass.

*Bledsoe, Caroline H. (1980) *Women and Marriage in Kpelle Society.* Stanford, Calif.

Blumberg, Rae Lesser (1982) 'Females, Farming, and Food: Rural Development and Women's participation in Agricultural Production Systems, in Barbara Lewis (ed.), *Invisible Farmers: Women and the Crisis in Agriculture,* Washington, D.C., pp. 24-102.

Bohannon, Laura (1968) 'Dahomean Marriage: A Revaluation', in Paul Bohannon and John Middleton (eds), *Marriage, Family, and Residence,* Garden City, N.Y., pp. 85-107.

*Boserup, Ester (1970) *Woman's Role in Economic Development,* New York.

Brain, James L. (1976) 'Less than Second Class: Women and Rural Settlement Schemes in Tanzania', in Nancy Hafkin and Edna Bay (eds.), *Women in Africa: Studies in Social and Economic Change,* Stanford, Calif., pp. 265-84.

Brain, James L. (1978) 'Symbolic Rebirth: The Mwali Rite Among the Luguru of Eastern Tanzania', *Africa,* **48** 2, 176-88.

*Breidenbach, Paul (1979) 'The Woman on the Beach and the Man in the Bush: Leadership and Adepthood in the Twelve Apostle Movement of Ghana', in Bennetta Jules-Rosette(ed.), *The New Religions of Africa,* Norwood,N.J.,pp.

99-125.

Brooks, Charlotte K. (1974) (ed.), *African Rhythms*, New York.

Brown, Barbara B. (1980a) *Women, Migrant Labor, and Social Change in Botswana*. African Studies Center Working Paper No. 41.

Brown, Barbara B. (1980b) 'Women's Role in Development in Botswana', *Rural Sociology Report Series*, No. 17, Gaborone.

Bruce, Judith and Staudt, Kathleen (1981) 'Training for Development Planning and Women: A Course Outline Taught at the Eastern and Southern Management Institute, Arusha', The Population Council, New York.

Bryceson, Deborah (1980) 'Proletarianization of Tanzanian Women', *Review of African Political Economy*, **17**, 4-17.

Bryceson, Deborah Fahy and Mbilinyi, Marjorie (1980) 'The Changing Role of Tanzanian Women in Production', in A. O. Anacleti (ed.), *Jipemoyo 2*, Uppsala.

Bryson, Judy (1981) 'Women and Agriculture in Sub-Saharan Africa: Implications for Development', in Nici Nelson (ed.), *African Women in the Development Process*, London, pp. 28-46.

Bujra, Janet M. (1975) 'Women "Entrepreneurs" of Early Nairobi', *Canadian Journal of African Studies*, **9** 2, 213-34.

Bujra, Janet M. (1977) 'Production, Property, Prostitution: Sexual Politics in Atu', *Cahiers d'Etudes Africaines*, **17**, 13-39.

*Bukh, Jette (1979) *The Village Woman in Ghana*, Uppsala.

Bunger, Robert L. (1973) *Islamization Among the Upper Pokomo*, Syracuse, N.Y.

Cabral, Amilcar (1974) *Return to the Source: Selected Speeches*, New York.

Calame-Griaule, Geneviève (1965) *Ethnologie et Langage: la parole chez les Dogon*, Paris.

Caldwell, John C. (1968) *Population Growth and Family Change in Africa*, Canberra.

*Caplan, Patricia and Bujra, Janet (1979) *Women United, Women Divided*, New York.

Caplan, Patricia (1981) 'Development Policies in Tanzania—Some Implications for Women', in Nici Nelson (ed.), *African Women in the Development Process*, London, pp. 98-108.

Carr, Marilyn (1978) *Appropriate Technology for African Women*, Addis Ababa.

Casely-Hayford, Gladys (1967) 'Freetown', in Donatus Ibe Nwoga (ed.), *West African Verse*, London, p. 6.

Caughman, Susan (1981) 'Women at Work in Mali: The Case of the Markala Cooperative', Boston University African Studies Center Working Paper No. 50, Boston, Mass.

(Cereals II) (1980) 'Senegal Cereals Production Project II, Project Paper', AID mimeo, Washington, D.C.

Chagnon, Napoleon A. (1968) *Yanomamo: The Fierce People*, New York.

Chaliand, Gerard (1971) *Armed Struggle in Africa*, New York.

Chaney, Elsa M. (1980) 'Women in International Migration', WID/AID, Washington, D.C.

Chauncey, George Jr. (1981) 'The Locus of Reproduction: Women's Labor in the Zambian Copperbelt, 1927-1953', *Journal of Southern African Studies*, **7** 2, 135-64.

Churucheminzwa, Sarudzai (1974) 'Why I Joined ZANLA's Women's Detachment', *Zimbabwe News*, Maputo, June 1977.

Ciancanelli, Penelope (1980) 'Exchange, Reproduction and Sex Subordination Among the Kikuyu of East Africa', *Review of Radical Political Economy*, **12** 2, 25-36.

Clark, Carolyn (1980) 'Land and Food, Women and Power in Nineteenth

Century Kikuyu', *Africa,* **50** 4, 357-70.

Cliffe, Lionel (1976) 'Rural Political Economy of Africa', in P. Gutkind and I. Wallerstein (eds.), *The Political Economy of Contemporary Africa,* London.

Cliffe, Lionel and Moorsom, Richard (1979) 'Rural Class Formation and Ecological Collapse in Botswana', *Review of African Political Economy,* **15/16,** 35-52.

Clignet, R. and Sween J. (1969) 'Social Change and Type of Marriage,' *American Journal of Sociology,* **75,** 123-45.

Cloud, Kathleen (1978) 'Sex Roles in Food Production and Distribution in the Sahel', *Proceedings and Papers of the International Conference on Women and Food,* **3** Jan., University of Arizona, Tucson.

Cohen, Abner (1969) *Custom and Politics in Urban Africa,* London.

*Cole, E. (1967) *House of Bondage,* New York.

Collier, Jane and Rosaldo, Michelle, (1981) 'Politics and Gender in Simple Societies', in Sherry Ortner and Harriet Whitehead (eds.), *Sexual Meaning,* Cambridge, UK, pp. 275-329.

*Colligan, Paddy (1981) *Soweto Remembered: Conversations with Freedom Fighters,* New York.

*Collins, Carol (1977) *This is the Time: Interview with Two Namibian Women,* Chicago.

Collins, Carol (1978) 'The Women Militants', in Liberation Support Movement, *Namibia: SWAPO Fights for Freedom,* Oakland, Calif.

Comhaire-Sylvain, S. (1969) *Femmes de Kinshasa,* Paris.

Condé, Maryse (1981) *Saison à Rihata* (Season in Rihata), Paris.

Conti, Anna (1979) 'Capitalist Organization of Production Through Non-Capitalist Relations: Women's Role in a Pilot Resettlement in Upper Volta', *Review of African Political Economy,* **15/16,** 35-52.

Cornwall, Barbara (1972) *The Bush Rebels,* New York.

Cronise, Florence M. and Ward, H. W. (1903) *Cunnie Rabbit, Mr Spider, and the Other Beef: West African Folktales,* London.

Cross-Upcott, A. R. W. (1955) 'Barikiwa Pottery', *Tanganyika Notes and Records,* **40** Sept., 24-9.

D'Azevedo, Warren L. (1976) 'The Setting of Gola Society and Culture: Some Theoretical Implications of Variations in Time and Space', *Krober Anthropological Society Papers,* **21,** 43-125.

Deere, Carmen (1976) 'Rural Women's Subsistence Production in the Capitalist Periphery', *Review of Radical Political Economics,* **8** 1, 9-17.

DeLancey, Viriginia (1977) 'Women at the Cameroon Development Corporation: How Their Money Works', Paper presented at the 1977 African Studies Association Annual Meeting.

Denzer, LaRay (1981) 'Constance A. Cummings-John of Sierra Leone: Her Early Political Career', *Tarikh,* **25,** 20-32.

De Thé, Marie-Paule (1970) 'Des associations secrètes aux associations modernes: la femme dans la dynamique de la société Beti, 1887-1966', Thèse pour le doctorat de troisième cycle, Ecole Pratique des Hautes Etudes, Paris.

Dhlomo, Herbert I. E. (1935) *The Girl Who Killed to Save: Nongqase the Liberator,* Lovedale, South Africa.

Dikobe, Modikwe (1973) *The Marabi Dance,* London.

Dirasse, Laketch (1978) 'The Socio-economic Position of Women in Addis Ababa:The Case of Prostitution', unpublished Ph.D. thesis, Boston University.

Dixon, Ruth B. (1980) 'Assessing the Impact of Development Projects on Women', AID Program Evaluation Discussion Paper No. 8., Washington, D.C.

Dobert, Margarita (1970) 'Liberation and the Women of Guinea', *African*

Report, **15** 7, 26-8.

D'Onofrio-Flores, P. M. and Pfafflin, S. M. (1982) (eds.), *Scientific-Technological Changes and the Role of Women in Development,* Boulder, Colo.

Donohugh, Agnes C. L. and Berry, Priscilla (1932) 'A Luba Tribe in Katanga: Customs and Folklore', *Africa,* **5,** 176-83.

Dorjahn, V. R. (1959) 'The Factor of Polygyny in African Demography', in W. R. Bascom and M. Herskovits (eds.), *Continuity and Change in African Cultures,* Chicago, pp. 87-112.

Draper, Patricia (1975) '!Kung Women: Contrasts in Sexual Egalitarianism in Foraging and Sedentary Contexts', in Rayna Reiter (ed.), *Toward an Anthropology of Women,* New York, pp. 77-109.

Duerden, Dennis and Pieterse, Cosmo (1974) (eds.), *African Writers Talking,* London.

Dugast, Idelette (1955) *Monographie de la Tribu des Ndiki: Banen du Cameroun,* Paris.

Dulansey, Maryanne (1976) 'Can Technology Help Women Feed their Families? Post Harvest Storage, Processing and Cooking — Some Observations', *Women and Development,* Final Report of AAAS Workshop for US Department of State, Washington, D.C., Mar. 1976.

Dupire, Marguerite (1971) 'The Position of Women in a Pastoral Society', in Denise Paulme (ed.), *Women of Tropical Africa,* Berkeley, Calif.

(EAP, NLC) East African Protectorate (1913) *1912-13 Native Labour Commission, Evidence and Report,* Nairobi.

Ehrenreich, Barbara and English, Deirdre (1979) *For Her Own Good: 150 Years of Experts' Advice to Women,* Garden City, N.Y.

*Ekwensi, Cyprian (1961) *Jagua Nana,* New York.

Elkan, Walter (1957) 'The Employment of Women in Uganda', *Bulletin de l'Institut Interafricain du Travail,* **4** 4, 8-23.

El-Saadawi, Nawal (1981) *The Hidden Face of Eve: Women in the Arab World,* Boston, Mass.

Emecheta, Buchi (1976) *The Bride Price,* London.

Emecheta, Buchi (1977) *Second-Class Citizen,* London, 1974; repr. 1977.

*Emecheta, Buchi (1979) *The Joys of Motherhood,* New York.

Epstein, A. L. (1967) 'Urbanization and Social Change in Africa', *Current Anthropology,* **8** 3, Oct., 275-95.

Etienne, Mona (1980) 'Women and Men, Cloth and Colonization: The Transformation of Production-Distribution Relations among the Baule (Ivory Coast)', in Mona Etienne and Eleanor Leacock, (eds.), *Women and Colonization,* New York, pp. 214-38.

Evans-Pritchard, E. E. (1965) *The Position of Women in Primitive Societies and Other Essays in Social Anthropology,* London.

Fazan, S. H. (1932) 'Memo on the Rate of Population Increase of the Kikuyu Tribe', cyclostyled, Nairobi.

Federal Republic of Nigeria, National Manpower Board (1968) *Labor Force Sample Survey—1967,* I. Lagos.

Finnegan, Ruth (1970) *Oral Literature in Africa,* Oxford.

Fisher, Allan G. and Fisher, Humphrey J. (1971) *Slavery and Muslim Society in Africa,* New York.

Fortmann, Louise (1978) 'Women and Tanzania Agricultural Development', Economic Research Bureau Paper 77.4, mimeo, University of Dar es Salaam.

Fortmann, Louise (1979) 'The Plight of the Invisible Farmer: The Effect of National Agricultural Development Policy on Women', in *Women and Development,* Final Report of AAAS Workshop for US Department of State, Washington, D.C.

Fugard, Athol (1969) *Boesman and Lena*, Cape Town.
Geertz, Clifford (1966) 'The Rotating Credit Association: A "Middle Rung" in Development', in I. M. Wallerstein (ed.), *Social Change: The Colonial Situation*, New York, pp. 420-46.
Gemery, Henry and Hogendorn, Jan (eds.) (1978) *The Uncommon Market: Essays in the Economic History of the Atlantic Slave Trade*, New York.
Gessain, Monique (1971) 'Coniagui Women (Guinea)', in Denise Paulme (ed.), *Women of Tropical Africa*, Berkeley, Calif., pp. 17-46.
Ghana, Census Office (1961) *1960 Census—Special Report A*, Accra.
*Glaze, Anita (1975) 'Women Power and Art in a Senufo Village', *African Arts*, 3, 25-9; 65-8.
Goody, Jack (1973) 'Polygyny, Economy, and the Role of Women', in Jack Goody (ed.), *The Character of Kinship*, Cambridge, pp. 175-90.
Goody, Jack and Buckley, Joan (1973) 'Inheritance and Women's Labour in Africa', *Africa*, 43, 108-21.
Gordon, David (1972) *Women of Algeria*, Cambridge, Mass.
Gordon, Elizabeth 'An Analysis of the Impact of Labour Migration on the Lives of Women in Lesotho', in Nici Nelson (ed.), *African Women in the Development Process*, London, pp. 59-76.
Griaule, Marcel (1938) *Jeux Dogons (Dogon Games)*, Paris.
Grindle, Merilee, (ed.) (1980) *Political and Policy Implementation in the Third World*, Princeton, NJ.
Guyer, Jane (1978) 'The Food Economy and French Colonial Rule in Central Cameroun', *Journal of African History*, 29 4, 577-97.
Guyer, Jane (1980) 'Food, Cocoa, and the Division of Labour by Sex in Two West African Societies', *Comparative Studies in Society and History*, 22 3, 355-73.
Guyer, Jane (1981) 'The Raw, the Cooked, and the Half-Baked: A Note on the Division of Labor by Sex'. *Boston University African Studies Center Working Paper No. 48*, Boston, Mass.
*Hafkin, Nancy and Bay, Edna (eds.) (1976) *Women in Africa: Studies in Social and Economic Change*, Stanford, Calif.
Hahn, Theophilus (1881) *Tsuni-//Goam, The Supreme Being of the Khoi Khoi*, London.
*Hanna, W. J. and Hanna, J. L. (1972) *Urban Dynamics of Black Africa*, Chicago.
Hansen, Karen Tranberg (1979) 'When Sex Becomes a Critical Variable, Married Women and Extra-Domestic Work in Lusaka', Paper presented at the African Studies Association annual meetings in Los Angeles, Nov. 1979.
Harrell-Bond, Barbara (1975) *Modern Marriage in Sierra Leone*, The Hague.
Harris, Marvin (1959) 'Labour Migration Among the Mozambique Thonga: Cultural and Political Factors', *Africa*, 29 1, 50-65.
Haswell, Margaret (1975) *The Nature of Poverty*, London.
Hay, Margaret Jean (1972) 'Economic Change in Luoland: Kowe, 1890-1945', unpublished Ph.D. thesis, University of Wisconsin.
*Hay, Margaret Jean (1976) 'Luo Women and Economic Change During the Colonial Period', in Nancy Hafkin and Edna Bay (eds.), *Women in Africa; Studies in Social and Economic Change*, Stanford, Calif.
Hay, Margaret Jean (1982) 'Women as Owners, Occupants, and Managers of Property in Colonial Western Kenya', in Margaret Jean Hay and Marcia Wright (eds.), *African Women and the Law: Historical Perspectives*, Boston.
Hay, Margaret Jean and Wright, Marcia (eds.) (1982) *African Women and the Law: Historical Perspectives*, Boston, Mass.
Head, Bessie (1973) *A Question of Power*, London.

Hedlund, Hans (1979) 'Contradictions in the Peripheralization of a Pastoral Society: The Maasai', *Review of African Political Economy,* **15/16**, 15-34.

Hellman, E. (1948) *Rooiyard: A Slum in Johannesburg*, Cape Town.

Henn, Jeanne K. (1978) 'Peasants, Workers and Capital: The Political Economy of Labor and Incomes in Cameroon', unpublished Ph.D. thesis, Harvard University.

Herskovits, Melville J. (1938) *Dahomey: An Ancient West African Kingdom*, New York.

*High-Wasikhongo, Frieda (1980) 'Akwete Weaving and Patronage', *Africa Arts,* **13**, 62-6.

High-Wasikhongo, Frieda (1981) *Traditional African Art: A Female Focus*, Elvehjem Museum of Art, University of Wisconsin, Madison.

Hill, Polly (1963) *The Migrant Cocoa-Farmers of Southern Ghana*, Cambridge.

Hill, Polly (1969) 'Hidden Trade in Hausaland', *Man,* **4** 3, 392-409.

Hill, Polly (1977) *Population, Prosperity and Poverty: Rural Kano, 1900 and 1970*, Cambridge.

Hill, Polly (1978) 'Food-Farming and Migration from Fante Villages'. *Africa,* **48** 3, 220-30.

Hoch-Smith, Judith (1978) 'Radical Yoruba Female Sexuality: The Witch and the Prostitute', in Judith Hoch-Smith and Anita Spring (eds.), *Women in Ritual and Symbolic Roles*, New York, pp. 245-67.

Hoffer, Carol (1972) 'Mende and Sherbro Women in High Offices', *Canadian Journal of African Studies,* **6** 2, 151-64.

The Holy Bible, Revised Standard Version.

*Hosken, Fran (1979) *The Hosken Report*, Lexington, Mass.

Huber, Hugo (1968/69) 'Woman Marriage in Some East African Societies', *Anthropos,* **63/64**, 745-52.

Huntington, Suellen (1975) 'Issues in Woman's Role in Economic Development: Critique and Alternatives', *Journal of Marriage and the Family,* **37**, 1001-12.

(IFPRI) International Food Policy Research Institute (1980) 'Food Needs of Developing Countries: Projection of Production and Consumption to 1990', Washington, D.C.

(ILO) International Labour Organization (1975a) *Womanpower: The World's Female Labour Force in 1975 and the Outlook for 2000.* Geneva.

(ILO) International Labour Organization (1975b) *Yearbook of Labour Statistics, 1975.* Geneva.

(ILO) International Labour Organization (1977) *Labour Force Estimates and Projections, 1950-2000*, 2nd ed., Geneva.

(ILO) International Labor Organization (1978) 'Women, Technology, and the Development Process', mimeo paper prepared for the African Regional Meeting of UNCSTD, Cairo, July 24-29, 1978.

*Isaacman, Barbara and Stephen, June (1980) *Mozambique: Women, the Law, and Agrarian Reform*, Addis Ababa.

Jacobs, Alan H. (1975) 'Maasai Pastoralism in Historical Perspective', in Theodore Monod (ed.), *Pastoralism in Tropical Africa*, London.

Johnson, Cheryl (1981) 'Madam Alimotu Pelewura and the Lagos Market Women', *Tarikh,* **25**, 1-10.

Johnston, Hugh Anthony Stevens (ed. and trans.) (1966) *A Selection of Hausa Stories*, Oxford.

Jones, A. M. (1943) 'African Music', Rhodes-Livingstone Museum Occasional Paper No. 2.

Jones, Christina C. (1982) 'Women's Legal Access to Land', in Barbara Lewis (ed.), *Invisible Farmers: Women and the Crisis in Agriculture*, Washington, D.C., pp. 196-238.

*Jules-Rosette, Bennetta (1979) 'Symbols of Power and Change: An Introduction to New Perspectives on Contemporary and African Religion', in Bennetta Jules-Rosette (ed.), *The New Religions of Africa*. Norwood, N.J., pp. 1-21.

Kaberry, Phyllis (1952) *Women of the Grass Fields: A Study of the Economic Position of Women in Bamenda*, London.

Kamarck, Andrew (1967) *The Economics of African Development* New York.

Kéita, Aoua (1975) *Femme d'Afrique: La Vie d'Aoua Kéita racontée par elle-meme (African Woman: The Life of Aoua Keita as told by Herself)*, Paris.

Kenyatta, Jomo (1938) *Facing Mount Kenya: The Tribal Life of the Gikuyu*, London.

Kershaw, Greet (1975/1976) 'The Changing Roles of Men and Women in the Kikuyu Family by Socio-economic Status', *Rural Africana*, **29**, 173-94.

Kettel, Bonnie (1981) 'Gender and Class in Tugen-Kalenjin Social Organization', paper presented at African Studies Association Annual Meeting, 1981.

Kitching, Gavin (1980) *Class and Economic Change in Kenya*, New Haven, Conn.

Kjaerby, Finn 'The Dynamic History of the Subordination of Women in Classless African Societies', paper presented to the BRALUP Workshop on Women's Studies and Development, University of Dar es Salaam, 1979.

Klein, Martin and Robertson, Claire (eds.) (forthcoming) *Women and Slavery*, Madison, Wisc.

Koenig, Dolores B. (1977) 'Sex, Work, and Social Class in Cameroon', unpublished Ph.D. thesis, Northwestern University.

Krapf-Askari, E. (1969) *Yoruba Towns and Cities*, London.

Krug, A. N. (1949) 'Bulu Tales', *Journal of American Folklore*, **62**, 348-74.

Laburthe-Tolra, Phillippe (1977) *Minlaaba: Histoire et société traditionnelle chez les Beti du Sud Cameroun*, Paris.

Ladipo, Patricia (1981) 'Developing Women's Cooperatives: An Experiment in Rural Nigeria', in Nici Nelson (ed.), *African Women in the Development Process*, London, pp. 123-36.

Lambert, H. E. (1956) *Kikuyu Social and Political Institutions*, London.

La Pin, Deirdre (1977) 'Story, Medium and Masque: The Idea and Art of Yoruba Story-telling', unpublished Ph.D. thesis, University of Wisconsin.

Lapchick, Richard and Urdang, Stephanie (eds.) (1980) 'The Effects of Apartheid on the Employment of Women in South Africa', background paper for the UN World Conference on the United Nations Decade for Women, July 14-30, 1980, Copenhagen.

*Lapchick, Richard and Urdang, Stephanie (1982) *Oppression and Resistance: The Struggle of Women in Southern Africa*, Westport, Conn.

Laye, Camara (1959) *The African Child*, Glasgow, first published as *L'Enfant Noir*, Paris, 1953.

Leach, Edmund (1973) 'Complementary Filiation and Bilateral Kinship', in Jack Goody (ed.), *The Character of Kinship*, Cambridge, 1973, pp. 48-58.

Lebeuf, Annie M. D. (1971) 'The Role of Women in the Political Organization of African Societies', in Denise Paulme, (ed.), *Women of Tropical Africa*, Berkeley, Calif., pp. 93-120.

Leeuwenberg, Jef (1977) *Transkei: A Study in Economic Regression*, London.

Legassick, Martin (1977) 'Gold, Agriculture, and Secondary Industry in South Africa, 1885-1970', in Robin Palmer and Neil Parsons (eds.), *The Roots of Rural Poverty in Central and Southern Africa*, Berkeley, Calif., pp. 175-200.

Leith-Ross, Sylvia (1939) *African Women*, London.

*LeVine, Sarah (1979) *Mothers and Wives: Gusii Women of East Africa*, Chicago.

Lewis, Barbara (1976) 'The Limitations of Group Action Among Entrepreneurs: The Market Women of Abidjan, Ivory Coast', in Nancy Hafkin and Edna Bay (eds.), *Women in Africa: Studies in Social and Economic Change*, Stanford, Calif., pp. 135-56.

*Lewis, Barbara (1977) 'Economic Activity and Marriage Among Ivoirian Urban Women', in Alice Schlegel (ed.), *Sexual Stratification: A Cross-Cultural View*, New York, pp. 161-91.

Lewis, I. M. (1971) *Ecstatic Religion: An Anthropological Study of Spirit Possession and Shamanism*, Harmondsworth.

Liberation Support Movement (n.d.) *The Mozambican Woman in Revolution*, Richmond, B.C.

Liedholm, C and Chuta, E. (1976) 'The Economics of Rural and Urban Small-Scale Industries in Sierra Leone', African Rural Economy Paper No. 14, Michigan State University.

Little, Kenneth (1949) 'The Role of the Secret Society in Cultural Specialization', *American Anthropologist,* **51**, 199-212.

Little, Kenneth (1966) *West African Urbanization: A Study of Voluntary Associations in Social Change*, Cambridge.

Little, Kenneth (1972) 'Voluntary Associations and Social Mobility Among West African Women', *Canadian Journal of African Studies,* **6** 2, 275-88.

*Little, Kenneth (1973) *African Women in Towns*, London.

Llewelyn-Davies, Melissa (1979) 'Two Contexts of Solidarity Among Pastoral Maasai Women', in Patricia Caplan and Janet Bujra (eds.), *Women United, Women Divided*, New York, pp. 206-37.

Lloyd, P. C. *et al.*, (1967) *The City of Ibadan*, Cambridge.

*Longmore, L. (1959) *The Dispossessed*, London.

Lucas, Robert (1979) 'The Distribution and Efficiency of Crop Production in Tribal Areas of Botswana', African Studies Center Working Paper No. 20, Boston, Mass.

MacCormack, Carol Hoffer (1977) 'Wono: Institutionalized Dependency in Sherbro Descent Groups (Sierra Leone)', in Suzanne Miers and Igor Kopytoff (eds.), *Slavery in Africa: Historical and Anthropological Perspectives*, Madison, Wisc., pp. 181-203.

Machel, Josina (n.d.) 'The Role of Women in the Struggle', in Liberation Support Movement, *The Mozambican Women in Revolution*, Richmond, B.C.

Machel, Samora (n.d.) 'The Liberation of Women is a Fundamental Necessity for the Revolution' (1973), in Samora Machel, *Mozambique: Sowing the Seeds of Revolution, Speeches by Samora Machel*, London, c. 1974.

Machel, Samora (1977) 'Opening Address to the Second Conference of OMM, Maputo, 1976', in *Documents of the Second Conference of the Organization of Mozambican Women*, Maputo (Unofficial translation).

Maher, Vanessa (1974) *Women and Property in Morocco*, Cambridge.

Mandeville, Elizabeth (1979) 'Poverty, Work and the Financing of Single Women in Kampala', *Africa,* **49** 1, 42-52.

Manga Mado, Henri-Richard *Complaintes d'un forcat*, Yaoundé.

*Mann, Kristin (1982) 'Women's Rights in Law and Practice: Marriage and Dispute Settlement in Colonial Lagos', in Margaret Jean Hay and Marcia Wright (eds.), *African Women and the Law: Historical Perspectives*, Boston, Mass., pp. 151-71.

Manning, Patrick (1981) 'The Enslavement of Africans: A Demographic Model', *Canadian Journal of African Studies,* **15** 3, 499-526.

Mariotti, Amelia (1979) 'The Incorporation of African Women into Wage Employment in South Africa, 1920-1970', unpublished Ph.D. thesis, University of Connecticut, Storrs.

Matthews, Thomas (1977) 'Mural Painting in South Africa', *African Arts,* **10**, 28-33.

*Mba, Nina (1982) *Nigerian Women Mobilized: Women's Political Activity in Southern Nigeria, 1900-1965*, Berkeley, Calif.

*McGrath, Phyllis (1976) *The Unfinished Assignment: Equal Education for Women*, Washington, D.C.

McSweeney, Brenda Gael (1979) 'Collection and Analysis of Data on Rural Women's Time Use', *Studies in Family Planning,* 11 11/12, 379-83.

McSweeney, Brenda Gael and Freedman, Marion (1980) 'Lack of Time as an Obstacle to Women's Education: The Case of Upper Volta', *Comparative Education Review,* 24 2, part 2.

Meillassoux, Claude (1964) *Anthropologie économique des Gouro de Côte d'Ivoire*, Paris.

Meillassoux, Claude (1972) 'From Reproduction to Production: A Marxist Approach to Economic Anthropology', *Economy and Society,* 1, 93-105.

Meillassoux, Claude (1981) *Maidens, Meal and Money: Capitalism and the Domestic Community*, Cambridge.

Meinhoff, Carl (1921) *Africanische Märchen (African tales),* Jena, East Germany.

*Mernissi, Fatima (1975) *Beyond the Veil: Male-Female Dynamics in a Modern Muslim Society*, New York.

Michelmann, Cherry (1975) *The Black Sash of South Africa: A Case Study in Liberalism*, London.

Middleton, John (1981) 'Christianity', 'Islam', and 'Traditional Religion', in Roland Oliver and Michael Crowder (eds.), *Cambridge Encyclopedia of Africa*, Cambridge, pp. 406-12.

Middleton-Keirn, Susan (1978) 'Convivial Sisterhood: Spirit Mediumship and Client-Core Networks Among Black South African Women', in Judith Hoch-Smith and Anita Spring (eds.), *Women in Ritual and Symbolic Roles*, New York. pp. 191-205.

Miers, Suzanne and Kopytoff, Igor (eds.) (1977) *Slavery in Africa: Historical and Anthropological Perspectives*, Madison, Wisc.

Minon, P. (1960) *Katuba: étude quantitative d'une communauté urbaine africaine*, Liège.

Mitchell, J. Clyde (1961) 'Social Change and the Stability of African Marriage in Northern Rhodesia' in Aidan Southall (ed.), *Social Change in Modern Africa,* London pp. 316-29.

Molnos, Angela (1973) *Cultural Source Materials for Population Planning in East Africa, III: Beliefs and Practices*, Nairobi.

Moock, Peter (1976) 'The Efficiency of Women as Farm Managers: Kenya', *American Journal of Agricultural Economics,* 58, 831-5.

Mueller, Martha (1977) 'Women and Men, Power and Powerlessness in Lesotho', in Wellesley Editorial Committee (ed.), *Women and National Development*, Chicago, pp. 154-66.

Mugabe, Robert (1979) 'Opening Speech to the First Zimbabwe Women's Seminar, May 1979', Zimbabwe News, Maputo.

Mullings, Leith (1976) 'Women and Economic Change in Africa', in Nancy Hafkin and Edna Bay (eds.), *Women in Africa: Studies in Social and Economic Change*, Stanford, Calif., pp. 239-64.

Murray, Colin (1977) 'High Bridewealth, Migrant Labour and the Position of Women in Lesotho', *Journal of African Law,* 21 1, 79-96.

Murray, Colin (1979) 'The Work of Men, Women, and the Ancestors: Social Repro-duction in the Periphery of South Africa', in Sandra Wallman (eds.), *Social Anthropology of Work*, New York.

Murray, Jocelyn (1974) 'The Kikuyu Female Circumcision Controversy, with Special Reference to the Church Missionary Society's Sphere of Influence', unpublished Ph.D. thesis, University of California at Los Angeles.

Mutiso, Gideon (n.d.) 'Mbai sya Eitu: A Low Status Group in Centre-Periphery Relations', unpublished paper, University of Nairobi.

Nadel, S. F. (1942) *A Black Byzantium*, London.

Nelson, Nici (1979) ' "Women Must Help Each Other": The Operation of Personal Networks Among Buzaa Beer Brewers in Mathare Valley, Kenya', in Patricia Caplan and Janet Bujra (eds.), *Women United, Women Divided*, New York, pp. 77-98.

*Nelson, Nici (ed.) (1981) *African Women in the Development Process*, London.

Newland, Kathleen (1975) *Women in Politics: A Global Review*, Washington, D.C.

Newland, Kathleen (1980) *Men, Women, and the Division of Labor*, World Watch Paper No. 37, Washington, D.C.

Ngugi wa Thiong'o, (1977) *Petals of Blood*, London.

Nketia, J. H. Kabwena (1969) *Funeral Dirges of the Akan People*, New York.

Nwapa, Flora (1966) *Efuru*, London.

Nwapa, Flora (1970) *Idu*, London.

Nyerere, Julius K. "Socialism and Rural Development," in Julius K. Nyerere, *Ujamaa: Essays on Socialism*. London and New York, 1968.

Nzula, A., Potekhin, I. I. and Zusmanovich, A. Z. (1979) *Forced Labour in Colonial Africa*, London.

O'Barr, Jean (1972) 'Cell Leaders in Tanzania', *African Studies Review,* **15**, 437-66.

O'Barr, Jean (1975a) 'Making the Invisible Visible: African Women in Politics and Policy', *African Studies Review,* **18**, 19-28.

O'Barr, Jean (1975b) *Third World Women: Factors in their Changing Status*, Durham, N.C.

O'Barr, Jean (1976) 'Pare Women: A Case of Political Involvement; *Rural Africana,* **29**, 121-34.

Obbo, Christine (1976) 'Dominant Male Ideology and Female Options: Three East African Case Studies', *Africa,* **46** 4, 371-89.

*Obbo, Christine (1980) *African Women: Their Struggle for Economic Independence*, London.

Oboler, Regina (1980) 'Is the Female Husband a Man?' *Ethnology,* **19** 1, 69-88.

Ochieng', William R. (1975) 'Editorial', *Kenya Historical Review,* **3** 2, i-iv.

Ogot, Grace (1964) 'The Rain Came', in Ellis Ajitey and Ezekiel Mphahlele (eds.), *Modern African Stories*, London, 180-9.

O'Kelly, Elizabeth (1973) *Aid and Self-Help*, London.

Okeyo, Achola Pala (1979) 'Women in the Household Economy: Managing Multiple Roles', *Studies in Family Planning,* **10**, 337-43.

Okeyo, Achola Pala (1980a) 'The Joluo Equation', *Ceres*, May-June, 37-42.

Okeyo, Achola Pala (1980b) 'Daughters of the Lakes and Rivers', in Mona Etienne and Eleanor Leacock (eds.), *Women and Colonization: Anthropological Perspectives,* New York, pp. 186-213.

Okonjo, Kamene (1976) 'The Dual Sex Political System in Operation: Igbo Women and Community Politics in Midwestern Nigeria', in Nancy Hafkin and Edna Bay (eds.), *Women in Africa: Studies in Social and Economic Change*, Stanford, Calif., pp. 45-58.

O'Laughlin, Bridget (1974) 'Mediation of Contradiction: Why Mbum Women Do Not Eat Chicken', in Michelle Rosaldo and Louise Lamphere (eds.), *Women, Culture, and Society*, Stanford, Calif., pp. 301-18.

*Oppong, Christine (1974) *Marriage Among a Matrilineal Elite*, Cambridge.

Owuor, Henry (1967) 'Luo Songs', in Ulli Beier (ed.), *Introduction to African Literature*, London, 50-6.

(Pala Okeyo *see* Okeyo, Acola Pala)

Parkin, David J. (1969) *Neighbors and Nationals in an East African City Ward*, Berkeley, Calif.

Parkin, David J. (1972) *Palms, Wine, and Witnesses*, San Francisco, Calif.

Paulme, Denise (ed.) (1971) *Women of Tropical Africa*, Berkeley, Calif., first published as *Femmes d'Afrique Noire*, Paris, 1960.

*p'Bitek, Okot (1966) *Song of Lawino: An African Lament*, Nairobi.

p'Bitek, Okot (1970) *Song of Ocol*, Nairobi.

Pélissier, Paul (1966) *Les Paysans du Sénégal*, Saint-Yrieix.

Pellow, Deborah (1977) *Women in Accra*, Algonac, Mich.

Perham, Margery (1937) *Native Administration in Nigeria*, London.

Poewe, Karla (1978) 'Matriliny in the Throes of Change: Kinship, Descent and Marriage in Luapula, Zambia', *Africa*, **48** 3, 205-18.

Pons, V. (1969) *Stanleyville*, London.

*Potash, Betty (1978) 'Some Aspects of Marital Stability in a Rural Luo Community', *Africa*, **48** 4, 380-97.

Poynor, Robin (1980) 'Traditional Textiles in Oyo, Nigeria', *African Arts*, **14**, 47-51.

Priebatsch, Suzanne and Knight, Natalie (1978) 'Traditional Ndebele Beadwork', *African Arts*, **11**, 24-7.

Public Broadcasting System, 'N!ai, The Story of a !Kung Bushwoman', a film produced for the Odyssey Series, distributed by Documentary Educational Resources, Watertown, Mass.

Quarcoo, A. K. and Johnson, Marion (1968) 'Shai Pots: The Pottery Tradition of the Shai People of Southern Ghana', *Baessler-Archiv*, **16**, 47-88.

Quimby, Lucy (1979) 'Islam, Sex Roles, and Modernization in Bobo-Dioulasso', in Bennetta Jules-Rosette (ed.), *The New Religions of Africa*, Norwood, N.J. pp. 203-18.

Quinn, Naomi (1977) 'Anthropological Studies of Women's Status', *Annual Review of Anthropology*, **6**, 181-225.

Ranger, T. O. (1972) 'Missionary Adaptation of African Religious Institutions: The Masasi Case', in T. O. Ranger and Isaria Kimambo, (eds.), *The Historical Study of African Religion*, London, pp. 221-51.

Raum, O. F. (1973) *The Social Functions of Avoidances and Taboos Among the Zulu*, Berlin and New York.

Reisman, Paul (1980) 'The Fulani in a Development Context', in Stephen P. Reyna (ed.), *Sahelian Social Development*, Abidjan, pp. 71-186.

Remy, Dorothy (1975) 'Underdevelopment and the Experience of Women: A Nigerian Case Study', in Rayna R. Reiter (ed.), *Toward an Anthropology of Women*, New York, pp. 358-71.

Republic of Kenya (1978) Ministry of Finance and Economic Planning, Central Bureau of Statistics, *Women in Kenya*, Nairobi.

Richards, Audrey, I. (1939) *Land, Labour and Diet in Northern Rhodesia*, London.

*Richards, Audrey, I. (1956) *Chisungu: A Girls' Initiation Ceremony Among the Bemba of Northern Rhodesia*, London.

Richards, Audrey I., Sturrock, Ford and Fortt, Jean M. (1973) *Subsistence to Commercial Farming in Present-Day Buganda: An Economic and Anthropological Survey*, Cambridge.

Ritzenthaler, Robert E. (1960) 'Anlu: A Women's Uprising in the British Cameroons', *African Studies*, **19** 3, 151-6.

Robertson, Claire (1976) 'Ga Women and Socioeconomic Change in Accra, Ghana', in Nancy Hafkin and Edna Bay (eds.), *Women in Africa*, Stanford, Calif.

Robertson, Claire (forthcoming) *Sharing the Same Bowl: A Socioeconomic History of Women and Class Formation in Accra*.

Rogers, Barbara (1981) *The Domestication of Women: Discrimination in Developing Societies*, London.

*Rogers, Susan G. (1980) 'Anti-Colonial Protest in Africa: A Female Strategy

Reconsidered', *Heresies,* **9** 3, 22-5.

Rogers, Susan, G. (n.d.) 'Efforts Toward Women's Development in Tanzania: Gender Rhetoric vs. Gender Realities', unpublished paper.

Rohrmann, G. F. (1974) 'House Decoration in Southern Africa', *African Arts,* **7,** 18-21.

Ropa, Teurai (1978a) 'Our Women are Women of Action', *Zimbabwe News,* Maputo, Jan.-Feb.

Ropa, Teurai (1978b) 'Women Have Total Involvement in Struggle', *Zimbabwe News,* Maputo, May-June.

Rosaldo, Michelle and Lamphere, Louise (eds.) (1974) *Women, Culture, and Society,* Stanford, Calif.

Rosberg, Carl G. and Nottingham, John (1966) *The Myth of 'Mau Mau': Nationalism in Kenya,* New York.

Rouch, Jean, and Bernus, E. (1959) 'Notes sur les prostituees "toutous" de Treichville et d'Adjamé', *Etudes Éburnéenes,* **6,** 231-42.

Roy, Christopher (1975) 'West African Pottery Forming and Firing Techniques', unpublished M.A. thesis, Indiana University.

Rubin, Barbara (1970) 'Calabash Decoration'. *African Arts,* **4,** 20-5.

Rubin, Gayle (1975) 'The Traffic in Women: Notes on the 'Political Economy' of Sex', in Rayna R. Reiter (ed.), *Toward an Anthropology of Women,* New York, pp. 157-210.

Ryan, Mary P. (1981) *Cradle of the Middle Class: The Family in Oneida Country, New York, 1790-1865,* New York.

Sacks, Karen (1979) *Sisters and Wives: The Past and Future of Sexual Equality,* Westport, Conn.

Schapera, Isaac (1971) *Married Life in an African Tribe,* Harmondsworth, first published 1940.

Scheub, Harold (1977) 'Performance of Oral Narrative', in William R. Bascom (ed.), *Frontiers of Folklore,* Boulder, Colo., pp. 54-78.

Schildkrout, Enid (1978) *Peoples of the Zongo,* New York.

Schlegel, Alice (ed.) (1977) *Sexual Stratification,* New York.

*Schuster, Ilsa M. Glaser (1979) *New Women of Lusaka,* Palo Alto, Calif.

(SEDES) Société d'Etudes pour le Développement Économique et Sociale (1965) *Région de Korhogo,* 9 vols, Paris.

*Sembène, Ousmane (1970) *God's Bits of Wood,* trans. Francis Price, London, 1970, first published as *Les Bouts de Bois de Dieu,* Paris, 1960.

Shields, Nwanganga (1980) 'Women in the Urban Labor Markets of Africa: The Case of Tanzania', World Bank Staff Working, Paper No. 380.

Sibisi, Harriet (1977) 'How African Women Cope with Migrant Labor in South Africa', *Signs,* **3** 1, 167-77.

Sieber, Roy (1972) 'Kwahu Terracottas, Oral Traditions, and Ghanaian History', in Douglas Fraser and Herbert Cole (eds.), *African Art and Leadership,* Madison, Wisc., pp. 173-83.

Simon, J. (1974) *The Effects of Income on Fertility,* Monograph No. 19, Carolina Population Center, Chapel Hill, N.C.

Skinner, Elliott P. (1965) 'Labor Migration Among the Mossi of the Upper Volta', in Hilda Kuper, (ed.), *Urbanization and Migration in West Africa,* Berkeley, Calif., pp. 60-85.

Skinner, Neil (ed. and trans.) (1969) *Hausa Tales and Traditions: An English Translation of 'Tatsuniyoyi na Hausa',* originally compiled by Frank Edgar, London.

Smith, Fred (1978a) 'Gurensi Basketry and Pottery', *African Arts,* **12,** 78-81.

*Smith, Fred (1978b) 'Gurensi Wall Painting', *African Arts,* **11.**

*Smith, Mary (1981) *Baba of Karo: A Woman of the Muslim Hausa,* New Haven, Conn., first published 1955 with introduction by Michael G. Smith.

Smith, Michael G. (1957) 'The Social Functions and Meaning of Hausa Praise-Singing', *Africa,* 27, 26-43.

Smock, Audrey C. (1977a) 'Ghana: From Autonomy to Subordination', in Janet Giele and Audrey Smock (eds.), *Women: Roles and Status in Eight Countries,* New York, pp. 173-216.

*Smock, Audrey C. (1977b) 'The Impact of Modernization on Women's Position in the Family in Ghana', in Alice Schlegel (ed.), *Sexual Stratification: A Cross-Cultural View,* New York, pp. 192-214.

Sofola, Zulu (1977) *The Sweet Trap,* Ibadan.

Sousa, Noémia de (1975) 'If You Want To Know Me', in Wole Soyinka (ed.), *Poems of Black Africa,* London, pp. 84-5.

Southall, A. W. (1961a) 'Kinship, Friendship and the Network of Relations in Kisenyi, Kampala', in A. Southall, (ed.), *Social Change in Modern Africa,* London, pp. 217-29.

Southall, A. W. (ed.) (1961b) *Social Change in Modern Africa,* London.

Southall, A. W. (ed.) (1973) *Urban Anthropology,* New York.

Southall, A. W., and Gutkind, P. C. W. (1957) *Townsmen in the Making,* Kampala.

Spencer, Dunstan S. C. (1976) 'African Women in Agricultural Development: A Case Study in Sierra Leone'. Overseas Liaison Committee, American Council on Education, Paper No. 9, Washington, D.C.

Spies, S. B. (1980) 'Women and the War', in Peter Warwick (ed.), *The South African War: the Anglo-Boer War, 1899-1902,* London, pp. 161-85.

Spring, Anita (1978) 'Epidemiology of Spirit Possession Among the Luvale of Zambia', in Judith Hoch-Smith and Anita Spring (eds.), *Women in Ritual and Symbolic Roles,* New York, pp. 165-89.

Stamp, Patricia (1975/1976) 'Perceptions of Change and Economic Strategy Among Kikuyu Women of Mitero, Kenya', *Rural Africana,* 29, 1975-1976, 19-43.

*Staudt, Kathleen (1975/1976) 'Women Farmers and Inequities in Agricultural Services', *Rural Africana,* 29, 81-94.

Staudt, Kathleen (1978) 'Agricultural Productivity Gaps: A Case Study of Male Preference in Government Policy Implementation', *Development and Change,* 9, 439-57.

Staveley, Jennifer L. (1977) 'Prostitutes and Prostitution in Africa: The Development of Women's First Wage Earning Activity', unpublished M.A. paper, University of Waterloo.

Steady, Filomina Chioma (1975) *Female Power in African Politics: The National Congress of Sierra Leone,* Munger Africana Notes No. 31, Pasadena, Calif.

*Steady, Filomina Chioma (1976) 'Protestant Women's Associations in Freetown, Sierra Leone', in Nancy Hafkin and Edna Bay (eds.), *Women in Africa: Studies in Social and Economic Change,* Stanford, Calif. pp. 183-212.

*Stichter, Sharon (1975-76) 'Women and the Labor Force in Kenya, 1895-1964', *Rural Africana,* 29, 45-67.

Storgaard, Birgit (1975/1976) 'Women in Ujamaa Villages', *Rural Africana,* 29, 135-55.

Strobel, Margaret (1976) 'From Lelemama to Lobbying: Women's Associations in Mombasa', in Nancy Hafkin and Edna Bay, *Women in Africa: Studies in Social and Economic Change,* Stanford, Calif.

*Strobel, Margaret (1979) *Muslim Women in Mombasa, 1890-1975,* New Haven, Conn.

Strobel, Margaret (1982) 'Review Essay: African Women', *Signs,* 7, 109-31.

*Sudarkasa, Niara (1973) *Where Women Work: A Study of Yoruba Women in the Marketplace and in the Home,* Ann Arbor, Mich.

Sundkler, B. G. M. (1961) *Bantu Prophets in South Africa,* first published 1948, reprint London and New York, 1961.

Sundkler, B. G. M. (1945) 'Marriage Problems in the Church in Tanganyika', *International Review of Missions,* **34** 135, 253-68.

Sutherland, Efua Theodora (1967) *Foriwa,* first published 1964, reprint Accra-Tema, 1967.

Swanson, Maynard W. (1977) 'The Sanitation Syndrome: Bubonic Plague and Urban Native Policy in the Cape Colony, 1900-1909', *Journal of African History,* **18** 3, 387-410.

*Tadesse, Zenebework (1982) 'Women and Technology in Peripheral Countries: An Overview', in P. M. D'Onofrio-Flores and S. M. Pfafflin (eds.), *Scientific-Technological Change and the Role of Women in Development,* Boulder, Colo.

*Thompson, Robert (1969) 'Abatan: A Master Potter of the Egbado Yoruba', in Daniel Biebuyck, (ed.), *Tradition and Creativity in Tribal Art,* Berkeley, Calif., pp. 120-82.

Thornton, John (1980) 'The Slave Trade in Eighteenth Century Angola: Effects on Demographic Structures', *Canadian Journal of African Studies,* **14** 3, 417-27.

Tiffany, Sharon W. (1978) 'Models and the Social Anthropology of Women: A Preliminary Assessment', *Man,* **13**, 34-51.

Tiger, Lionel (1969) *Men in Groups,* London.

Tinker, Irene and Bramsen, M. B. (eds.) (1976) *Women and World Development,* Washington, D.C.

Tremearne, A. J. N. (1913) *Hausa Superstitions and Customs,* London.

Tsele, Lindiwe Mimi (1981) *Women in Chimurenga: A Personal Account of the Experience of Some of the Women of Zimbabwe,* London.

Tutuola, Amos (1958) *The Brave African Huntress,* New York.

Uchendu, Victor C. (1965) *The Igbo of Southeast Nigeria,* New York.

(UN) United Nations (1978) 'Report to the Secretary-General, Development and International Economic Cooperation: Effective Mobilization of Women in Development', A/33/238. New York, Oct. 26, 1978.

United States Department of Commerce, Bureau of the Census (1980) *Illustrative Statistics on Women in Developing Countries,* Washington, D.C.

(UNVF) United Nations Voluntary Fund, *Progress Reports 1978, 1979, and 1980 for Swaziland Rural Development Projects,* and Personal Communication, Margaret Snyder, UNVF.

*Urdang, Stephanie (1979) *Fighting Two Colonialisms: Women in Guinea-Bissau,* New York.

(USAID) United States Agency for International Development (1981) Office of Development Information and Utilization, *Selected Statistical Data by Sex,* Washington, D.C.

(USDA) United States Department of Agriculture (1981) *Food Problems and Prospects in Sub-Saharan Africa,* Washington, D.C.

U'Tamsi, Tchikaya (1970) *Selected Poems,* ed. and trans. Gerald Moore, London.

Vail, Leroy and White, Landeg (1977) ' "Tawani Machambero!": Forced Cotton and Rice Growing on the Zambezi', *Journal of African History,* **19** 2, 239-63.

Van Allen, Judith (1972) 'Sitting on a Man: Colonialism and the Lost Political Institutions of Igbo Women', *Canadian Journal of African Studies,* **6** 2, 165-81.

Van Allen, Judith (1974) 'Memsahib, Militante, Femme Libre: Political and Apolitical Styles of Modern African Women', in Jane Jacquette (ed.), *Women in Politics,* New York, pp. 304-21.

*Van Allen, Judith (1976) ' "Aba Riots" or Igbo "Women's War": Ideology,

Stratification, and the Invisibility of Women', in Nancy Hafkin and Edna Bay (eds.), *Women in Africa: Studies in Social and Economic Change*, Stanford, Calif., pp. 59-85.

Van Onselen, Charles (1982) 'Prostitutes and Proletarians, 1886-1914', in C. Van Onselen, *Studies in the Social and Economic History of the Witwatersrand 1886-1914*, vol. 1, 'New Babylon', London, pp. 103-43.

Van Zwanenberg, R. M. A. (1972) 'History and Theory of Urban Poverty in Nairobi: The Problem of Slum Development', *Journal of East African Research and Development,* 2 2, 165-203.

Vaughn, James (1973) 'Kyagu as Artists in Marghi Society', in Warren d'Azevedo (ed.), *The Traditional Artist in African Societies*, Bloomington, Ind., pp. 162-93.

Vincent, Jeanne-Françoise (1976) *Traditions et Transition: Entretiens avec des Femmes Beti du Sud Cameroun*, Paris.

Waane, S. A. C. (1977) 'Pottery-Making Traditions of the Ikombe Kisi, Mbeya Region, Tanzania', *Baessler-Archiv,* **25**, 251-317.

Wachtel, Eleanor (1975) 'Economic Enterprises of Women in Nakuru, Kenya', paper presented at the annual meeting of the Canadian Association of African Studies, York University, Feb. 1975.

Wachtel, Eleanor (1975/1976) 'A Farm of One's Own: The Rural Orientation of Women's Group Enterprises in Nakuru, Kenya', *Rural Africana,* **29**, 69-80.

*Wachtel, Eleanor (1976) 'Minding Her Own Business: Women Shopkeepers in Nakuru', *African Urban Notes,* 2 2, 27-42.

Wahlmann, Maude (1972) 'Yoruba Pottery-Making Techniques', *Baessler-Archiv,* **20**, 313-46.

Wahlmann, Maude (1974) *Contemporary African Arts*, Chicago.

*Walker, Rosalyn (1976) *African Women African Art*, an Exhibition of African Art Illustrating the Different Roles of Women in African Society. The African-American Institute, New York, Sept. 13—Dec. 31, 1976.

Walker, Sheila (1979) 'Women in the Harrist Movement', in Benetta Jules-Rosette, (ed.), *The New Religions of Africa*, Norwood, N.J., p. 87-97.

Welch, Charles E. and Glick, Paul (1981) 'The Incidence of Polygamy in Contemporary Africa', *Journal of Marriage and the Family,* **43**, 191-3.

*Wellesley Editorial Committee (eds.) (1977) *Women and National Development: the Complexities of Change*, Chicago.

Werner, Alice and Hichens, William (eds.) (1943) *Utendi wa Mwana Kupona (Advice of Mwana Kupona upon the Wifely Duty)*, Medstead, UK.

White, Luise S. (1979) 'Wages and Reproduction in Nairobi, 1909-1950', paper presented at the African Studies Association annual meetings, Los Angeles, 1979.

White, Luise S. (1983) 'A History of Prostitution in Nairobi, Kenya, *c.* 1900-1952', unpublished Ph.D. thesis, University of Cambridge.

Whitely, Wilfred H. (1964) *A Selection of African Prose, I: Oral Literature*, Oxford.

Whyte, Martin King (1978) *The Status of Women in Pre-Industrial Societies*, Princeton, N.J.

(WID) Women in Development Office, *AID Report on Women in Development*, reports submitted to the Committee on Foreign Relations, US Senate, and to the Speaker of the House of Representatives, Washington, D.C., 1978 and 1980.

Williams, Denis (1973) 'Art in Metal', in S. O. Biobaku (ed.), *Sources of Yoruba History*, Oxford, pp. 140-64.

Wilson, Monica and Mafeje, Archie (1963) *Langa*, Cape Town.

Wipper, Audrey (1972) 'African Women, Fashion, and Scapegoating', *Canadian Journal of African Studies,* **6** 2, 329-49.

Wipper, Audrey (1975/1976) 'The Maendeleo ya Wanawake Movement in the Colonial Period: The Canadian Connection, Mau Mau, Embroidery, and Agriculture', *Rural Africana, 29*, 195-214.

Wipper, Audrey (1975/1976) 'The Maendeleo ya Wanawake Organization: the Co-optation of Leadership', *The African Studies Review, 18* 3, 99-120.

Wisner, Ben (1982) 'Mwea Irrigation Scheme, Kenya: A Success Story for Whom?', *Anthropological Research Council Newsletter*, Boston.

World Bank (1978) *Recognizing the 'Invisible' Woman in Development: The World Bank's Experience*, Washington, D.C.

Wright, Marcia (1975) 'Women in Peril: A Commentary on the Life Stories of Captives in Nineteenth Century East-Central Africa', *African Social Research, 20*, 800-19.

Youssef, Nadia H. (1981) 'A Cautionary Note Regarding the Use of Employment Statistics for Women' in USAID, Office of Development Information and Utilization, *Selected Statistical Data by Sex*, Washington, D.C.

Notes on contributors

Lisa Aronson is assistant professor of art history at the University of Wisconsin, Stevens Point. Thus far her studies have focused on women's weaving traditions in Southern Nigeria, examining the impact of trade on designs, technology and economic organization. Her published works include: 'Patronage and Akwete Weaving', *African Arts* (1980); 'History of Cloth Trade in the Niger Delta: A Study of Diffusion', in *Textiles of Africa*, ed. Dale Idiens (1980); and 'Popo Weaving: The Dynamics of Trade in Southeastern Nigeria', *African Arts* (1981).

Jane I. Guyer is assistant professor of anthropology at Harvard University. She has carried out field research on the history and organization of agriculture in Western Nigeria and Southern Cameroon. Her publications include papers on economic history: head tax (*Cahiers d'Etudes Africaines*, 1980), colonial food policy (*Journal of African History*, 1978), the Depression (*African Economic History*, 1981); local farming systems (*Africa*, 1980; *Comparative Studies in Society and History*, 1980); and a review of the literature on household and community (*African Studies Review* 1981).

Margaret Jean Hay is publications editor of the African Studies Center and lecturer in history at Boston University. Her principal interests include agrarian history and the changing economic roles of African women. Her published work include 'Luo Women and Economic Change During the Colonial Period', in Edna Bay and Nancy Hafkin, eds, *Women in Africa: Studies in Social and Economic Change* (Stanford, 1976): 'Peasants in Eastern African Studies', *Peasant Studies* (1979); and *African Women and the Law: Historical Perspectives* (with Marcia Wright, Boston, 1982).

Jeanne Koopman Henn, assistant professor of economics at Northeastern University in Boston, lived in Cameroon and Tanzania for seven years while conducting reserach on rural work and incomes and teaching economic development at the University of Dar es Salaam. She gratefully acknowledges the helpful comments of friends in the Women's Study Group at the University of Dar es Salaam on an earlier version of her chapter. Special thanks to May Matteru, Marjorie Mbilinyi, Bertha Koda, Enos Bukuku, and Rosemary Ganley.

Deirdre LaPin has taught African literature at the University of Ife and is currently associate professor of English and folklore at the University of Arkansas, Little Rock. She lived and conducted field research in Nigeria from 1972 to 1977 and again in 1982. Her publications reflect combined interests in African folklore, comparative literature, and anthropology; they include 'Narrative as Precedent in Yoruba Tradition', in *Oral Traditional Literatures*, ed. John M. Foley (1981); 'Tale and Trickster in Yoruba Verbal Art' *Research in African Literatures* (1981); *Words and the Dogon World*, a translation with introduction of Geneviève Calame-Griaule's *Ethnologie et language: la parole chez les Dogon* (forthcoming, Philadelphia, 1983), and *Story, Medium, and Masque: A Festschrift for Albert Bates Lord* (Bloomington, forthcoming).

Barbara Lewis completed her doctoral degree in political science at Northwestern University in 1970, and now teaches comparative politics at Rutgers University.

Her dissertation focused on the politics of the truckers' association of the Ivory Coast; subsequent field work includes a study of rotating credit associations among Abidjan market women and a survey of fertility and labor force participation among Ivorian urban women. Her publications include 'The Limitations of Group Action Among Entrepreneurs: The Market Women of Abidjan, Ivory Coast', in Nancy Hafkin and Edna Bay, eds, *Women in Africa: Studies in Social and Economic Change* (Stanford, 1976), she has served as editor of the *African Studies Review of Books*, and is the editor of *Invisible Farmers: Women and the Crisis in Agriculture* (Washington, D.C., 1982). She is currently studying public policy and domestic food crop production in Cameroon.

Jean O'Barr is the director of women's studies and an associate professor of political science at Duke University. A graduate of Indiana University, she earned her Ph.D. in political science from Northwestern University in 1970. Her published works include 'Making the Invisible Visible: African Women in Politics and Policy', *African Studies Review* (1975), 'Pare Women: A Case of Political Involvement', *Rural Africana* (1976), *Third World Women: Factors in Their Changing Status* (Durham, N.C. 1975), and *Perspectives on Power* (Durham, N.C., 1982).

Claire Robertson has a Ph.D. in African history from the University of Wisconsin, and is a faculty research associate in the African Studies Program at Indiana University. Her chief research interests concern socioeconomic change and the position of women, particularly the relationships between gender, class, mode of production, and the sexual division of labor. Her publications include *Sharing the Same Bowl: A Socioeconomic History of Women and Class in Accra, Ghana* (Bloomington, forthcoming), *Women and Slavery in Africa*, co-edited with Martin Klein (Madison, in press) and *Women and Class in Africa*, co-edited with Iris Berger (in preparation).

Sharon Stichter is associate professor of sociology at the University of Massachusetts, Boston, and research associate at the African Studies Center, Boston University. She is currently working on a study of economic and family roles among middle- and low-income women in Nairobi. Her publications include 'Women and the Labor Force in Kenya, 1885-1965', *Rural Africana*, (1975-76), and *Migrant Labor in Kenya: Capitalism and African Response, 1895-1975* (London, 1982).

Margaret (Peg) Strobel is director of the Women's Studies Program and associate professor of women's studies and history at the University of Illinois at Chicago. Her book *Muslim Women in Mombasa, 1890-1975* (Yale University Press, 1979) was co-winner of the Herskovits award from the African Studies Association in 1980. Her other publications include 'Review Essay: African Women', *Signs* (1982); and 'Slavery and Reproductive Labor in Mombasa', in Claire C. Robertson and Martin A. Klein, eds, *Women and Slavery in Africa* (Madison, forthcoming). She is currently completing, with Sarah Mirza, a manuscript of the texts of three oral histories of women from Mombasa in Swahili and English.

Stephanie Urdang is a journalist and researcher with a special interest in the roles of African women, and is an editor of *Southern Africa* magazine, New York. Her published works include *Fighting Two Colonialisms: Women in Guinea Bissau* (New York, 1979) and, with Richard Lapchick, *Resisting Oppression: The Struggle of Women in Southern Africa* (Westport, Conn., 1982). She has been a consultant to the International Labor Office and the World Conference of the United Nations Decade for Women.

Luise White is assistant professor of history at Rice Unviersity, and has taught African history and women's history at Occidental College, California State

University at both Fullerton and Northridge, and the University of Southern California. Her doctoral dissertation is on the history of prostitution in Nairobi, 1900-1952, for Cambridge University. Her main research interests are African women's history and labor history.

Audrey Wipper is an associate professor of sociology at the University of Waterloo in Canada. She has edited *The Roles of African Women: Past, Present and Future*, a special issue of the *Canadian Journal of African Studies* (1972), and *Rural Women: Development or Underdevelopment?*, a special issue of *Rural Africana* (Winter, 1976). Her articles on Third World Women include: 'Equal Rights for Women in Kenya?' *The Journal of Modern African Studies* (1971); 'The Politics of Sex', *African Studies Review*, (1971); 'Riot and Rebellion Among African Women: Three Examples of Women's Political Clout', in Jean O'Barr, ed., *Perspectives on Power* (Durham, N.C., 1982); and 'The Underside of Development', *Rural Africana* (1976).

Index

Aba riots, 70-72; see also
Igbo women's protest
Abatan, Yoruba woman
potter, 128-129, 132
Abeokuta, 44-45
Abeokuta Women's
Union, 45
Abidjan, 34, 35, bf 36,
37, 40, bf 41, 44
Accra, 33, bf 36, 37, 38,
bf 41, 44, 48-48
administrative and
managerial occupations,
women in, 192
*Advice of Mwana Kupon
Upon the Wifely Duty,
The*, 98
African Child, The, novel
by Camara Laye, 112
African National Congress
(ANC), 150, 156
African Party for the
Independence of Guinea
and Cape Verde
(PAIGC), women's roles
in, ch. 10: 156-169
African clergy, role of, 95
age at marriage, 56-57
age groups, 8-9
age-set organizations, 69
agricultural extension, and
women farmers,
177-178, 187
agricultural land, women's
access to, 43
agriculture, 1-2, 3, 4-5,
'13-14, 10-14, 23-26, ch.
2: 9-32
cash-crop production,
11, 13-14, 23-26
cooperative work in, 70
hoe agriculture, 2
raising productivity, 16
source of government
revenue, 20
staple food crops, 21
subsistence, 13; as
women's
responsibility, 74
subsistance production
vs. cash-crop
production, ch. 2:
19-32
women's role in, 60-64
agronomic research, 183
Aidoo, Ama Ata,
Ghanaian author, 110

Akwete, women's weaving
in, 121, 123-124,
132-138
Alakija, Aduke, bf 151
Albert, Ethel, 6
Alfonso, king of the
Kongo, 92
Algerian women, and
nationalist struggle,
149-150
All-Muslim Women's
Association, in
Freetown, 85
alternative fuel sources,
179
Amalgamated Muslim
Women's Movement, in
Freetown, 85
American missionaries, 92
Anglo-Boer war, women's
roles in, 150
Angola, 189, bf 190
Angola, 54
Angola, nationalist
struggle in, 156
Anlu Uprising, among the
Kom, 71-72, 146-147
Anlu, women's
associations in
Cameroon, 71-72
Anowa, play by Ama Ata
Aidoo, 110
apartheid, problems of
women under, 90-91 (see
also South Africa)
apprentices, 24, 35;
apprentice weavers, 123
appropriate technology,
183-184
Arab culture, see Islamic
influences
architecture, 124-125
armed struggle, women in,
ch. 10: 156-169
art, religious significance
of, 130-131
arts, women in, ch. 8:
119-138
associations, precolonial,
11
authority, vs. power, 142
autonomy, women's, 19

Bâ, Mariama, Senegalese
author, 117
Bamako, 34, bf 36, 37, bf
41
Bamenda, 17
Banu Saade, women's
dance group in
Mombasa, 84

barren wives, 62
basket-weaving, 121
Baumann, Hermann, 2-3
beaded garments, among
Ndebele women, 124
beer brewers, and beer-
brewers' associations,
22, 35, 64-65, 81
Benin (Dahomey), 2
Beti, 13
Biafran War, 123
bilateral descent, 55-56
birth rate, 49
Black Sash, 150
blacksmiths, 121, 122
blue-collar jobs, women
in, 191, bf 192
body decorations, 126
Boer War, see Anglo-Boer
War, 150
Boesman and Lena, play
by Athol Fugard, 113
bookkeeping skills,
women's lack of, 83
bori, Hausa women's
spirit cult, 97
Botswana, 15, 27-28, 189,
bf 190, 193, bf 194
*Brave African Huntress,
The*, novel by Amos
Tutuola, 109
Brazzaville, prostitutes'
associations in, 79
brewers, women as, see
beer brewers
Bride Price, The, novel by
Buchi Emecheta,
114-115
bride price, see
bridewealth
bridewealth, 9, 14, 15, 17,
56, 59, 62, 105, 127,
159
Brooks, Angie Elizabeth,
bf 151
budgets, household, 47-48
Bukh, Jette, 23-26
Bukoba District, 62-63
bureaucracies, and
planning for women,
175
burial of babies, conflict
over, 97
Burundi, 6
Bushmen, see San

Cabral, Amilcar, founder
of PAIGC, 165
calabashes, decoration of,
124
Cameroon, 13, 17, 20,

215